W9-BWN-999

TOURO COLLEGE LIBRARY
Kings Hwy

WITHDRAWN

Sowing the Seeds of Character

Recent Titles in
Educate US
David Gerwin and Terry A. Osborn, Series Editors

Portrait of a Profession: Teaching and Teachers in the 21st Century
David M. Moss, Wendy J. Glenn, and Richard L. Schwab, editors

Language and Cultural Diversity in U.S. Schools:
Democratic Principles in Action
Terry A. Osborn, editor

Educating the First Digital Generation
Paul G. Harwood and Victor Asal

SOWING THE SEEDS OF CHARACTER

The Moral Education of Adolescents in Public and Private Schools

TOURO COLLEGE LIBRARY
Kings Hwy

Judd Kruger Levingston

Educate US
Terry A. Osborn and David Gerwin, Series Editors

Westport, Connecticut
London

KH

Library of Congress Cataloging-in-Publication Data

Levingston, Judd Kruger.
    Sowing the seeds of character : the moral education of adolescents in public and private schools / Judd Kruger Levingston.
        p. cm. — (Educate US, ISSN 1551–0425)
    Includes bibliographical references and index.
    ISBN 978–0–313–35191–4 (alk. paper)
    1. Moral education (Middle school)—United States.   2. Moral education (Secondary)—United States.   I. Title.
    LC268.L46   2009
    370.11'5—dc22   2009010331

British Library Cataloguing in Publication Data is available.

Copyright © 2009 by Judd Kruger Levingston

All rights reserved. No portion of this book may be reproduced, by any process or technique, without the express written consent of the publisher.

Library of Congress Catalog Card Number: 2009010331
ISBN: 978–0–313–35191–4
ISSN: 1551–0425

First published in 2009

Praeger Publishers, 88 Post Road West, Westport, CT 06881
An imprint of Greenwood Publishing Group, Inc.
www.praeger.com

Printed in the United States of America

The paper used in this book complies with the Permanent Paper Standard issued by the National Information Standards Organization (Z39.48–1984).

10 9 8 7 6 5 4 3 2 1

10/1/10

To Hillary,
How delightful to share our lives, our love and our laughter
To Ivan, Miranda, and Serena,
Each one of you a cornucopia of character

Sow a habit and you reap a character;
Sow a character, and you reap a destiny.

Samuel Smiles, Life and Labor, *1887*

Contents

Series Foreword

It is a rare week in which an issue in education fails to make headlines in the United States. Parents, policymakers, educators, and taxpayers have a stake in the developments regarding schools and schooling. However, though the public is increasingly sophisticated in its understanding of the intricacies of education, popular media venues offer little opportunity for an in-depth treatment of the relevant points related to the vital decisions that are made in boardrooms, classrooms, homes and voting booths. Educate US is a series presenting a comprehensive discussion of issues in a forum that minimizes technical jargon as it explores the various facets of the problems and potential in U.S. education. The authors and contributors to this series are those whose concerns about the health and welfare of education in the United States are translated into activism. Scholarship is not merely about the gaining of expertise; it includes an inherent component of advocacy. The nature of education in a democracy requires one to take a well-advised position and then to let one's voice be heard. This activity is at least as important as—in many ways so much more vital than—the technical aspects of the scholar's craft.

Judd Levingston passionately advocates for viewing schools as inherently moral spaces, even as he develops a variety of moral stances that a school, and developing adolescents, can adopt. He brings us along on school visits, into classrooms and teacher workrooms, and we accompany him as he follows some teenagers through their school day. We examine dilemmas he has faced as a principal, rabbi, classroom teacher and parent, and changes in his own views on moralizing. At every point he turns a discerning eye on the situation, and introduces us to history and theory in moral education that illuminate the range of options a school, parent, teacher or student might have for framing an issue or taking action. By the end of the book we gain a broader view of what it means to be moral in schooling, a richer vocabulary for describing how we might balance tradition, community, and personal conscience in our lives, with our families, and what stances we might wish in schools for our children. We may try to reshape a school where find ourselves, look for a school that more closely matches our vision for moral schooling, or create something new in our community. In this book Judd Levingston helps us develop our own positions on moral schooling and the means to articulate and act on them.

To participate in a meaningful and beneficial way, therefore, we all must recognize that deeper than questions of election year politics, accountability, and slogans, many decisions regarding education are essentially moral in nature. Choices that seem expedient, or fit ideologically charged models designed to appeal to the masses may nevertheless be harmful to our society, and ultimately our children. If Educate US convinces series readers to weigh choices in that vein, it will have achieved its purpose. Living in a time of daily concerns related to homeland security and prosecuting numerous wars, we would do well to remember the words of Mark Twain, "It is curious—curious that physical courage should be so common in the world, and moral courage so rare." Curious, indeed.

Terry A. Osborn and David Gerwin, Series Editors

Acknowledgments

I would like to express my deep thanks to the many individuals who encouraged my work on this book. My editor David Gerwin sowed the first seeds of this book and has been a trusted sounding board from the book's inception; Jonathan Engel provided guidance in the early stages of my writing. In preparing the manuscript, I received invaluable assistance from my dear mother, Eleanor Levingston, who can spot a misplaced comma from her office, 300 miles away. Amy Cohen also read early drafts, helping me to shape the argument in this book. Elisheva Urbas thoughtfully guided me through the final drafts of the manuscript. It was a pleasure to work with Robert Hutchinson, senior editor at Praeger, who shepherded this from proposal to manuscript and then to publication. I also wish to thank the people at Apex for their editorial assistance.

I am grateful to the many administrators, teachers, and students who welcomed me so warmly to "John Adams High School," "Templeton High School," "Amesbury High School," "Hanford Day School," "Al-Quds Islamic Academy," "Fairhill Friends School," "Academy of the Sisters of St. Theresa," "Meiguo Chinese Academy," "Haym Solomon High School," and "Joe Louis Elementary School." This book would not have been written without the enthusiastic support, encouragement, and release time I received from middle school principal Susan Friedman and from head of school Jay Leberman at the "Jerusalem School." Mindy Harris and Arden Bell provided helpful administrative support. My wonderful colleagues at the "Jerusalem School" and Rachel Hollander, a thoughtful student teacher this year, all provided support and encouragement, and they inspire me to think about moral issues every day in my work as a teacher.

Thomas Lickona, Carol Ingall, Peter Kuriloff, Joan Goodman, Marc Harwood, and Joel Fish provided guidance as I began to sharpen my thinking about ethnographic research, moral education, character education, and play. Muhammad abdul Lateef Hayden, Jing Xinnan, Sydney White, Andrew Weller, and Devorah Lissek provided leads, colleagueship, and additional suggestions. The interlibrary loan staff of the Free Library of Philadelphia, the Paley Library staff at Temple University, and my colleagues in the Department of Religion at Temple University, Khalid Blankenship and Lucy Bregman, provided guidance as well. I am grateful to Danielle Miller and Lorraine Peterson for support at home. I also appreciate the moral support of my family and friends, especially my parents, Howard and Eleanor Levingston and Lewis and Laura Kruger. This book is dedicated to my wife and children who have been in my cheering section from start to finish.

I believe that this book accurately represents the schools I visited and the teachers and students I met. I bear responsibility for any misrepresentations.

Philadelphia, Thanksgiving 2008

Introduction: From Baseball Fields to Schools

"I want a ballplayer with guts enough not to fight back!
You've got to do this job with base hits
and stolen bases and fielding ground balls, Jackie.
Nothing else!"

—Branch Rickey to Jackie Robinson in Alan Axelrod,
Profiles in Audacity

By the time Branch Rickey hired Jackie Robinson to join the Brooklyn Dodgers Major League Baseball organization in 1945, the seeds of character already had been sown in both men. Branch Rickey had played professional baseball and had seen black players face discrimination in games and in hotels; he was determined to change that climate. He had heard about a player named Jackie Robinson who had played in the Negro Leagues under a contract with the Kansas City Monarchs, and his physical prowess and his temperament indicated that he had the potential to play and excel in an integrated game if only the color line could be crossed.

Branch Rickey's decision to sign Jackie Robinson was a moral decision that would further some of the changes already underway in racial relations in the United States. The Commissioner of Baseball himself, Albert B. "Happy" Chandler, who had served as Governor of Kentucky, suggested that a racially integrated game of baseball should be a natural consequence of the service African Americans had given to the United States in war: "If they can fight and die on Okinawa [and] Guadalcanal . . . they can play ball in America."[1] During this same postwar period, a commission appointed by President Harry S. Truman began to explore the desegregation of the United States armed forces and the commission's work culminated in the eventual desegregation and integration of the armed forces, which was 95 percent complete by October 1953.[2]

Playing baseball thus became more than a physical contest: it also became a moral contest when the Dodgers traveled and faced the fans in different cities, some of whom shouted racial epithets, throwing things at the team, occasionally putting Jackie Robinson in physical danger, wearing down the resolve of the team, and challenging the commitment to integration. Rickey and Robinson became important partners and role models for their partnership in integrating baseball and challenging the prejudices of Americans.[3]

After Robinson signed a contract with Branch Rickey, he crossed the color line by playing first for the Brooklyn Dodgers minor league team in Montreal, and then by rising to the major leagues as a rookie in 1947. He had a stellar first year, leading the National League in stolen bases and hits and earning the title of Rookie of the Year. Hiring Jackie Robinson turned out to be a good business decision that improved revenue for the Dodgers by drawing in many new fans who were excited about seeing such a successful black player. Jackie Robinson also raised awareness about civil rights, helping to pave the way in the following decades for efforts to integrate buses and lunch counters in the American South, calling attention to unjust inequalities in American society that needed to be addressed publicly in legislatures and courts of law.

This introduction begins with baseball because the seeds of character are sown in the crucible of relationships, conflicts, life-changing decisions, and everyday moments. Students cannot merely sit in a classroom and learn to be moral people: they have to study great moral decisions, and they have to understand the process of moral reasoning. Branch Rickey made a moral decision because he was sensitive to the injustices of fellow players who were African American, and his background had steeled him to expect conflict and to stare it down for the right cause. Jackie Robinson made a moral decision as well, because he was willing to use his talent and serve as an example for others, even putting his talent on the line to advance the cause of a more open society, following the moral teachings of his mentors and teachers, from his mother to his pastor, Karl Everette Downs, at Scott United Methodist Church in Pasadena.[4] Jackie Robinson was prepared to accept Branch Rickey's offer because his background taught him to appreciate his athletic gifts and to trust the moral clarity that he felt at the moment.

THE ROOTS OF MORAL DECISION MAKING

Just as we might ask what pushed Branch Rickey to hire Jackie Robinson in 1947 and not to wait any longer, we also might ask what it would take to push a child to decide to stick up for an isolated and seemingly friendless classmate? It takes the accumulation of messages and convictions from years of practice. Families and schools give young people frequent messages about their behavior, helping them to develop moral convictions. Parents teach their children through countless routine moments ("Say please!" "Look at someone when they are talking to you!" "Have you asked Grandma how *she* is?" "David, it's your duty to take out the trash!"). Many families choose the public and private schools their children attend on the basis of factors like geography, affordability, convenience, what their family and friends are doing, and on basis of the values and outlooks that the school espouses. In some areas, nearly everyone attends the local public school, and in other areas, families have a range of choices, and they are more inclined to choose a school on the basis of its sense of purpose or mission.

Branch Rickey and Jackie Robinson faced the moral decision of a lifetime, and one might say that a lifetime of moral training prepared them to seize the moment and to collaborate on the integration of Major League Baseball long before public water fountains and lunch counters would be integrated throughout the entire United States.

To some people, moral education may seem like a luxurious use of time, like teaching art and music in poor neighborhoods with students whose reading and math abilities are far below grade level. Or, for wealthier schools, moral education may seem extraneous because it is already part of a school's sense of mission, or it takes time away from students' readying their academic profiles in preparation for college, or because it implies that there might be something immoral that needs to be corrected. I remember being at a faculty meeting about moral education when a colleague remarked, "Everything we do is moral!" He added that he didn't think it necessary for us to go to great lengths to work with young people on moral issues because they already had many positive role models in their parents and teachers. I argued then, as I argue here in these pages, that moral education is not a luxury, nor is it a frivolous by-product of an education in the arts and sciences. It is a self-conscious and deliberate attempt to make sure that young people learn about integrity, respect, care for oneself, care for the world, and principles of justice and freedom. As Richard Kahlenberg wrote in a *New York Times* opinion piece, public education and public schools "have a special rationale: to provide a common education to children from all backgrounds that teaches not only skills but also American history, culture and democracy."[5] This call to civic responsibility has moral overtones: public, private, and parochial schools are obliged not just to teach skills, but also to introduce students to the moral principles that guide this country.

Moral education, character education, and religious education address ways of training young people through their years of schooling to make choices and to act according to religious and secular traditions that represent integrity and right, whether at school, at home, or in public life. The rough and tumble of school playgrounds and classrooms everywhere offers opportunities for moral decisions and moral growth through modes as varied as ball games, word games, number games, historical reenactments, laboratory experiments, foreign language role play, dramatic play, musical improvisation, and artistic exploration. This book presents ways in which institutions and individuals express a moral outlook and specific moral positions as they face murky issues for which there may be no right answer. When a friend breaks a rule, for example there are many possible responses. Which is more important: to be loyal to the friend and to protect the friend from punishment, or to be honest with adults and to protect one's own reputation? Could there be another way to resolve the same moral problems?

Public discussion about moral education has become more urgent than before. The two major party candidates for president in 2008 both called on public education systems to improve test scores, student discipline, and the overall moral climate. In the run-up to the 2008 presidential election, moral perspectives on issues as diverse as the banking system, foreign policy, professional sports, and education became widely discussed with a sense of immediacy.[6] In advance of the election season, in October 2007, a bill came to the U.S. Congress cosponsored by then Illinois Senator Barack Obama and his fellow legislators from Illinois, Senator Dick Durbin and Representative Phil Hare, seeking to improve student behavior in schools. The bill sought to direct funds to schools with innovative programs that would reduce the number of suspensions, keeping students in school and improving the overall climate.[7] Earlier in his career, while serving as a member of the Illinois Senate, Obama served as a board chairman for the Chicago Annenberg Challenge, which provided significant funds for struggling schools, giving Obama credibility as someone interested in reform that would improve academic achievement and provide enrichment programs.[8] These enrichment programs and trips to museums and concerts did not promise to raise test scores, but the Annenberg Challenge was created in part to shape the taste and character of students in an age heavily dominated by commercial media.

The 2008 Democratic Party platform included a moral call both for a shared sense of responsibility that would lead to improvement in schools at every level, from preschool programs to institutions of higher education: "We must prepare all our students with the 21st-century skills they need to succeed by progressing to a new era of mutual responsibility in education."[9]

Republican presidential candidate John McCain spoke in 2008 about the importance of maintaining a moral role for teachers. In the speech, given at his alma mater, Episcopal High School in Alexandria, Virginia, McCain said that schools "should be able to compete for dedicated, effective, character-building teachers, hire them and reward them."[10] The Republican Party platform included a call for civic education that would prepare young people for "responsible citizenship in a free society."[11] McCain's specific proposals for schools were less ambitious than those of his rival, Barack Obama, focusing on after-school tutoring and support for voucher programs for families wishing to choose private schools. Both McCain and Obama supported merit pay for successful teachers.[12]

In the present era, national and state testing often leads teachers to focus on making sure that their students get the right answers to objective questions; this trend may hinder a teacher's efforts to engage students and to sow the seeds of character.[13] The moral role of the teacher is all the more important because of the many forces that can either enhance or undermine the moral development of young people. The Internet is one such force, for example. It has created an urgent need for teachers and parents to help students navigate the vast resources available that broaden a student's knowledge with the most recent scientific findings. The Internet also has required teachers and parents to teach young people about staying within boundaries of appropriate discourse in cyberspace. One multiyear study that began in 2005 supports Internet-based socializing and learning, but it is equally important to know that Internet-based bullying and abuse has led, in at least one case, to a teen suicide. In another case, misuse of the Internet led to the defamation of a teacher in a New York City independent school after a student used a Facebook page to defame her. This created a campus-wide conflict about the limits of free speech and Internet use.[14] Some schools and teachers are embracing technology more than ever, and others are retreating from it and avoiding it.[15]

As much as the new technologies succeed in capturing our imaginations (and the attention of school disciplinarians), familiar issues such as cheating, drug abuse, and teenage sexual activity may seem old-fashioned in comparison, but they have not gone away. One study indicates that adolescent sexual activity in the United States declined between 1991 and 2007, but some sexually transmitted diseases, such as HIV disease, have increased, and teenage birthrates have risen.[16] Some teenagers feel that pregnancy should be avoided while others see it as a rite of passage.[17] According to a UNICEF study, in 1998, the United States had the highest teenage birthrate among wealthy industrialized nations.[18]

In schools, some research indicates that cheating has continued to increase over the last 20 years.[19] Educators studying the roots and implications of cheating suggest that a school culture that respects integrity may stem the increases in cheating; a University of Connecticut professor launched an academic study to compare cheating rates at public and private schools at different income levels to see what kinds of interventions will reduce cheating. After this study was described in a *New York Times* Editorial Observer comment, the newspaper published several letters to the editor blaming the educational system, blaming a decline in values, and even blaming teachers for the decline in morals and the high levels of cheating today.[20]

Cheating affects the academic integrity and moral climate of a school, while risky behaviors threaten the safety and stability of the student population. National studies indicate that drug abuse began to increase toward 2002, and then it returned to lower levels that had not been seen for a decade.[21]

The landscape of our schools is changing. It would be insulting to earlier generations of educators to suggest that our schools have become more moral than they were before, as if what happened in the past was frankly *immoral* or indifferent to moral questions and moral behavior. On the contrary, stories about children being rapped on the knuckles by their schoolteachers in earlier years of the 20th century make it clear that teachers have taken their moral authority seriously and that they continue to see themselves in the important role of making students learn to behave and to respect authority and lived experience.[22] The rise of high school community service requirements and the new public schools opening with explicit moral missions point to ongoing interest in secular schools that are prepared to play a role in shaping the moral outlook of their students.

Many charter schools have opened since the first charter schools were established in 1992 in the state of Minnesota. As of May 2008, over 1.2 million students are enrolled in more than 4,000 charter schools in 40 states and the District of Columbia.[23] Charter schools provide a public school education under a charter from the local government that grants a release from many locally mandated curricular standards. Charter schools vary widely, and they include inner-city charter schools that require uniforms and that set their own calendars, charter schools with a cultural focus, and charter schools guided by themes such as technology, the sea, and the environment. In Wisconsin, teachers at environment-focused charter schools introduce children to concepts such as the moral stewardship of the earth and its natural resources. Many of these charter schools promote academic excellence with a moral focus, and in particularly dangerous school districts, many promise to provide both psychological and physical safety.[24]

Home schooling has continued to increase as well in recent years, with more than 1 million students receiving their education at home, up from approximately 100,000 in 1983. Families are choosing home schooling for two central reasons: to provide greater safety, especially from peer pressure, and to provide religious or moral instruction along with academic instruction.[25] The current climate has allowed families to become consumers with an array of options including neighborhood public schools, charter schools with a particular area of focus, private schools, faith-based schools, and home schooling.

FROM "THOU SHALT NOT MORALIZE" TO "SOWING THE SEEDS OF CHARACTER"

My professional experience as a school principal and classroom teacher has given me ample time to think about moral education as it can be practiced in schools, and my personal experiences as a parent also have contributed to my thinking. My wife and I are in the thick of our child-rearing years, observing our three children in their three different schools. They regularly present moral issues around the dinner table regarding such early childhood issues as sharing toys; middle childhood issues such as sharing friends, developing skills, learning to trust one's own academic judgment; and the challenges of the teenage years that include sharing information, relating to adults as mentors, self-advocacy, forming one's own identity, and confronting questions about human existence that may be unanswerable.

I first became interested in moral education when I was teaching at a school for girls in Baltimore. I found myself wanting to spend classroom time on great moral and ethical issues. In Comparative Religion, a class I taught to 12th-grade students, we discussed whether all religions say the same thing in their respective versions of the Golden Rule, from Confucius, who said, "What you do not wish yourself, do not unto others"; to Jesus, who said in the Gospel according to Luke, "And as you wish that men would do to you, do so to them"; to the Jewish sage Hillel, who spoke in a commentary on Leviticus 18:19 ("You shall love your neighbor as yourself, I am the Lord your God"), "What you hate, do not do to your neighbor. This is the whole Torah in its entirety, and everything further is its commentary. Now go and learn."[26] In another 12th-grade elective that I taught, called Third World Politics, and in 7th-grade Geography, we could not avoid moral issues when discussing the imbalance of wealth and power that led to unfair trading practices, slavery, and corruption. As the European sphere increased its wealth, the developing world began to acquire new problems it hadn't sought. In a class on European history, to give an example, I wanted to raise the discussion level beyond comprehension of the phases of the French Revolution: I wanted my students to evaluate Napoleon as a moral leader, and then, when we studied the 1930s and 1940s, to consider questions about the appeal of Fascism in so many countries. The school, which I call the "Carey School," was not at all opposed to discussions about these moral issues but curricular demands, limited time for discussion. I also was intrigued by the honor code at the all-boys school around the corner. The students signed an affirmation of their honesty on the completion of every paper, quiz, and test, and I wondered whether the boys saw it as little more than a necessary routine or whether they saw it as a reminder not to cheat.

At a Jewish after-school program that I directed in New York in the mid-1990s, students and I often exchanged ideas both in class and in school-wide assemblies about the moral imperative of maintaining cultural ties and a strong sense of cultural identity. When I was a high school principal at a Jewish day school in New York and then at an independent all-boys school in Philadelphia, I could see that moral issues arose almost daily. Students and I often spoke about moral leadership, often around how the older students could treat the younger students with a spirit of generosity and about how older students have the capacity to set the tone for the rest of the school. The conversations and assemblies with guest speakers raising issues of integrity often help students to find voices for their own conscience. Students don't always see the immediate benefits of these kinds of experiences until much later when they attribute a decision they made to words they heard some time earlier from a teacher, guest speaker, or parent.

As a rabbi, coming from a faith tradition that cares deeply about moral behavior and about character development, I feel grateful for the opportunities I have had to teach about moral education in my own community and to learn about moral education in other communities. I find that being a rabbi adds a layer of insight to discussions about morality that I have with my students. In my present classroom as a middle school teacher, my 6th, 7th, and 8th grade students and my advisees and I often speak about taking responsibility for homework and for behavior, and about how we use language to cultivate friendship or to express our differences. Over the years, when a student has done something

praiseworthy or, just as often, when a student has violated an important principle or school rule, I have tried to take advantage of what educators often
call teachable moments. Instead of keeping a conversation with a student in
the moment, I try to make time for the student's action to open a constructive discussion about Jewish tradition, about how the action might be viewed
in a positive or negative light by the ancient sages, and about how the action
might weigh on the student's conscience as an affirmation or as a negation
of love and of God's presence. Working with young people during the course
of a full day at school, I feel obliged to be aware of eyeballs rolling when the
kids want to move on; they don't want to labor over every moment in the rush
of a school day! Moral behavior involves far more than sitting quietly in an
assigned seat: it involves grappling with options, thinking through outcomes,
and being willing to accept that sometimes there might not be a correct moral
answer.

This book represents the culmination of a shift in my thinking. Originally
titled *Thou Shalt Not Moralize,* I had intended for this book to give voice to the
conviction that schools must be places in which moral questions are welcomed,
raised, and debated by teachers and students, but that teachers should not be
in the business of moralizing, of administering doctrine by telling children
what to do or what to think. As my research got underway at Muslim, Roman
Catholic, Jewish, Quaker, and Chinese schools, and also at secular public and
independent schools with no ethnic or religious affiliation, I observed caring
teachers, including some who seized opportunities for moral discussion and
some who avoided moral discussion, choosing not to become diverted from
the regular curriculum. I spoke with students from poor and embattled neighborhoods who uphold the highest levels of generosity, and I also spoke with
students from the opposite end of the economic spectrum who came from
wealthier backgrounds and who are more suspicious and less forgiving. I also
met suburban students who credited their teachers with instilling in them a
willingness not to be a bystander when something destructive is taking place.

I heard students quoting the good things that their teachers taught them;
students occasionally hear a former teacher's voice the way that they might
hear a parent's voice and use that voice to guide them through a particularly
difficult moment. As a result, I began to give up the idea that teachers should
not "moralize." I worry about any adult wielding too heavy a hand, so when
teachers seek to govern student behavior with doctrine without leaving much
room for students to reason on their own, the students give up the capacity
to become independent moral actors. As I write in chapter 1, people may be
disposed toward certain character traits, and a teacher may not always be able

to establish that character trait in a child, but the teacher can join a young person's family and friends as a partner in trying to sow the seeds of character, giving children a vocabulary for discussion and action that will help them to face the murky issues that lack clear and ready answers. Teachers also have to moralize with a sense of humility, because the answers a teacher gives a child one year might not serve the child later on in school and in life.

Many individuals play a role in sowing the seeds of character in young people: parents, teachers, and, for teenagers, peers and workplace supervisors. As much as I would have liked to see how moral development is influenced by all of these individuals, I did not visit students at their homes or workplaces, so this study is limited to the ways in which schools provide the field in which the seeds of character are sown.[27]

THE NATURE OF THIS PROJECT

I use the word *character* to describe a broad range of moral habits, virtues, and dispositions. Thomas Lickona and Matthew Davidson describe character in several dimensions, including virtue, habits, psychological "muscle," the way in which we function in relationships, and the way in which we develop personality traits,[28] For example, a teenager with a strong character may have a predisposition to behave respectfully toward authority figures, to summon courage in times of fear, and to act with humility even in a moment that could be more self-aggrandizing. Character education may sound more specific than moral education because it focuses on an individual's development. Character education happens in conjunction with moral education when students have opportunities to focus on questions about human behavior toward one another, about issues of citizenship and dignity, and about the great questions of human existence.[29]

Research for this book took place in two phases. In the 1998–99 school year, I visited four schools in the New York area (where I was living at the time); at each school, I shadowed one or more students and interviewed the students to learn about their moral outlook. One student, whom I call "Tamar," attended a large regional suburban public high school that I call Amesbury High School; another student, whom I call "Jeffrey," attended a highly selective public high school that I call John Adams High School, located in one of the outer boroughs of New York; another student, whom I call "Gadiel," attended a relatively small private school in Manhattan that I call Hanford Day School. Two students, whom I call "Jared" and "Felicia," attended a small public high school in Manhattan that I call Templeton High School, which was founded for highly motivated students who did not have the high scores necessary to enter the most exclusive New York City public high schools. At each school, I attended classes with my host student, interviewed teachers and administrators, and wrote extensive field notes based on my observations. Much of that research became the basis for my doctoral dissertation and for several articles.[30]

During the second phase of research for this book, from 2007 to 2008, I visited several other schools where I observed classes and conducted student and teacher interviews, including a Muslim school that I call the Al-Quds Islamic Academy; a Roman Catholic school that I call the Academy of the Sisters of St. Theresa ("ASST"); a large public high school located in an inner-city Philadelphia neighborhood, which I call Haym Solomon High School; a Quaker school that I call Fairhill Friends School; and a private Jewish day school that I call the Jerusalem School; I also visited a Sunday-only Chinese language school that I call Meiguo Chinese Academy, where moral education is part of Chinese language studies and authentic folk stories and historical narratives are taught with a moral message to instill ethnic pride and personal convictions.

I approached my school visits using some of the methods that anthropologists use when they are doing ethnographic studies. As an ethnographer, I adopted a nonjudgmental stance, and I took extensive notes on the conversations I heard, the student-teacher interactions, the different classroom settings, and the overall atmosphere in each school building. By looking at documents from each school (admissions brochures, student newspapers, Web sites), I was able to gather data about how the school presents itself in official terms before seeing daily life and the many informal moments of a school day.[31] When I visited each school, I would observe several classes, passing through the halls with my host students or teachers. I often found that by the time of my second visit, a few students would recognize me and even wave to me in a friendly greeting. This meant that I was less of a curiosity, so I could trust that students were acting naturally around me. Most of the students and adults I met at each school could function as *key informants,* that is, they were not outliers; they were comfortable speaking about their schools and about their own personal values, and others regarded them as effective representatives of their schools.[32] I occasionally became a participant observer, joining in a few classroom and hallway conversations, but the limited time I had in each school required me to stay focused on taking copious descriptive notes that I could use later on when I would begin to prepare this book. My findings are presented in a series of vignettes, inspired in part by the work of Sara Lawrence Lightfoot, who created vivid portraits of schools and who has developed a methodology called *Portraiture* for crafting her ethnographic findings into a coherent picture of a place and the people in it.[33]

THREE MORAL OUTLOOKS

Morality is a multidimensional feature of human life involving feelings, behavior, and ideas. The child-development expert Jerome Kagan identifies empathy, fear, and guilt as the earliest moral emotions that begin to shape a child's life. By adolescence, young people begin to integrate what they have learned and experienced, and they develop their own moral philosophy.[34] Morality in one culture may be very different from morality in another culture or in another region of the world. Even within the same teenage culture in the United States, moral attitudes vary from one school to another. In light of the many different institutional and personal voices that I encountered, I found that I tended to hear three different sets of moral ideas, themes, and language. I will introduce them briefly here, and I will expand on them later in the coming pages.

The first moral outlook may be considered the most traditional: institutions that bear this outlook tend to be standard-bearers for a cause or for a tradition. Students and teachers who share this outlook speak with confidence about their faith, their expectations from others, and about their sense of responsibility. I call this outlook "Authentic and Assured."

I call the second moral outlook "Bridging and Binding" to describe those who agree on a commitment both to tradition and to the development of their own independent voices. Students and teachers learn and speak the language of their respective traditions, while also seeking to figure out how to negotiate conflicts between the tradition and contemporary life. Their approach to precedent is in keeping with the 20th-century rabbi and scholar Mordechai Kaplan, who saw individual religious observance as an indication of one's commitments to the community.[35]

The most liberal of the three outlooks may also be seen as the most permissive, so I call it "Constructing and Considering." People with this outlook strive to articulate their own values and voices. Driven less by a sense of obligation to the community, and less by tradition, Constructing and Considering people are moved to say yes and to respond to the needs and factors in the moment, even if that response may contradict or go against the grain of tradition or precedent. Critics may call this permissive outlook the least principled, while others may find Constructing and Considering people to be the most creative because of their flexibility. Freedom from a tradition allows for new combinations of ideas, like people I know who combine the Eastern physical and religious discipline of yoga with the Western religious discipline of regular Jewish prayer.

Just as there is no single school that is more successful than any other, especially now, with so many different approaches to education, I believe also that there is no single most successful approach to moral education. The three outlooks introduced in this book describe and express the aspirations and ideals of different communities. My research leads me to feel concerned that the pressure on schools to prepare students for standardized testing may be limiting student opportunities for open-ended, broad discussions about moral issues. Although one may criticize private, parochial, and charter schools and accuse them of undermining the melting-pot ideal in American society by drawing students away from public schools, they tend to be freed up from the constraints that public schools face. Students at private and parochial schools enjoy the luxury of being able to spend the extra day on a study of the Civil War, to wrestle with questions about the long-term impact of slavery and Reconstruction in American history, or to study the human reproductive cycle in biology classes and to discuss birth control, abortion, and child rearing.

STRUCTURE OF THE BOOK

In chapter 1, "Did You Ask a Good Question Today? Questions at the Heart of Moral Education," I introduce what I refer to as the heart of moral education: questions in the classroom and expressions from teachers of moral right and caring. Chapter 2 introduces the three moral outlooks that I observed and came to understand at the schools I visited. Using examples from my interviews of students, teachers, and administrators, chapters 3, 4, and 5 introduce these three outlooks: Authentic and Assured, Bridging and Binding, and Constructing and Considering.

In chapter 6, "Play: Getting into Character," I explore ways in which play represents an essential form of moral education that transcends institutional loyalty and any single moral outlook. After teaching at a variety of levels for over 20 years, it wasn't until I became a full-time middle school teacher that I discovered the effectiveness of play in stimulating character development. Play allows children to traverse the safe and meaningful zone between a world of rules and authority on one side, and a world of chaos and anarchy on the other side. When children play, they exercise different ideas, trying them on, discarding them, ultimately deciding which ideas and values to keep. Schools provide moral education of the deepest sort when they allow children to test their commitments, to develop their identities, and to challenge one another in the classroom, out on the fields, and in extracurricular activities. Teachers can provide feedback to young people and help them to stretch their imaginations, to learn to work with others, and to enter new areas of knowledge. Students may come to experience moral education the way they approach a game they haven't played before: anxious to learn the rules, excited about new challenges, eager to excel, and happy to identify with success. Teachers who feel empowered both to nurture a sense of play and to be role models and agents of their students' moral development may discover that their words have inspired children to become a Branch Rickey or a Jackie Robinson who acts with moral fiber when the opportunity presents itself.

I hope that this book helps to reopen the excitement of inquiry, open-ended moral questions, and play that foster the development of young moral actors who grow into adults of character.

Did You Ask a Good Question Today? Questions at the Heart of Moral Education

Isidor I. Rabi, the Nobel laureate in physics was once asked, "Why did you become a scientist, rather than a doctor or lawyer or businessman, like the other immigrant kids in your neighborhood? 'My mother made me a scientist without ever intending it. Every other Jewish mother in Brooklyn would ask her child after school: 'Nu? Did you learn anything today?' But not my mother. She always asked me a different question. 'Izzy,' she would say, 'Did you ask a good question today?' That difference—asking good questions—made me become a scientist.'"

—Donald Sheff, *"Letter to the Editor,"* New York Times, *January 19, 1988*

Imagine yourself walking through the hubbub of a middle school or high school, noticing the hubbub when classes are changing and stopping by the busy classrooms along the hallways. Some classes are tackling math problems, while others are conducting science experiments, listening to folk music and contemporary music, and developing vocabulary in a foreign language. When you poke your head inside some of the classrooms, you glimpse student-teacher interchanges that are quick and provocative and that raise moral issues. You also hear quite a few interchanges about sitting up straight, about not forgetting to do the homework, and about making sure that pencils and pens and notebooks are ready. Some teachers may have dimmed the lights to highlight the computer projectors, and some laptops are powering up. And now as you walk by eight classrooms, you observe moral education in eight creative and different ways:

Claryce, ¡Por favor! It is wonderful if you already know the answers, but please be patient and don't call out vocabulary words even when you know them! ¡Ahora! Roberto: commençar, por favor.

Sydney, would you please explain what scientists have learned about how human activities have been harming the environment?

Kyle, how do you think the experience of slavery shaped African American art and music?

Rosa, now that we have looked at the Declaration of Independence, how do you think Thomas Jefferson was informed by religious beliefs when he wrote about "inalienable rights"?

Keisha, do you think there is a finite number for pi? Can you imagine a universe in which pi has a definite value?

Daniel, do you know what has happened to Siddhu? He hasn't been here since Monday. Since you live near him, would you please bring today's homework to him when you get home? And tell him we miss him!

Fa-Ping, how would you describe the evolving friendship between Piggy and Ralph in Lord of the Flies? Is it a friendship based on convenience, politics, or mutual affection?

Jean-Paul, I see you are napping! Please wake up and conjugate our verb in the future perfect tense! You must pay better attention next time!

I will admit that in the final comment to Jean-Paul, conjugating a verb does not constitute a form of moral education, though the study of a foreign culture is part of one's moral development, and the way in which a teacher criticizes a student raises moral issues as well! The first six examples here involving Claryce, Sydney, Kyle, Rosa, Keisha, and Daniel are more typical of moral education that is deliberate and planned by the teacher.

This imaginary walk through a school helps to introduce moral education as a process, not a product. When I walk through a school and when I enter a class, I listen for these kinds of interchanges that demand different levels of student involvement. Not only do they have to understand the facts and central ideas around each topic they are studying, but they also have to stretch into areas of experience and thought that might not always be comfortable.

FOUR TYPES OF QUESTIONS

While doing doctoral research, Katherine Simon of Stanford University, identified four kinds of moral questions and activities that took place in the classroom. She describes the four general kinds of moral questions in her book *Moral Questions in the Classroom*:

1. Questions about behavior
2. Questions about the meaning of human existence
3. Questions about things unknown
4. Questions about universal existential concerns and principles[1]

Once we start looking closely at the kinds of questions teachers ask students, we can see how often moral issues arise in everyday classrooms. When the teacher asks Claryce to be patient and, in effect, for Claryce to be less demanding, it is a matter of classroom conduct, common courtesy, and reasonableness. From a practical standpoint, the teacher cannot afford to lavish so much attention on just one student. On a deeper level, the teacher is asking the student to be kind, generous, mindful and ethical toward others. The question to Sydney about the environment calls into question the moral behavior of our species in the larger communities of the plant and animal kingdoms.

Simon's second area of questions includes the teacher's question to Kyle, in which he is asked to enter the mind of a slave and to imagine how deprivation and the loss of dignity find expression in music and art. When the teacher asks Rosa about rights and about Jefferson's religious beliefs, Rosa has to consider a weighty existential issue: why does human existence require a sense of entitlement for inalienable rights, including "life, liberty and the pursuit of happiness"? By raising these issues of human dignity and civil rights, the teacher opens up the possibility that other moral questions will arise about the degree to which lawmakers show respect for the humanity of others and whether our society maximizes the ability of each citizen to thrive.

Simon's third area of questions, questions about things unknown, may seem more like speculation than like a category of moral inquiry. These kinds of questions engender a sense of humility as a student confronts the limits and extent of knowledge; they can inspire a sense of wonder about what is possible for an individual to know and to accomplish. In a faith-based school, these kinds of questions might foster a sense of awe and an appreciation for the good in the world. Like the teacher's question to Keisha about a finite number for *pi*, questions with unknown answers stretch students' minds, sometimes leading to questions about good and evil. These kinds of questions and conversations may be rare, and most math classes I have observed focus on teaching students how to find a known answer, not an unknown answer. Nevertheless, when students experience unanswerable and open-ended questions, they experience a lack of certainty that illuminates something about the human condition. Many contemporary novels and earlier works, such as Goethe's poem *Dr. Faustus,* are about the wicked bargains people are willing to make to learn something that usually sits beyond their reach.

When the teacher asks about Siddhu, the teacher shows that a school exists not only to impart academic information but also to reinforce a child's citizenship in a community. By charting a student's attendance or truancy, a school not only fulfills city and state laws, but it also makes sure that each child can be valued and held accountable. When teachers become involved by showing concern, they teach a moral lesson that the classroom constitutes a small community that is diminished by the absence of any one citizen. It is an everyday example of Simon's fourth category of moral questions, questions about universal existential concerns and principles, because Daniel is being asked to come forward as Siddhu's friend and classmate. To give a deeper example of this category, picture the question to Fa-Ping about the relationship between Piggy and Ralph, or imagine an even more complicated question, asking a student to consider the despair and hate felt by the boys lost on the island in William Golding's *Lord of the Flies*.[2] These kinds of questions leave room for interpretation, and although one answer may not necessarily be more correct than another, they lead students to consider weighty issues that could have an impact on their own understanding of friendship, love, hate, conflict, and peace.

These kinds of moral questions are sticky and sometimes awkward, not only because there are no correct answers to questions about rights and about the feelings we project onto people who lived long before our own time, but also because sometimes the answers to these kinds of questions may be contradictory. Sometimes, one might argue, everyone should be entitled to enjoy life, liberty, and the pursuit of happiness. During World War II, however, the opposite was true: the concern for security led young people to feel patriotic about giving up the feeling of entitlement when they blackened their windows and saved wrappers and rubber tires; the same concern for security also led to the unconscionable incarceration of Asians in American internment camps.

Students and teachers are not always ready for far-reaching questions with serious moral implications. In an era dominated by standardized tests that require a single answer, some level of impatience is inevitable, especially if the class bell rings right in the middle of a student comment, cutting off discussion just when things are getting good. It can be challenging for a teacher to launch and then to wrap up a far-reaching conversation in the 40- to 50-minute period that is typical of most American middle and high schools. From a moral education perspective, however, these kinds of questions are worth asking because they engage students deeply by asking them to come to terms with an understanding of the human experience. When these kinds of questions arise in the context of the academic curriculum, the questions may be abstract, but they are not tangential at all.[3]

There are times when students turn the tables, raising moral issues for their teachers to consider. Students often have a knack for putting their teachers on the spot with stealthy and insightful questions. Here are some questions with moral overtones that students might pose during the course of a day in school:

> *Mrs. Cavalieri, why didn't Abraham Lincoln fight harder to free the slaves sooner in his administration, and then 100 years later, why did President John F. Kennedy wait for more than two years before doing much about civil rights?*
>
> *Dr. Dimmock, if Marie Curie knew that her discovery of radium could produce dangerous results that might make herself and other people sick, why didn't she stop what she was doing?*
>
> *Ms. Chen, why do the French make so many words masculine instead of feminine? And why did Napoleon change the French calendar and the names of the months?*

Each of these questions projects a student's curiosity, and if Mrs. Cavalieri and Dr. Dimmock and Ms. Chen were to give straightforward and factual responses, then they probably would satisfy the average student. After all, Lincoln did not fight to end slavery in the early days of his presidential administration because he did not want to lose his political allies or an opportunity possibly to bring the South back into the Union. Dr. Dimmock could attribute Marie Curie's scientific pursuits to sheer determination, and Ms. Chen could dismiss the student's question as a diversion from the real business of language study, and she could attribute Napoleon's actions to delusions of grandeur.

Alternatively, these three teachers could listen to these questions as moral questions. Mrs. Cavalieri could speak about the ambivalence of many in the early 19th century about slavery and about whether the slaves living on plantations should be entitled to the same rights and privileges as their white masters or the whites living in the North. Dr. Dimmock could speak to the ways in which people sometimes are willing to sacrifice themselves for a cause, be it scientific or political. And Ms. Chen could speak about the dangers of power and about the unique ways in which language study enables us to glimpse other cultures.

Katherine Simon discusses these kinds of questions in her book in the chapter "We Could Argue About That All Day," recalling the moments when students raise questions of a moral nature that often have to be set aside. Teachers face pressures to keep covering new material and to prepare students for classroom and state-mandated tests, so they may feel reluctant to open up controversial topics that could lead to conflict. To be fair, teachers may defer discussion also because they feel that the students do not have enough background information to respond to one another from a knowledgeable position. Simon concludes, "It seems to be neither pedagogically nor politically easy to dedicate class time to discussions that are controversial yet constructive, flexible yet focused, and grounded in what matters morally and existentially as well as in factual evidence."[4]

EACH SCHOOL HAS ITS OWN APPROACH

Moral education takes place not only in the questions that fly between teachers and students, but also in the presence (or lack thereof) of a school's institutional leadership. The Moral Life of Schools project, led by Philip W. Jackson and several partners, spent countless hours in classrooms, hallways, and in conversations with school leaders. The findings of the Moral Life of Schools project are worth discussing at length here. The authors of the project came to identify eight levels, or categories, of moral instruction and behavior in school. Parents may recognize these categories from visits to their children's classrooms, assemblies, athletic events, performances, recess periods, and graduation ceremonies. Here are the eight categories of moral instruction with descriptions drawn from my observations at a variety of schools:

1. *Moral instruction as a formal part of the curriculum.* Faith-based schools often include courses of study in the sponsoring faith tradition; secular schools may offer courses on ethics or life issues without necessarily giving preference to a single ethical tradition. At the Al-Quds Islamic Academy in Philadelphia, for example, students take a class called Islamic Studies, in which they learn about Muslim moral and ethical traditions. At the Academy of the Sisters of St. Theresa, a Roman Catholic K–8 school, also in the Philadelphia area, students take classes in religious studies, in which they study the Bible and learn about Roman Catholic traditions.

2. *Moral instruction within the regular curriculum.* At the Hanford Day School in New York City, students also devoted time in their English classes to the moral implications of war as part of their study of the Vietnam War novel *The Things They Carried.* Similarly, in a class in Language Arts at the Jerusalem School in Philadelphia, students read from the text of a play about Anne Frank and her family, who hid from the Nazis in a small apartment, pausing every few minutes to discuss how they might have behaved if they had been under a similar level of duress.

3. *Rituals and ceremonies.* At John Adams High School in New York City, the year begins with a recitation of the Ephebic Oath, an oath in which young people

pledge citizenship and integrity, following the text of an oath adapted from ancient Greek society. At the Jerusalem School, as part of the morning prayer services that take place every day during the school's second period, students have opportunities to offer musical interpretations, discuss current events, develop Hebrew prayer skills, and share insights from other Jewish literature.

4. *Visual displays with moral content.* Students at Haym Solomon High School in Philadelphia regularly walk to the nearby Joe Louis Elementary School, where they pair up with 2nd graders in reading activities. The halls and classrooms at Joe Louis are decorated with many large posters guiding students in appropriate behavior and exhorting them to stretch their minds and strive to learn new things every day.

5. *Spontaneous interjections of moral commentary into on-going activity.* During the reading activity at Joe Louis Elementary School, "Mr. Wesley," the lead high school teacher from Haym Solomon High School, offered a supervisory presence along with words of encouragement as he circulated throughout the room, affirming the ways in which the older students were positive role models for the younger students. At John Adams High School in New York City, the Latin teacher offered solace to his students struggling through a conjugation when he said, "Mastering Latin is like mastering brain surgery—it requires a lot of discipline." And then, wryly acknowledging that the rewards don't come in a paycheck, he added, "The problem is there isn't as much money in it." He also made a reference to cheating, reminding his students not to cheat while he distributed a quiz to his 10th-grade students. Moments of moral instruction occur throughout the school day, in the ways in which teachers establish and cultivate order and in the ways in which they use the curriculum to lead students in an exploration of issues of ethics and meaning. The apparent degree of trust and honesty between teachers and students also reveals a great deal about the moral climate of a school.

Jackson and his coauthors describe three other areas that serve as barometers for a school's moral life:

6. *Classroom rules and regulations.* At Joe Louis Elementary School, where high school students were tutoring the Joe Louis 2nd graders, and at Amesbury High School, a suburban high school about 35 miles outside of New York City, each room displayed the school rules for students to see (and presumably follow). At both schools, it is fair to assume that the teachers introduced the rules to the students at the beginning of the year and that once the year was underway, students could look at the walls for reminders of their own responsibilities and their teacher's expectations.

7. *The morality of curricular substructure.* At some Jewish day schools, the schedule gives priority to Jewish studies by holding those classes in the morning and by holding classes in general studies (such as English, history,

mathematics, science, and foreign languages) in the afternoon. In contrast, at the Jewish day schools where I have taught and served as an administrator, classes for all subjects were not restricted to any particular time of day, because the school did not want to prejudice one field over the other. As a result, a student can have a Bible class in between classes in evolutionary biology and world history. The structure of the curriculum and the schedule reflect a moral view about hierarchies of knowledge and the way in which students are expected to absorb each subject.

8. *Expressive morality within the classroom.* Teachers give expression to moral ideas constantly during the course of the day, sometimes directly and sometimes in subtle ways. The kindly tone of voice that Mr. Hurley uses with his students at the Academy of the Sisters of St. Theresa communicates concern, patience, and genuine affection for his student, and his students praise his accessibility and his standing as a moral role model.

Back-to-school nights and parent-teacher conferences can't convey the moral life of a school the way daytime classroom observations can. For those who have an opportunity to visit a school during the daytime, I recommend following the same process I follow when I want to gauge the moral life of a classroom: I look around at the classroom walls to see in what ways the teacher has created the setting for a productive atmosphere, and I observe classroom decorum to see in what ways the teacher establishes discipline and positive relationships with the students. When teachers correct students on their behavior and on their responses to questions of content, do the students look as if they are beleaguered, or do they look as if they are being given a fair chance? As a class period unfolds, I am interested to ask if the curriculum is oriented around college preparatory tests or state-mandated tests, or does the curriculum nurture intellectual inquiry from a variety of angles? Does class time allow for direct moral instruction, or does moral instruction take place on the side only when time allows? Do rules seem to exist for their own sake, or do they have support from a mission statement or from unifying moral principles? And when teachers give praise, does the praise feel genuine or insincere? How does the school present itself to outsiders, and how does it receive and then introduce new students to the school culture at whatever point they enter?[5]

KEEPING OUR TERMS STRAIGHT: MORAL EDUCATION, CHARACTER EDUCATION, AND RELIGIOUS EDUCATION

In public discussions, the terms "character" and "morality" may seem interchangeable, as if they refer to the same set of issues. It is easy to confuse the two terms while speaking about character education and moral education. To muddy the waters further, the terms cannot be isolated, because both depend on the other. Good character education cannot exist without strong morals, and strong morals are lived out in good character. Character education and moral education require the involvement of public leaders, parents, educators, and, ultimately, the students themselves.

Moral education is a broad field, and, as noted earlier, it can involve ethics and personal behavior, questions about dignity and civil rights, unknowns and mysteries, and meaning and values. A commitment to moral education might inspire a biology unit on politics and the environment; a unit that introduces literature of reflection; and debates in history classes when students analyze great decisions and leadership. In some faith-based settings, moral education aims to indoctrinate, and in other faith-based settings and in secular school settings, moral education may be part of an open process that doesn't necessarily lead students to a single conclusion.

This presents a complicated curricular challenge for any group of educators, citizens, and young people to identify an ideal set of values and character traits that should become part of a school's formal and informal educational program. In a pluralistic nation such as the United States, where there are already competing demands for high levels of achievement in the arts, sciences, and languages, some see moral education, character education, and religious education as vehicles for curricular enrichment, but others may see those fields as threatening academic freedom by establishing the answers before each child can answer the set of moral questions for himself or herself.

Professor Thomas Lickona of the State University of New York, Cortland, writes passionately about moral education, calling for recognition of the "clear and urgent need" for values education. In the present time, in which families have been playing less of a role in the moral development of children, it is essential that schools provide moral education.[6] Professor Emeritus Larry Nucci of the University of Chicago argues that moral education should not avoid highly charged topics. He writes that moral education needs to include large philosophical and universal moral concepts such as human welfare, justice, and compassion.[7]

Character education can take place at any moment and in any classroom, because it can shape a child's outlook regardless of the subject matter being taught. Even in the heat of a conflict, a middle school principal I know once said that she saw her job as teaching young people how to be oppositional without losing a sense of courtesy. It is in their nature to be oppositional, she conceded, but the school could help them to develop their character by encouraging them at least to behave "oppositional courteously."[8] Teachers are in a unique position to help students each day, sometimes to establish a set of values and sometimes to activate values that will carry them through new—and sometimes uncomfortable—situations.

One's moral framework is shaped in a community. As Ryan and Bohlin write, "By engaging students in moral discourse, they learn to take moral themes seriously and to take others seriously, listening to and considering thoughtfully what each of them says."[9] Or, as William Damon writes, moral education promotes reasoning that enables a student "to apply basic moral values to unfamiliar problems, and to create moral solutions when there is no one around to give the child direction." He adds that it is likely that we all believe that children need to avoid drugs and dangerous situations, but we may not be able to touch upon every single issue. Instead, we can promote "the ability to detect moral issues in complex situations."[10] The psychiatrist Robert Coles relates a good working definition of character that is based on personal strength and not on external feedback: "Character meant being kind and good, even when there was no one to reward you for being kind and good."[11]

Good character (honesty, integrity, courage, etc.) is not restricted to any single moral outlook. Character produces an attitude, a stance, and a way of entering into a situation. Joan Goodman and Howard Lesnick's fictional character Hardie Knox offers a particularly helpful definition of character to his junior colleague Maria Laszlo:

> To me, character traits are connected to moral activity, but not the same as it. To use an overworked analogy, character traits—well-established, permanent, structural capacities—are like the computer's hard drive, whereas moral acts—diversified, contextually complex, requiring flexibility—are its programs. Character is often morally neutral. I mean we say benevolence and respect are good, but as you obviously know benevolence can become infantilization, respect can become blind suspicion and courage can be used to ignoble ends. Character traits for me are dispositions.[12]

It seems that some dispositions, such as a tendency to cheerfulness, shyness, or even an inclination toward risk-taking may be inborn and difficult to acquire, and it seems that some other dispositions, such as the inclination to be honest and to find willpower in times of uncertainty can be taught. Students can be taught about character traits, acquire them and then incorporate those traits into their personal disposition. Neither character nor morality comes to full expression without being tested, lived, and experienced. This is consistent with the ideas of John Dewey, the pre-eminent early 20th century educational philosopher, who wrote that morality "is as much a matter of interaction of a person with his social environment as walking is an interaction of legs with a physical environment."[13] In a similar vein, Professor Nucci sees character as a description of the self. It is "not a constellation of personality traits or virtues, but, rather, the operation of the moral aspects of the self in relation to the self as a whole."[14]

There are choices that adults face throughout the years for which they are unprepared. Even a school with a great character education program that focuses on a different character trait each year cannot prepare students for every kind of moment, but it is possible for teachers to help students to establish a set of values for guidance in new situations.

Educators who wish to strengthen character education in their schools have many tools available to them. Thomas Lickona and several colleagues developed a handbook for school leaders and teachers who wish to bring their commitment to character education not only to each classroom but also to each school community. Character education isn't meant to serve only a narrow goal of cultivating courage and honesty and other virtues. As Professor Lickona wrote to me in an e-mail, character education encompasses a broad outlook that has to be part of a child's moral education: "We think of 'character development' as, at least ideally, being the broader process, since we define character to encompass knowing, feeling, and doing—the head, the heart, and the hand."[15]

To answer to the obvious question about what morals and values a school should teach, Lickona cites the ancient philosopher Aristotle who described good character "as the life of right conduct—right conduct in relation to other persons and in relation to oneself."[16] In this competitive and test-focused era in which character education might seem less important than, say, science education, Lickona offers 10 reasons why character education is more important than ever in one of his most influential books, *Educating for Character*:

1. There is a clear and urgent need.
2. Transmitting values is and always has been the work of civilization.
3. The school's role as moral educator becomes even more vital at a time when millions of children get little moral teaching from their parents and where value-centered influences such as church or temple are also absent from their lives.
4. There is common ethical ground even in our value-conflicted society.
5. Democracies have a special need for moral education, because democracy is government by the people themselves.
6. There is no such thing as values-free education.
7. The great questions facing both the individual person and the human race are moral questions.

8. There is broad-based growing support for values education in the schools.
9. An unabashed commitment to moral education is essential if we are to attract and keep good teachers.
10. Values education is a doable job.[17]

Focusing not only on values, but also on virtues, Kevin Ryan and Karen E. Bohlin, in their book, *Building Character in Schools: Practical Ways to Bring Moral Instruction to Life*, present ways in which schools can implement programs that cultivate virtue. Although public schools are not in a position to prescribe that students hold any one particular moral outlook, they can cultivate virtues in the students. As Ryan and Bohlin write, virtues and virtuous behavior provides "the social glue we need to survive together peaceably." To illustrate this, the authors describe a school in Arizona with a motto that promotes three virtues beginning with the letter, "P." Students at the school aspire to live out Purpose, Pride, and Performance. Virtues such as honesty and a sense of responsibility have the capacity to fuel many kinds of thoughtful action.[18] While anybody can give a dollar to a homeless person or plant a tree on a whim, if opportunities to develop character in the classroom are created and practiced, then those "P" virtues will be meaningful.

There are times when schools and communities create and enforce standards of behavior that represent conventions and customs, though they are upheld, sometimes enforced and sometimes celebrated as if they represent moral values. Moral education involves philosophical principles such as fairness and tolerance, while conventions involve agreed-upon customs from dress codes to rules for behavior during assemblies. Schools may give their conventions a layer of moral meaning, calling the dress code, for example, a set of rules designed to elevate students' morals, putting students on the same level to reduce competition. Since one school's dress code may be more or less formal than another, one is no more correct than another, so both are conventions that simply reinforce the values of a school or religious community.[19] At one school I visited, for example, students were expected to keep their hair neat and their shirts tucked in as part of an effort to promote values of self-care, respectful conduct, and dignity. Boys who had hair down to their shoulders were questioned about their ability to conform and to follow school guidelines. Most of the time, the school encouraged independent thinking, but in this case, when it came to discussions about the dress code, it was important that students follow the school rules. There is nothing necessarily moral about hair guidelines and dress codes; they represent conventions that adults and families agree to uphold when they enroll in the school, reinforcing the school or religious community.[20]

As Larry Nucci explored these connections between conventions, faith, and morality, he heard a particularly interesting perspective from an Amish boy whom he calls Joseph. The young man spoke about religious conventions that he believes have a moral meaning. In Joseph's community, the young man explained, if a girl does not wear a head covering, it would be considered a refusal to submit to God. Joseph said, "Well, in the Bible it says that the woman is supposed to keep her head covered and I think that if a girl is going by the standards of the Bible, then she should wear it." Later he spoke about the powerful theology behind his community's unusual dress, saying that it is a witness to the power of God; he and other Amish behave in ways that help them to identify more with God than with other people in the secular world.[21] The reader may wonder where in the Bible it says that women should cover their hair; is it a direct commandment or is it an interpretation of a passage in the Hebrew Bible or in the Christian New Testament? Whatever the origins of the custom, Joseph believes that the convention of head coverings holds moral meaning about submission to God and about group identification. To draw an analogy about conventions from public life, at a baseball game there is nothing necessarily moral about the convention of wearing a baseball hat. It might be to cover a bad hair day, to keep the sun off of one's head or out of one's eyes, or to express an affiliation with a particular team. In the Amish community, however, the convention of a head covering is the fulfillment of moral education about women's roles and about modesty toward God.

Religious education does not necessarily exclude humanistic values and virtues such as honesty and courage, but it is grounded in traditions and beliefs about God and personal destiny, and it seeks to elevate the individual to develop personal faith and / or religious practice. Some faith-based schools begin the process of moral education through units on value concepts such as charity, while other faith-based schools begin religious studies with faith concepts and rituals. Morality is closely tied to religion, so in some faith-based schools, religious beliefs serve as a foundation for moral education, and children learn to talk about God and then to act on those beliefs. In other faith-based schools, it is the opposite, and moral education serves as a springboard for religious beliefs, and through action the children come to believe in a divine power that is behind them and that inspires them to continue to do good. Harry Wong and Rosemary Wong write that teachers in secular schools and religious schools alike replicate a biblical dynamic in the first days of school when they present themselves as authority figures who have the power of judgment and academic knowledge. They explain that when teachers call young people on their behavior, raising issues of sin and repentance, rebellion and authority, falsehood and truth, the same issues that are at the root of the divine-human relationship in the first chapters of the biblical Book of Genesis.[22]

Robert Coles explores how children from Jewish, Christian, and Muslim families describe their own faith and desire to submit to God in two of his well-known books, *The Moral Life of Children* and in *The Spiritual Life of Children*. He found a close connection between religious faith and moral behavior among children from many different faith traditions. In *The Moral Life of Children*, Coles thoughtfully describes the remarkable steps taken by six-year-old Ruby Bridges who crossed the proverbial Color Line and an actual line of racist protesters in 1960 to integrate an elementary school in New Orleans, Louisiana. On her first walk to the school, Robert Coles describes her having such strong moral fiber that she prayed for the people who were taunting her.[23] In *The Spiritual Life of Children*, a girl named Ilona speaks about this from a Jewish perspective when she said, "God wants us to do all we can to make the world just a little better while we're here."[24] In the same book, a Muslim child speaks about heaven as a reward from God: "You only go to heaven if you've proven to Allah that you belong there, and it's hard to get there, because He won't let you in unless He *knows* you're good, and you believe what He wants you to believe, and you bow to Him, and if He wants you to do something, you do it, and you don't complain."[25] These three girls from the three most prominent monotheistic faith traditions draw from their beliefs about God to help them not only to survive, but also to behave with high moral standards.

The religious studies curricula that I observed at the Jewish, Roman Catholic, and Muslim schools all tended to be organized around textual studies (scriptural and other scholarly writings) and instruction about proper observance of religious rites. Moral education was part of the religious studies curriculum at each school through informal channels in advisory programs, in everyday teacher-student interactions, and also in more formal channels that allow teachers to work with students on issues of character and behavior. Religious education is one of a few ways for someone to learn to become a decent person while also feeling elevated in the relationship with the larger community.[26]

Of these three processes—character education, moral education and religious education—did one evolve before the other? One can imagine moral education in a field, on a hunt, while preparing food, while learning how to take care of children, and, one might even say, from the first moments of life while a child was surrounded by friends and family who felt a deep investment in the child's well-being and development. Even in the present era, when farms are fewer and day-care programs are more common, families and communities still play a significant role in the educational process. William Damon, an influential thinker in moral education, considers a child's respect for parental authority to be "the single most important moral legacy" of the child-parent relationship because it establishes a precedent for the child's relationship with other adults during the early years before adulthood and citizenship.[27]

As much as a school institutionalizes policies and practices that promote the moral development of children through character education, moral education, and religious education, the moral guidance and instruction that children receive at home continues to remain a primary frame of reference. In today's world, parents set moral expectations when they ask children to assume responsibility for picking up their own toys, attending to their own hygiene, and, later, when they are asked to contribute to the family through yard work, food shopping and through bringing money home from paying jobs. After reading books about early American life and after listening to stories from grandparents about life during the Great Depression of the 1930s, my own children have pointed out that today's tame household jobs (emptying a dishwasher or folding a load of laundry, for example) seem more like a nuisance than a moral responsibility. Mowing the lawn does not seem as essential to the family welfare as mowing hay, chopping wood, and feeding the coal stove, the kinds of chores children did in earlier eras.

Schools function as moral systems in which there are appropriate roles that need to be fulfilled both in the informal curriculum and in the formal curriculum. Schools can cultivate virtue in several domains, from hallways to study halls, cafeterias, and, of course, classrooms. Moral education does not need to wait for a special assembly or for the principal; it can take place within a school at any moment. Parents looking at a school need to remember that moral education needs to be age appropriate. Even the most earnest and well-meaning teacher may not be able to help a 10-year-old understand that fair doesn't necessarily mean the same thing as equal and that it might be fair for one student to have six questions to answer while another student only has two. At the high school level, a 15-year-old might not be ready to understand some of the abstract issues of constitutional justice, but she might be ready to understand that certain laws protect the rights of minorities.

Each school needs to establish how to carry its mission forward and implement character education, moral education or religious education. Some curricula are content-based, focusing on history and then turning a student's attention outward, and some are more personal, asking students to draw from their experiences and from their imaginations while they develop faith, a moral outlook, and a strong character. It is not enough to agree that moral education is important; educators have to make major curricular decisions that will shape what happens in classrooms, hallways, cafeterias, and athletic fields.

CURRICULAR INITIATIVES

Facing History and Ourselves is one such curriculum that teaches historical material appropriate for standard history classes required by schools while also
fostering moral-reasoning skills in students. The program, first developed in
the 1970s, introduces students to the causes, events, and implications of Nazi
brutality as it unfolded in Europe from the 1920s to the 1940s. The curriculum focuses not only on the destruction of European Jews, Roma, Jehovah's
Witnesses, homosexuals, and people of conscience, as any historical program
should, but it also explores the implications of being a bystander while democracy is challenged and undermined. Students explore the implications of
personal power and political power. Jan Darsa, the director of Jewish Education for Facing History and Ourselves, describes the moral implications of the
curriculum:

> Having students think about how their identity is formed, their core values,
> and the factors that push them off their moral centers are questions with which
> adolescents are grappling. When teens contemplate the moral decision-making
> of that period—by looking at the roles of victim, bystander, perpetrator, rescuer
> and resister—they begin to see themselves as players in a historical process, and
> they understand their role and responsibility as citizens in the society in which
> they live.[28]

The students participate in content-oriented moral discussion that may not
always have clear answers when they are faced with some of the dilemmas
around personal survival and Nazi power. These kinds of discussions have
the capacity to shape students' character at the same time that the students
acquire a body of knowledge about a tragic and complicated series of events
during wartime a few decades ago.

The Jerusalem School implements a program called *Second Step* for health
and moral education through the lower school and continuing into the middle school. Based in lower school homerooms and middle school advisory
groups, classroom teachers (not just the school counselors) lead students in
discussions about empathy, self-advocacy, problem solving, and healthy decision making. The program takes its name, *Second Step*, from the idea that
one's First Step takes place at home, while the Second Step is taken at school
with nonfamily teachers and peers.[29] As I have grown accustomed to visiting
schools and to seeing young people making decisions, extending friendships,
and learning new things, I often have wished that I could visit their homes to
see how families foster the moral development of their children.

Another character education program, *The Responsive Classroom*, developed in Massachusetts and used in other areas of the United States, encourages students to develop social skills that will make them better learners and better members of the community. Debra Viadero describes the program as leading each student to "pledge every morning to 'play with everyone' and to 'treat others the way I want to be treated.' " She writes that researchers have found that students who participate in *The Responsive Classroom* with trained teachers strengthen their character in five areas: cooperation, assertion, responsibility, empathy, and self-control. The studies also have found a positive correlation between character development and academic achievement.[30] Kevin Ryan uses this correlation in a call to action that appeared in *Education Week:*

> [L]et us recognize the obvious link between good character and academic achievement. While some children are intellectually gifted, most have to pay attention, study the material, and do their homework carefully if they are to achieve in high school. These behaviors don't come naturally. They have to be practiced and gradually integrated into a person's character.
>
> . . . Don't wait around for years until some massively expensive research study reports the obvious: Students with the good habits that constitute good character do well in school.[31]

The Haym Solomon High School in Philadelphia uses an additional program called *Journey of a Champion,* initiated by an organization called Champions of Caring, founded by Barbara Greenspan Shaiman. Her family's experience of persecution in Nazi Europe inspired her to support the work of teenagers to improve the world and "to make our world a more caring and compassionate one." Students learn about women's suffrage in the United States, about resistance to North American slavery on the Underground Railroad, about the systematic destruction of European Jews during World War II, and about treatment of Asian Americans in the United States during the 20th century. Through service to others and study of their own communities, students gather enough information to consider how to overcome conflict, to bridge cultural differences, and to take on a leadership role.[32]

The success of these programs, whether *Second Step, The Responsive Classroom,* or *Journey of a Champion,* depends on the degree to which teachers establish a moral rapport with their students. One of the teachers who uses *The Responsive Classroom* regretted that she did not spend enough time on character education in the fall, so the time spent on more traditional academic material in her 5th-grade classroom was less successful, and the students were not able to learn as much.[33]

These character education programs like *Second Step* may be acclaimed for helping children to develop listening skills and self-advocacy skills, but they also can be criticized for putting students in awkward situations in which they role-play conflicts and resolutions that could unmask existing tensions among students. A teacher could unwittingly pair students together to role-play a theft scene or a gossip scene in which past experience might intrude, opening up old wounds that had never completely healed. The trigger films in each unit depict students from different ethnic groups that may lead to conversations about ethnic stereotypes instead of about bullying and bystander behavior. Teachers may not feel equipped to help students to talk about differences between ethnic groups and about the damaging stereotypes, so discussions can easily get out of hand if they are not monitored carefully. These limitations do not necessarily mean that *Facing History and Ourselves, Second Step,* and *The Responsive Classroom* should not be used; teachers simply have to be aware of the limitations and potential triggers to conflict and acknowledge them to the students.

In religious education, educators give children feedback in keeping with the conventions or rules of particular religious traditions, but in secular education they are not permitted to become advocates for particular religious traditions.[34] Importantly, this does not mean that teachers should create a morally neutral environment: William Damon writes that democratic society requires citizens who can "think, argue, and freely make choices. Schools can provide such relationships for their students, and indeed must do so if they are to be effective forums for moral education."[35] In moral education, as in character education and religious education, success rarely comes in measurable outcomes. A successful classroom inspires and welcomes questions. It cultivates habits of mind for young people to grow up and to know where to turn to answer their questions.

Character Studies: Three Moral Outlooks and the Role of Gender

A *moral outlook* is not just an opinion or a perspective on a particular issue, nor is it merely a personality or a set of preferences. A personality may be lively, bitter, outgoing, cautious, responsive, or absent-minded, and, due to one's personality, one may prefer vanilla to chocolate or rap music to classical music, but an outlook is more complicated, encompassing a combination of religious faith, political inclinations, and view of human nature. A moral outlook is close to a "sensibility," what David Hansen describes as a combination of emotions and reason. Hansen writes that a sensibility is "not like a tool that a teacher pulls out of a box and then replaces once she or he has done the sensible and sensitive thing."[1] A teacher's sensibility may be shaped by her emotional availability and sense of mission toward the students. A moral outlook, shaped by a sensibility, tends to be informed by community ideals about what should be taught, how it should be taught, and by the kind of thinking processes required for engagement in class.

There is a risk when a school asks its students to conform to a specific image or a single outlook. Teachers in a school may vary widely in their backgrounds, beliefs, and goals for their students. Students want to see themselves as original thinkers and not as conformists. I found a version of this phenomenon in the 1980s when I was working at the Carey School, a girls' school with a uniform requirement. The girls requested occasional cut days when they could come to school without having to wear the uniform skirt and top. "We want to express our individuality," one girl explained to me during my first year. The school conceded and gave them a once-a-month break from the uniform. On each official uniform cut day, nearly every girl was wearing jeans! I had to smile at the irony that the girls had exchanged one uniform for another, with one difference: the students had chosen the uniform of jeans, while the school had chosen the uniform skirt and the white Peter Pan–collar blouse. Of course no self-respecting teenager wants to be described as part of a trend, so I couldn't point out the irony to the students or they would have accused me of being patronizing. Instead, I came to conclude that teenagers love to see themselves as unique individuals, as young people with original ideas. Even if their *clothes* do seem to represent the interchangeable clothes of a generation, they don't want their *ideas* to be reduced or simplified.

At the risk of betraying those teenagers, I have concluded that it does not take away from a student's individuality if I describe groups of adolescents and their teachers not only by their clothes and their taste in music, sports, and books but also by their moral outlooks. I have found that the teenagers I have met over the last decade tend to cluster their values at one of three points along a continuum marked at one end by individualism and at the other end by a sense of obligation to the community. While any study has its limitations, I feel privileged to have heard students speak with integrity about their convictions.

As a parent, I know that I am privileged to hear some information from my children that they never would share with anybody else; as a teacher and researcher, I also know that students share things with me as an unrelated adult that they wouldn't share with their families. Young people (like adults!) censor themselves, too, especially when they are describing more risky behavior that has taken place out of sight of the adults who know them.

After sifting through transcripts and notes from my conversations with the adolescents and teachers I met, I believe that my findings will be helpful for parents, teachers, and others who spend time with adolescents. Once I began to hear and identify the differences from one student to another and from one teacher to another, I could begin to see the ways in which an outlook could inform learning and teaching from one classroom to another.

When I set out to complete research about moral education, I knew that I would find moral education taking place in a variety of modes (classroom interactions, hallway interactions, conversations among students, decorations on the wall), so each time I entered an unfamiliar school, I would quickly review my surroundings as a parent, teacher, and researcher. Like the archaeologist I worked for when I was in college who could show me a two-inch potsherd and extrapolate the shape of the pot and the level of technology of a culture, I found that by observing moments in the life of a school, I could gain a sense of the general atmosphere, school mission, and moral climate. Any parent preparing to send a child to kindergarten or to a new school at any level can take note of some of the same things that I did:

- How guests are welcomed and given credentials as visitors
- How adults speak with one another both in and out of earshot of students
- How adults speak to students in the halls
- Courtesy in the hallways, holding open the door, polite language
- The rise and fall of intellectual energy in the classrooms
- The rise and fall of classroom and hallway noise
- The engagement of students in classrooms
- The cleanliness and accessibility of public spaces
- The degree of comfort and psychological safety for the youngest students and for students on the social margins
- School spirit, whether expressed in announcements, in student activities, special clothing, or in hallway decorations
- Celebrations of student achievement in announcements, in classes, and in the hallways
- Parent involvement, whether appropriate or intrusive
- Intrusions from the school office, whether done at random times or on a set schedule, with a sense of humor or with an embattled tone
- And, perhaps, the most important question: Do teachers look like they care about their students and about the subjects they teach?

Some elements in a school culture are difficult to gauge on a first or even second visit. It takes some time to learn, for example, about the extent to which parents and administrators support the teachers in the school. Do they put pressure on the school to follow a particular ideology or to be more academic, more athletic, or more oriented toward the arts? Do parents tend to speak first with teachers when issues arise, or do the parents feel empowered to go straight to the principal's office when they feel that something is wrong? For parents whose children attend a public school, how do they feel about being in the particular school district, and for nonpublic school parents, did they choose their school for its location, program, or mission?

It can take time also to learn about the educational climate for teachers: To what degree do teachers feel pressure to raise their students' test scores? Do teachers have room to develop their own curricular materials and to answer their students' spontaneous questions? What are their relationships like with the students both inside and outside of the classroom walls?

Although some of these questions are beyond the scope of this book, I believe that a school's approach to moral education is a good indicator of the degree to which school leadership, faculty and staff, parents and students are all in agreement about the school mission and about how that mission is carried out. These pieces all contribute to an institutional outlook.

To learn about the moral outlooks of teachers and students, I briefly contemplated a method of study used by Mihaly Csikszentmihalyi and Reed Larson in their study of adolescent life. The authors gave pagers to their adolescent collaborators in the research, enabling them to go about their daily classes and activities unselfconsciously. The researchers checked in with the students by paging them at various intervals and by having them complete a brief timesheet describing what they were doing and how they were feeling, whether they were at home or at school, with their friends at night or on the weekends, or in transition from one activity to another.[2] Although I had to concede that my research would not allow me to achieve that level of intimacy with the students who participated in my research, I still aspired to achieve that level of trust with the students.

I began by listening to the student voices before imposing a scrim of theory between what they said and what I heard. Having listened to the students with an open mind before drawing my conclusions, I came to believe that the students were honest and that they were not trying to tell me what they thought I wanted to hear. In fact, one of the teachers declared that if the students had been modifying their stories in any way at all to impress me (which he doubted, anyway), the students might have been more likely to try to show off by telling me stories that showed a more *immoral* side! They wouldn't have wanted to appear as too goody-goody! To make sure that my findings represented the institutions and the teachers, I shared early drafts of the manuscript with administrators and teachers who were more than willing to collaborate with me to ensure the accuracy of my findings.

In observing the moral culture of the schools and students I came to know, I tended to hear Western language about the roles of respect, authority, obligations to others, and perspectives on the Golden Rule. For pointing out the subtleties in language, I owe an intellectual debt to Robert Bellah and his team of researchers who explored different kinds of moral language in the 1980s and who described their findings in their landmark book *Habits of the Heart*. They found that many Americans spoke about how much they value a sense of community, about feeling duty-bound to serve their country, and about feeling a sense of responsibility to society. Bellah and his coauthors call this a "biblical" or "republican" outlook (meaning participation in the Republic, not necessarily in the Republican Party). They also found that many Americans are more inwardly focused, looking to fulfill their own destinies whether in business, the workplace, the arts, or religious practice with fewer communal obligations. Bellah and his coauthors describe these people as "utilitarian individualists" for the way that they seek their own individual fulfillment, and those whom they describe as "expressive individualists" focus on their own self-expression, on their desire to "get ahead," and on determining much of their own moral system.[3]

I have found somewhat similar attitudes in my research with adolescents. The 14- to 18-year-olds whom I have met and interviewed tend to express a moral outlook that falls somewhere along a continuum between, at one end of the continuum, a sense of duty and obligation to community, tradition, school, or team, and, on the other end of the continuum, a desire to "be myself" and to find acceptance on their own terms after considering their options. The authority of a religious tradition guides some teenagers, while an individual and independent sense of what is right guides others. In other language, I could describe the young people as standing between the two poles of *heteronomy* (guidance by an external authority) and *autonomy* (guidance by one's internal sense of authority), and a third group works to bridge the two.

The three moral outlooks that I have identified do not constitute fully developed moral philosophies; after all, does any one of us know a teenager with a fully developed moral philosophy that could withstand poking and prodding from serious academic criticism? Rather, these outlooks represent three waystations on a continuum of moral life and moral possibilities. These moral outlooks are not predictive; they are explanatory. These moral outlooks are nonjudgmental attempts to describe the lenses through which adolescents assess a moral dilemma, plot a course of action, and make choices about how they will spend their lives.

Instead of using language of heteronomy and autonomy, I have named the three outlooks "Authentic and Assured," "Bridging and Binding," and "Constructing and Considering."[4] The first of my three outlooks probably bears the closest resemblance to traditional cultures. Those who express the Authentic and Assured outlook seem to be the most receptive to authority figures from school or home or from other settings (athletics, the arts, the clergy). They seek religious or moral authenticity, feeling part of a chain of tradition. For one student, that meant loyalty to Jewish tradition; for another student, it meant not letting down his family. I also found that these students often spoke with confidence and self-assurance; they were not plagued with doubt about their respective roles in their families, schools, or society, nor did they doubt the rightness of their convictions.

Social and moral philosophy turned out to provide a useful vocabulary to describe each of these three outlooks. The Authentic and Assured perspective is inspired in part by the fictitious character of Joe Gorman in *Habits of the Heart*[5] who sees himself as the standard-bearer of old-time values in his small town of Suffolk, Massachusetts. In spite of his republican values and his desire for community, Gorman cannot escape being a creature of the modern age whose flag-waving comes in part because his espousal of community comes in an era of its decline. Teenagers who are Authentic and Assured rely on a variety of values from the secular republican values of Joe Gorman to the Jewish and Muslim dietary laws, religious prescriptions regarding daily prayer, and moral laws prohibiting premarital sex. Many of these standards can be considered objective because they appear in sources of religious law, not as a guideline, but as prescribed commandments. This parallels the philosopher Henry Sidgwick's "generic and authoritative" notion of "good and duty."[6] The individual withholds the right to some independence in moral decision making, following and relying instead on already-established laws. The 20th-century moral philosopher John Rawls describes "natural duties" that flow from an implicit contract between people and human civilization. Rawls explains that these natural duties are inherent in the human condition and that they lead people to promote justice, to show benevolence toward others, and even to perform acts of self-sacrifice and heroism.[7]

Someone who is Authentic and Assured also sees himself or herself as a partner in a moral contract or covenant with a nation, religious community, local community, friendship group, or God. This contract imposes obligations and responsibilities above and beyond adherence to a set of rules. Bearing responsibility for the fulfillment of certain duties places the Authentic and Assured individual in continuum with the Enlightenment philosopher Immanuel Kant and the duty he describes to fulfill a categorical imperative. Kant explains the categorical imperative as the understanding that any particular action might be seen as if it were at the status of a law for all to follow (or not to follow). If I pick up a piece of paper from the classroom floor, for example, I do it as if it were a law that everyone should pick up paper; likewise, if I use a tissue and drop it on the same floor, should it also be an example of something for all of humanity to do?[8]

The 20th-century educational philosopher and psychologist Lawrence Kohlberg described young people who accept authority as living in a conventional stage of morality because they comply with conventions or rules of their group. Some conventions might be superficial and specific to their generation, like the jeans they wear and the music they listen to. Other religious and secular conventions require that the individual relinquish some autonomy. The daily prayer required by Islam and Judaism, for example, requires that an individual stop and pray at a specific time alone or in a community. A school honor code is a kind of secular convention that commands obedience even in the case of a temptation to cheat. Students at this stage, in which they accept conventions, tend to be entering the thick of adolescence, taking loyalty issues seriously and weighing moral issues carefully so as not to jeopardize their membership in a group. Calling attention to themselves as good students and as good citizens is supposed to bring positive recognition from adults, but it often brings negative feedback and even some forms of ostracism from their peers for appearing to stand out as too much of a do-gooder. That might be enough to dissuade some students from doing good works and even from heeding an honor code. This presents a challenge to adults to reward good citizenship while also coaching the rest of the peer group to aspire to the same high levels of social skills and good moral behavior.[9]

At this stage, individuals also recognize that their membership in a group may mean that they have to give up some of what they enjoy (and might even prefer to do) as individuals. I remember encountering this firsthand one afternoon when I was a teaching intern at a summer boarding-school program, and a student wanted to put his stereo system in his window to blast his music at full volume for the entire courtyard to hear. When I mustered the authority to tell him that he couldn't, he objected: "But that's not fair!" When I explained that fairness to him would not have been fairness to others if he blasted his speakers so loudly that they would not have been able to study quietly, he understood what it meant to sacrifice his interests for the good of the group.[10]

Kohlberg would view this boy's willingness to conform to the conventions of the group as representative of the fourth stage of moral development. Similarly, he also would view a Jewish or Roman Catholic or Muslim student's willingness to sacrifice their own personal prayers or interpretations and to accept the words of the classical interpreters as typical of this fourth stage of moral development. Those who have reached what he refers to as the fifth stage of moral development, a stage of postconventional commitments to justice and the law, have moved beyond convention and rules, and those at the sixth stage are committed to universal values that express common ground across specific religious traditions.

One Authentic and Assured student who participated in my research, Darshona, spoke about issues of authenticity. Her Christian faith provided continuity and stability, while chaos seemed to govern her neighborhood. She wrote and published poetry about how her authentic faith offered a vision of a better world; she stayed focused on school, chose her friends carefully, and, as she put it in an interview, "My mom and my dad are my top 24/7."[11]

Another Authentic and Assured student, Tamar, participated in a Jewish youth group that requires its youth leaders to sign a pledge of honor that they will not date people who are not Jewish. She was willing to conform to religious and family based expectations like that pledge; at home, she was willing to assume regular responsibility for her sister because, as she put it, "you should." Because of her strong Jewish convictions, she did not expect her large suburban comprehensive public high school to provide an environment that would stimulate or challenge her moral outlook. Amesbury High School seeks to uphold rigorous standards of behavior and achievement, but the large student population and the heavy teaching load makes it difficult for teachers to become mentors to students. It seemed that some of the most positive adult-student relationships I observed were between students and security guards. Tamar seemed assured of her role at school, at home, and in her religious community.

Students and families with an Authentic and Assured outlook often look to the school to set standards of behavior for them, so they do not object to school uniforms. At some schools, such as the Carey School, a girls' school, the uniform represents the Authentic and Assured outlook, but the curriculum tends to foster the third outlook, Constructing and Considering. At the Roman Catholic school that I discuss in the following chapter, the uniform is an outward expression of the physical and spiritual discipline that is expected from the students. The uniform at the Academy of the Sisters of St. Theresa required shoes on the feet, khaki pants for the boys, gray and white checked skirts for the girls, and white shirts or polo shirts for everyone. A second school in this category, Al-Quds Islamic Academy, offers rigorous instruction in Arabic language to ensure that students study the Qur'an in its original language; courses in Islamic studies emphasize textual studies, clarification of behavioral precepts, and ways of practicing those precepts. The students at Al-Quds wear a uniform as well, with dark pants and white shirts for the boys and full modest dress for the girls.

Students who express the outlook I call Bridging and Binding tend to move comfortably between worlds, negotiating their home traditions on their own terms while also finding a way to be part of popular culture and new traditions. The philosopher Charles Taylor describes this kind of negotiation in his book *Sources of the Self*. In modern life, people grow up as part of a "web of interlocutors";[12] that is, people are part of a community with a shared vocabulary, but they differentiate themselves when they leave home for work, college, or study abroad and then begin to define a new set of values that emerge from the earlier set.

Young people often negotiate and seek to bridge the gender roles of their parents with the gender roles of their peers. Carol Gilligan describes the intense way in which young women tend to see morality as part of a larger set of issues that cannot be separated from relationships with other people. She quotes one college undergraduate who sees morality as a set of obligations that flow together, derived from membership in the larger community. The college student says, "I usually think of [morality] as conflicts between personal desires and social things, social considerations, or personal desires of yourself versus personal desires of another person or people or whatever. . . . A truly moral person would always consider another person as their equal."[13] This principled position leads an individual such as this student to weigh many different considerations when making decisions. She might agree with the philosopher Charles Larmore who explains, "Morality is not the same thing as self-fulfillment or the good life."[14] In modern life, there are always competing needs, expectations, obligations, and viewpoints, and one must make moral choices in a marketplace of ideas by negotiating one's way through many different influences.

Students who were successful at Bridging and Binding were comfortable both with a language of obligation and with a language of individualism. A 10th grader named Jeffrey Schochet at John Adams High School straddles the tradition-oriented approach and the more individualistic moral approach. He described being a moral person as "mixing what you feel is right with what is traditionally right according to your family and your culture." He added, "Basically, you have to be loyal to who you are, and loyal to where you come from. And I think that when you accurately follow those two principles, you can't go wrong morally."

Erik Erikson describes the socialization of adolescents in his work on adolescent psychology, and he especially took note of the tension at what he calls Stage 4, when young people who are in the midst of adolescence come to define their identity and their role in the world. Adolescent identities become crystallized around their interests and areas of competency. They identify themselves as soccer players, artists, musicians, scientists, yearbook people, and drama people. Sometimes they accept negative identities as well; in the same way that the adult gay and lesbian community has appropriated the word *queer* as a label to be spoken with pride, a girl I taught would speak with mischievous pleasure when she called her friends "fellow nerds" or "geeks."[15] The other half of Erikson's stage description, role confusion, describes the ways in which adolescents negotiate their new sense of self. Although they may attain a driver's license at 17 years of age, empowering them to travel farther than they ever have before, they may still be limited by the amount of money on their credit cards or by state requirements that they still attend school.

This moral confusion is depicted with irony, innuendo, and romantic suspense in the film *The Breakfast Club*.[16] Although it cannot claim to be the most accurate depiction of adolescent life, the film feels especially familiar to those of us who came of age in suburban American public schools in the 1970s and 1980s. In the movie, the school's vice principal is not a convincing disciplinarian for the five teenagers who come to be described as a princess, a criminal, a brain, an athlete, and a basket case. The students neither respect him (they laugh behind his back) nor do they heed his warnings from the first minutes of their Saturday morning detention, when they cover for John Bender, the 12th-grade criminal who leads them in some just-under-the-radar-screen rule breaking. Together the students smoke, traverse gated corridors, and develop a strong sense of friendship. Together they face moral dilemmas about breaking rules, and they also face larger existential issues of identity and meaning. While the athlete confides, "Being bad sure feels pretty good," he is afraid of jeopardizing an athletic scholarship (what he calls a "ride") to college, and they all have to come to terms with the implicit rules of high school socializing. If a burnout like John were to date a jock or a prom queen like Claire, then the two lovers both would lose status in their respective groups. How much would they be willing to sacrifice? Can a jock, a burnout, a socialite, a brain, and even a self-proclaimed weirdo and kleptomaniac befriend someone who is different without compromising their personal dreams and aspirations? The movie's uplifting end offers a decidedly moral answer to that dilemma: Yes, the process of socialization provides moral grounding. Yes, one can transcend one's initial moral framework.

The Jewish day school where I teach Jewish studies, the Jerusalem School, promotes a pluralistic approach to Jewish studies that helps students to strengthen their sense of Jewish identity. The Jewish studies classes tend to be directed toward providing students with study skills that enable them to enter into traditional Jewish texts each day in their classes; yet the students are not expected to become conversant in Jewish doctrine. The students are required to participate in daily communal prayer each morning, and the daily prayer services offer a moment of connection between the students and the tradition. Sometimes the prayer services have a traditional structure with traditional melodies, and on other days of the week, students have an array of choices, including meditation, current events, poetry and prayer, and the traditional service. The array of choices for the daily services (meditation, current events, poetry, and traditional prayers) leads me to conclude that the Jerusalem School nurtures a Bridging and Binding school environment.

To use Charles Taylor's language, students at the middle school level come to feel embedded in a web of ancient rabbinic interlocutors. When they come to classrooms to study rabbinic literature from 2,000 years ago, found in texts called *Mishnah* and *Talmud*, they ask, for example, why do the rabbis begin a discussion about the celebration of the holiday of Passover by pointing out that poor people are entitled to the same privileges of wealthier individuals? As part of their studies, they also discuss ways to Bridge this early precedent with more recent practices they might recognize in their home communities.

Schools are in a pivotal position to nurture student efforts to Bridge, to Bind, and also to feel bound. When I observed classes at Templeton High School in New York, a public high school, I saw how teachers affirm each student's individuality, showing respect for the family and ethnic values of the students while also helping them to negotiate the academic demands of high school and college.[17]

Young people who express the third moral outlook, which I call, Constructing and Considering, seek positive experiences, but they are not necessarily tied to tradition, community expectations, or any single ideology.[18] These young people make less of an effort to be bound to the past or to affirm the authority of duty-based traditions that some consider more authentic. These students who are Constructing and Considering may not be so assured as some of their peers, and they may not necessarily possess the moral confidence of their peers who affirm a particular tradition. Their decisions may be motivated by psychological factors such as parental influence, feelings about avoiding or confronting conflict, and feelings about approval and disapproval.[19] Students who are Constructing and Considering do not necessarily embrace pure anarchy and chaos, but they are not necessarily looking for a vocabulary from a specific tradition either. They seek to achieve something close to the "unencumbered self," which the political philosopher Michael Sandel describes as a state of being free of constraint, free to determine which fashions or styles to ignore or to follow.[20] The social philosopher Charles Taylor describes this moral state in similar terms when people make independent decisions, determining their own purposes without interference from external authorities.[21] To be Constructing and Considering, an individual relies on intuition and on a sense of what is right for any particular moment. This sounds like utilitarianism because pleasure is not necessarily deferred, and, instead, the individual seeks to maximize his or her personal satisfaction in the moment.[22]

One of the students who participated in my research, Gadiel Himmelfarb, exemplifies this third outlook. He told me that he seeks to live by the Golden Rule. It is important for him to create music, and, as he put it, just "being who you are" is important in his moral outlook. The Golden Rule is an objective standard for him, in part because people around him (especially his older brother!) frequently violated it, but Gadiel is not an activist who worries about how he treats others, nor is he an activist who loses sleep about troubles elsewhere in the world.

At the independent day school in New York that he attended, Hanford Day School, Gadiel felt at home with the relative informality of the school. He could play the keyboard, bring Billy Joel's music to an English class discussion about poetry, and be as competitive or as noncompetitive on the basketball court as he wished. He thrived in the nonjudgmental atmosphere of his Ethical Foundations class, which despite its being offered on a pass-fail basis, offered room for students to confront moral issues directly. Although the course was not especially rigorous (students faced minimal consequences if they did not complete the homework), the class and the school did foster an atmosphere of permission in which experimentation and diverse ideas could flourish. In the course, he expressed his relative ease with homosexuality and his support for untimed testing for students needing extra time to complete highly competitive standardized tests such as the SAT.

When I called him after his high school graduation to say hello and to explore whether his moral outlook had changed in the intervening years, I was not surprised to hear of his plans to attend college at a music school where he could flourish as a musician. Having attended a Jewish day school that might have encouraged him to Bridge and to feel Bound by the tradition, he looked back at the school as a place where he had succeeded in forging a strong but not necessarily binding Jewish identity. He was willing to live within the constraints of music, with its measures, scales, and chords, but he felt himself to be spiritually fulfilled through his participation in religious services at a synagogue that was known for its progressive politics, lively music, joyful dancing in the aisles, and extended singing of wordless melodies. Like students at more traditional Jewish, Christian, and Muslim schools, he studied a set of religious texts and religious values that added up to a rich form of character education, but as he verged on adulthood, he found flexibility, affirmation, and tradition in music, while religion seemed to continue to be overly structured. Once he left his Jewish day school after the 8th grade, Gadiel emerged with a moral and spiritual identity.[23]

Students who are Constructing and Considering are in the process of constructing meaning for themselves; this is something Jean Piaget identified and described in his work. His stages of psychological development identify the points at which children develop their ability to know and to understand new concepts. He used an experiment involving a beaker to see how young people made sense of abstract concepts such as volume. In the experiment, water was poured from a tall beaker into a short and stout beaker that had equal volume. Children who thought that the tall beaker was larger than the short one didn't understand the concept of volume yet, and instead constructed for themselves their own understanding of volume. He called this a *constructivist* process. This idea, that people construct ideas and meaning for themselves, has come to be translated into educational philosophies that encourage children to construct their own meaning, whether they are reading or formulating numerical, scientific, or religious ideas about how the world works.

In Piaget's fourth stage, when children reach middle and high school, they can think hypothetically and carry out formal operations. In literature and history classes, they have a greater capacity to anticipate literary and political twists and turns. They also have a new capacity for empathy, making them strong participants in moral discussions. Using Piaget's insights, teachers can anticipate when young people need concrete explanations and direct discipline and when they can handle more abstract, hypothetical discussions that could help them to develop their own moral concepts to guide their own moral behavior.[24]

In the same book, *The Moral Judgment of the Child*, Piaget explores the ways in which children play and develop a moral system around their games. As they live through the first stage of moral development, children aim to learn skills, which, at that point, are less important than rules. Children learn to move a ball by dribbling it or throwing it. During the second stage of moral development, they learn rules and come to regard them as "sacred and untouchable, emanating from adults and lasting forever. Every suggested alteration strikes the child as a transgression." Children at the third stage of development tend to understand that rules can be modified, so they begin to question rules and seek cooperation among the players to let those questions and modifications improve a game. The fourth stage involves the codification of rules.[25] With good communication, good social skills, and, when necessary, with the help of an adult teacher or coach, children develop rules that affirm their ability to be autonomous decision-makers who choose to follow conventions for the good of all, believing in the system of laws that they participated in establishing.[26] This level of democratic participation may naturally lead children to question any rule that has been handed down, whether it is a rule about how to play marbles or a rule about social and moral conduct. As Piaget writes,

> *The moment a child decides that rules can be changed, he ceases to believe in their endless past and in their adult origin. In other words, he regards rules as*

having constantly changed and as having been invented and modified by chil-
dren themselves. . . . Is it, then, the loss of belief in the divine or adult origin of
rules that allows the child to think of innovations, or is it the consciousness of
autonomy that dispels the myth of revelation?[27]

In other words, participatory democracy can lead to an awareness of bias and to great creativity, and it also can lead to a collapse of belief in the system. Children's play may be able to stand in, or at least serve as a metaphor for the ways in which a society constructs and lives out its moral system.

I should say a word about my own moral bias in this book: Although I was not able to study the family and cultural backgrounds of the students I interviewed, it is worth reviewing what other studies show about the influences of culture on morality. I am prepared to own up to my own bias in that the three moral outlooks that I describe in this book are distinctly Western in their focus on the relationship and the conflict that occasionally arises between individuals and communities, and between those who feel bound by tradition and those who want to be freed from the constraints of tradition.

I am not alone in this Western bias. Lawrence Kohlberg, for example, sees an affirmation of convention as a station on the way to postconventional universal thinking. Kohlberg's sixth stage focuses on large and universal ideals. Kohlberg would aspire for individuals to move beyond conformity to community norms; his models are Gandhi and Dr. Martin Luther King, Jr., two leaders who sought to transcend the boundaries that separate cultures and governments.

To draw a cultural contrast, two thinkers in the field of moral education, Elliot Turiel and Larry Nucci, found that Kohlberg's vision of universalism would not be very popular in traditional Indian culture. They focused their research on how young people become acculturated as they negotiate their roles in adult moral culture. In traditional Hindu Brahmin society, for example, personal obligations are quite different from those in contemporary American society. It is considered acceptable, for example, for a Brahmin parent to punish a son by caning him if he played hooky a second time from school after being warned against it by the parent. In the United States, this kind of physical punishment would be unacceptable.[28] William Damon points out that agrarian societies tend to expect conformity, because children had to behave and take care of things in the home while the parents were in the fields; technological society, in contrast, stimulates competition and a desire to call attention to oneself.[29]

As I continued to listen to the students who participated in my research, I became interested in my own bias. As I thought about it, the Authentic and Assured outlook accepts the conventions and norms imposed by the community. I suspect that if I were to research the moral outlooks of Hindu adolescents in India, I might define one outlook as "Ancestral," implying that the individual accepts without question the obligations imposed by the culture. I might define another outlook as "Freedom Seeker" for those individuals who question the traditional obligations and conventions. Laurence Kohlberg considers postconventional moral thinking to be at a higher level of moral development than conventional thinking. Traditional Hindu society regards the conventions of behavior to be at a much higher moral level than behavior that comes from thinking freely without constraint. More cross-cultural research needs to be done: other researchers such as Cecilia Wainryb have found it overly simplistic to label societies as either collectivist or individualist.[30]

THE ROLE OF GENDER

Interest in the relationship between one's gender and one's moral voice ebbs and flows. On one side of the discussion, almost any parent, can catalogue the differences that seemed ingrained, separating girls and boys in the way they speak to the way they play, share, and participate in the life of the home. On the other side of the discussion is the equally strong view that gender may not be so significant and that cultural factors shape one's moral voice. Having introduced the three moral outlooks I heard and observed while preparing this book, how does gender relate to moral education?

When I first defined moral education earlier in this book, I described it as concerning many areas: issues of ethics, issues of dignity and civil rights, and existential issues. The umbrella of moral education also covers the ways in which boys and girls are taught to express their gender identity. A child's gender identity appears to be cultivated at home from the first days of life, when parents name the baby, when blue or pink clothing and toys begin to arrive, and when children are first steered toward different kinds of activities. By the time children arrive in their kindergarten classrooms, they may already have a strong sense of masculinity or femininity.

Research indicates that the ways in which girls and boys are tracked at different levels may be influenced by prejudices about the abilities of each gender, whether in the cognitive ability to study math or a foreign language or in the physical ability to sit still in class. For this and other reasons, single-sex schools are enjoying a wave of popularity. Some cutting-edge brain research indicates that boys and girls learn differently, not only because they are socialized in different ways, but also because boys' and girls' visual and auditory systems appear to be constructed differently.

While it may be common knowledge that boys *like* a great deal of physical activity, teachers may not be aware that boys actually *need* the activity. The male nervous system craves activity. Boys are not programmed to sit still, however much their schools may ask and expect boys to work quietly at their desks. Many educators are advocating for single-sex schools in which the curriculum and classroom format can be modified to accommodate the differences between boys and girls. A cover article on single-sex education in the *New York Times Magazine* features David Chadwell, the South Carolina Department of Education coordinator of Single-Gender Initiatives, who calls upon teachers of boys to "get them up and moving. That's based on the nervous system. . . . So instead of having boys raise their hands, you're going to have boys literally stand up. You're going to do physical representation of number lines. Relay races. . . ." For girls, "If you try to stop girls from talking to one another, that's not successful. So you do a lot of meeting in circles, where every girl can share something from her own life that relates to the content in class."[31]

Single-sex schools are enjoying a wave of popularity. A Boston *Globe* editorial called for more single-sex schools, citing higher levels of academic achievement among boys and girls at single-sex schools. The editorial also explained that girls and boys in their single-sex environments have an opportunity to develop leadership skills and professional skills that they wouldn't necessarily receive in a coeducational setting.[32]

The letters to the editor that followed the article in the *New York Times Magazine* speak loudly to the moral issues surrounding education and gender. One writer equated single-sex education with facilities that were separate but equal during the era of racial segregation in the United States, claiming that segregation by gender constitutes a violation of civil rights. The writer, Michael Meyers, the executive director of the New York Civil Rights Coalition in New York, suggested that single-sex educational advocates are not so different from "public-school officials who argued vociferously that blacks could be effective and more active learners in black schools, and who argued as well that blacks not only did not need integration but that integration was a detriment to their self-esteem and fragile egos. . . ."[33]

Gender roles play an important role in moral development, shaping choices around clothing and the development of a personal voice. Carol Gilligan was one of the first psychologists to study and write about the ways in which a woman's moral voice may differ from that of a man. Nona Lyons, one of the research scholars in a study of girls at the Emma Willard School (a school for girls in Troy, New York), describes the ways in which the girls came to develop an ethic of care. She observed how girls reciprocated favors for one another. They became interdependent in the boarding-school community, relying on one another in academic and social situations. They became willing to sacrifice what might have been the right thing to do if it would have caused a conflict with a friend. In the girls' moral code, it might have been wrong to break a contract, but it would have been even more wrong to show a lack of understanding of a person's particular needs.[34]

In an acclaimed and somewhat controversial study about the lives of early adolescent girls, *Reviving Ophelia: Saving the Selves of Adolescent Girls*, Mary Pipher describes the ways in which girls begin to lose their energetic, fearless, adventurous, and even androgynous voice as they enter adolescence and begin to conform to adult norms. Girls face the moral challenge of bridging their childhood and their adulthood, leaving a world in which they were taught they could do anything and entering a world in which their mothers may be demonstrating what it is like to be dependent on others while repressing some of their own hopes and desires. Mothers introduce their daughters to mainstream culture without giving their daughters a vocabulary for separating from the culture when it is too oppressive.[35] Readers may not necessarily agree with everything in *Reviving Ophelia*, but it is difficult for parents and teachers to set the book aside without feeling discouraged that by the time many American girls reach adolescence, like Shakespeare's Ophelia, they lose their moral and emotional compass and the voice that once had carried them into adventures and into young adulthood.

There is compelling research on the other side, indicating that the wilting Ophelia is not necessarily the dominant paradigm for teenage girls. Lyn Mikel Brown's provocative book called *Raising Their Voices: The Politics of Girls' Anger* conveys the voices and spirits of white working-class and middle-class girls from Maine who are angry for many reasons. Many girls feel unable to relate to many of the adults around them, including their teachers in school. Some harbor a deep-seated anger about the ways in which the economic system limits economic and educational opportunities for girls of their social class, and others are angry about the ways in which boys their age "get away with so much" and expect that girls should be well-behaved, not overly intelligent, and sexually available.[36]

Another set of data that contradicts the Ophelia-like image of adolescent girls comes from Dan Kindlon, a clinical psychologist who teaches at Harvard

School of Public Health, who has described the phenomenon of what he calls "alpha girls," the girls who are successful athletes and students, who are less concerned about gender roles, and less prone to depression. Many of these alpha girls even are willing to engage in some of the rough-and-tumble play that boys traditionally enjoy. Kindlon describes the flexibility of the alpha girl psychology: she is free to choose whether to act in a more classically feminine manner, connected to her community, or whether to act in a more classically masculine manner, separate and psychologically distant. Not only does this have implications on college admissions (young women outnumber young men in college applications and at some colleges today), but it also has implications in the workforce as alpha girls grow up and compete with their peers for jobs.[37]

To protect the images of boys, some writers such as Christina Hoff Sommers and others have argued that the attention given to girls to support their different voice has meant that less attention is being paid to the voices of boys; educators like her argue for a focus on boys and their unique learning styles.[38]

When parents begin to raise their children with traditional expectations that are highly correlated with one gender or the other, giving their boys toy trucks and their girls dolls, it may not seem like a profound moral issue. When children and adults express discomfort with those gender expectations, as when boys show an interest in dolls and girls act like tomboys, the moral issues become complicated. Consider the complicated circumstances around a 3rd grader in Haverford Township in suburban Philadelphia, whose parents announced to his elementary school community that he wanted to be known and treated as a girl. While many of the children were reported to be accepting of the child, some of the parents objected to the relatively short notice given for a meeting that was called for the 3rd-grade class to discuss what it means to live as a boy but to feel like a girl, and some parents objected that the subject came up at all.[39] In another case in the Philadelphia area, an 18-year-old transgender teen named Ty has found acceptance as a boy four years after having revealed to his middle school classmates that although he was living as a girl named Tye, his identity was male and he wished to be treated as a male. The school responded by changing the name and gender on school records and by allowing the student, now called Ty, to use the nurse's bathroom during his years of transition. The acceptance by his peers has enabled him to thrive as a boy, and he has not experienced any bullying.[40]

Our gender does not bind us to any single moral outlook, though it may shape how we bridge our personal inclinations and outlooks with the schools and communities in which we live. Gender, like religion and family structure, is one of many identities that shape an individual's moral outlook. The philosopher Charles Taylor writes that one's identity is related to one's moral outlook. He writes, "To know who you are is to be oriented in moral space, a space in which questions arise about what is good or bad, what is worth doing and what not, what has meaning and importance for you and what is trivial and secondary."[41] As a young person interacts with family members and with nonfamily members of the same community, Taylor writes that we develop a "fundamental orientation in terms of who we are."[42]

The following chapters present three different moral outlooks, each with its own moral vocabulary. Some of the adolescents whom I met feel certain about their identity and their fundamental orientation, while others, as the title of this chapter suggests, like to study a character and try it on while they continue to develop their identity. Adolescents often do not have a fully formed character yet, and life experiences may yet shape their moral outlooks. Often they present a facade of certainty, so the first of the three outlooks is called "Authentic and Assured." Sometimes they feel in transition in their thinking and learning about an issue, or they feel themselves to stand in the ideological center, so I call the second outlook "Bridging and Binding." Still others see themselves as part of an ongoing conversation, so I call the third outlook "Consenting and Considering" to reflect their willingness to have some questions left unanswered. One can find a web of thoughtful interlocutors and outstanding educational institutions within each of the three outlooks. In each setting, the voices are compelling, so I have tried to represent as many of them as possible.

Authentic and Assured

MORE (*Moved*): *And when we stand before God,*
and you are sent to Paradise for doing according to your conscience
and I am damned for not doing according to mine,
will you come with me, for fellowship?

—Robert Bolt, A Man for All Seasons

How would I know what an Authentic and Assured student or teacher would look like? Would they wear red, white, and blue flag pins? Would they be fierce guardians of cultural, religious, and ethnic traditions? Would they be so convinced, so assured of the rightness of their values that they wouldn't have room for people whose ideas are different? Would they be open to the values of others?

Authentic and Assured moral leadership often flows from school principals and from teachers, and students may be influenced by the adults around them, or they may arrive at a set of authentic values on their own. I found in my interviews with students that following a tradition gives young people a sense of authenticity and support for their values. Some students whom I met spoke about tackling problems in society because they believed that they had a duty to improve the world; this feeling of obligation to contribute to society is anchored in a set of commitments and values. I met many young moral leaders and moral followers who speak with a vocabulary that suggests authenticity and self-assurance; some come from purely secular traditions and some come from specific religious traditions.

"YOU EXALTED CREATURES OF GOD!"
AL-QUDS ISLAMIC ACADEMY

Each year on the Martin Luther King, Jr., birthday weekend in January, the Jerusalem School participates in a community service project together with students from Al-Quds Islamic Academy. From that initial connection, I arranged to meet with Salim Farhat, the school's director, and Ahmed Habib Kerry, the school's principal. Ahmed Habib Kerry and I met one morning, and we spent a great deal of time in conversation in his office before he brought me to observe a class of high school seniors taught by Salim Farhat. On a return to the school, I visited several other classes and interviewed several students.

The school is located deep in a transitional neighborhood, and one of my colleagues expressed concern about my traveling by bicycle. When I bicycled to the school for each of my visits, the abandoned factories, boarded-up homes, and abandoned trolley tracks became markers on my route. The unkempt sidewalks and gutters gave the neighborhood an especially rough look. In contrast, the Al-Quds Islamic Society, which houses the school, is sparkling clean with a mosque on the ground floor and a set of steep steps leading to the upper floors and to the school. Security guards monitored the fenced-in parking lot, playground, and covered lunch area, so I locked my bike under their supervision, changed into my street shoes, and went inside the school.

Children greeted me, and a custodian held the door for me as we walked together up the stairs. The school had passed my First Impressions test! It was clear that the students felt a sense of belonging in the school that they could welcome me the way they did. After being guided to the school office by the custodian, I was greeted warmly, and if it could be seen as an indicator of the work ethic at the school, I wasn't certain which adult in the office was the principal. Was it the hearty man in his mid-50s, wearing a tie and a round embroidered cap? Or was it the man who had just dashed out the door and into the hallway, probably to catch a student?

I was offered a cold drink, and then the man in the cap, Ahmed Habib Kerry, introduced himself as the principal, immediately set down his folders, and took me into his office so that we could meet more privately. He recounted that the school was founded in 1991 with a deep sense of mission to be an urban school that includes students from different backgrounds. One of just four Muslim schools in Philadelphia, the school enrolls half of its students from Middle Eastern backgrounds and the other half from African American backgrounds. The principal explained to me that the school subscribes to a moderate understanding of Islam, and teachers speak often about the importance of charitable deeds. I learned, for example, that one of the teachers privately tutored a student on Saturdays; the student had a life-threatening disease. The tutoring enabled her to catch up to her peers, and now she is advancing in her studies. I also learned that when Salim Farhat, the director, heard about a person who needed a home and a refrigerator and other appliances, he arranged an apartment space for her and simply gave her the refrigerator from the school. He also saw to it that the school donated 400 prayer rugs to a prison ministry and corresponded with the prisoners. He is known for his generosity in the community.

Like any school with students for whom English is a second language, Al-Quds enrolls students who face linguistic challenges. Many students come from the Middle East and speak Arabic at home. These students tend to receive lower test scores and experience less academic success. Ahmed Habib said that when he taught in the public schools, he often focused on the bottom third of each class first in order to raise their self-esteem and academic achievement. From this practice, he is especially conscious of the students at this school who are struggling, and he goes out of his way to help them. The school has turned around some of these struggling students and brought them up to grade level. The school leadership hopes that with enough arms around a student's shoulder and with "lots of exhortation," any student can stay out of fights and succeed. Fortunately, the school does not face many of the disciplinary problems that plague large schools today. The principal joked that most of the school's behavioral and disciplinary problems are reminiscent of the 1930s: students often forget to get rid of gum, and in class they often forget to raise their hands. The reality is, of course, that the students face the challenges of urban youth: some of the students have family members in prison, they all have concerns about their own safety, and many are in the process of overcoming a range of motivational and behavioral issues.

The teachers and principal are proud of their success. In a personal e-mail message, the principal wrote that 99 percent of the graduating seniors are in college. "That's an enviable record," he wrote, especially because the school recently received recognition from the *Philadelphia Inquirer,* the local newspaper of record in Philadelphia; the school was ranked as one of the 10 most improved schools in various subjects. The school was rated number two and most improved in 11th-grade reading, and the 5th grade was ranked 8th in mathematics.[1]

Muslim faith pervades the curriculum and the atmosphere of the school. The school day begins at 8:35 A.M. with prayer and some kind of teaching and moral guidance for the students. Ahmed Habib told me that he begins the Friday assemblies following *jum'ah* prayers with an enthusiastic, *"A-Salaam-Aleikum,* You exalted creatures of God!" He wants to see the students join his enthusiasm. He wants the students to identify with their higher natural qualities rather than with the lower qualities. To extend this positive atmosphere, when teachers admonish students to behave themselves appropriately, and in more private counseling sessions, the students are told to remember their Creator. The science teacher brings in relevant passages from the Qur'an.

Students take one class in Islamic studies and a separate class in Arabic and in reading the Qur'an for 45 minutes each day. Some topics in the Islamic studies curriculum remind me of the Jewish studies curriculum at my own school: treating others fairly, purifying the heart, and deepening an understanding of prayer. The current political climate requires them to stay away from Middle Eastern politics in the curriculum so as not to raise any concerns (or suspicions) from outsiders. The school leadership also believes in the importance of extending students' appreciation for other cultures, especially Jewish culture, so students in the 9th grade read *The Diary of Anne Frank,* and they watch the film *Schindler's List.*

Ahmed Habib took me upstairs to visit classes. The upstairs classroom area and hallway, with its wooden plank floors and lockers lining the walls, reminded me of an old public school; but for the white uniform polo shirts and gray pants on the boys, and the full length navy dresses and kerchiefs on the girls, the hustle and bustle in the hall and the joking around could have been the sounds of high school students anywhere.

During the course of each class, I observed students nodding affirmatively, often appearing to be in agreement with the moralizing voices of their teachers. They did not appear to be trying to construct meaning for themselves. Their purpose was different: they were trying to become responsible citizens, literate in their faith, capable of acting with a strong conscience. They were learning to speak the authentic language of their tradition.

Teachers at the school expressed a commitment to cultivating students' moral values. At the front of the classroom I visited, where some teachers might have written the homework assignments or the activities planned for class, a white marker board was marked for a "Hadith [saying or teaching] of the day"; it was blank on the first of my visits, and it had a saying written on it during a later visit. I observed one class of high school seniors, taught by Salim Farhat, the director of the school's board of trustees. He shared with me that he gains contact time with the students by teaching moral and ethical issues once a week to seniors as part of their ongoing Islamic studies class.

It interested me that Salim Farhat's class was based both on material from Muslim tradition and on material from secular American culture. He shared with the students a film about the blue eye/brown eye experiment led by Iowa teacher Jane Elliot in 1968. To give her students the experience of prejudice, she created a hierarchy in the class based on eye color. In this famous experiment, the students with blue eyes were assigned certain privileges at the beginning of the school day, instantly lowering the self-esteem and the quality of the work of the students with brown eyes.

Salim Farhat saw himself in the role of conveying a religious message that bridged the secular experiment on film with the religious tradition at the foundation of the school. As the class discussion got underway about the blue eyes/brown eyes experiment, he offered moralization of his own. Not only did he instruct the students, "Don't call someone names," but he also went further, telling the students that world is large and that the meaning of labels can change overnight: "Yesterday, brown eyes were not meaningful and today it is negative. . . . You are all Muslims; you go to the outside world and you see different colors, different denominations."

Salim Farhat took his role as a teacher seriously, criticizing a student who came in late to the class, chiding him about the importance of being on time. He continued with deep moral messages about success in the eyes of God, telling his students that when they do good deeds, "God will reward you every time." He told the students that belief in God would give them confidence; as he put it, "Be smart to *not* get into trouble; not smart to get *out* of trouble!" Speaking to this mixed audience of boys and girls from different economic backgrounds, I sensed that he was guiding the students toward upward mobility, seeking to instill middle-class values. Having been in the United States for more then 35 years, he used his own experience as a guide for the students to find success as Muslims in the United States: "I never have one job: I have two jobs. . . . In this country, we are respected. You can believe me." Hoping that the students would carry his messages into the school culture, he encouraged the seniors to let the younger students walk by first and not to pick on them or to hurt their feelings. Taking one of the central issues in the film, self-respect and dignity, he closed the class with an anecdote about feeling confident and respected when he was just 10 years old and a 60-year-old cousin rose to shake his hand, treating him as a young adult. Salim Farhat wanted his students to absorb his moral messages about giving up prejudices, showing compassion, and developing self-respect.[2]

As much as I was moved by his moral biography, as I glanced around the room, I could see that the students were attending, but they were not being asked to respond to their mentor's words. Some eyes looked heavy and some looked distracted, and I recalled one of my own mentors cautioning me not to mistake student quiet for agreement. I would have liked to ask the students what they felt they were absorbing, but I did not think it necessary because their kindness to me as they left (nods and wishes for a good experience) led me to conclude that however the students may have heard their teacher's stories, they absorbed his messages about decency and self-respect. As I left the class, I found myself hoping that his students could absorb both his words about letting go of prejudice and about finding material success without giving up religious commitments.

It is unusual for a member of a board of trustees to teach in a school. Salim Farhat is not a trained teacher: he comes to the school for these weekly classes while managing a convenience store in another part of town, though it was clear that he took this class as seriously as he took any other work or volunteer responsibilities. He took seriously his role as a moral exemplar for his students.

When Salim Farhat was not in the classroom, his seniors had classes in Islamic studies with their regular teacher, Mrs. Hillal. She is responsible for teaching all of the 7th through 12th grade Islamic studies classes. Like Salim Farhat, she sees herself as a moral exemplar. Moral education is the point of departure for her curriculum; the textbook she uses is called *Teachings of the Qur'an for Children: Islamic Morals and Manners*.[3] When I observed Mrs. Hillal teaching Islamic studies with her 7th- and 8th-grade students, both of the classes concentrated on the Hadith (prophetic saying) of the day. The Hadith read as follows:

> *When a man dies, his acts come to an end, except for*
>   (i) *Sadaka ja'raiya,*
>   (ii) *Knowledge reaped, and*
>   (iii) *The dua (prayers).*

In the first class with 8th graders, she focused on doing good deeds every day, and she gave a number of examples. The students interacted a great deal with her, cross-examining and testing her and the principles in the Hadith. She said to the students, after giving them a minute to copy the Hadith into their notes, "It is very important to get out and to do good deeds. This is a continuous, daily affair. Every single day at this school, *Insha Allah*[4] will benefit." She encouraged students to give as much for *sadaqah* (charity/benevolence) as possible. It is important, for example, to build more *masjids* (mosques):

"[There are] not enough in our country . . . Our children need the education and we all need the blessings." One student asked what should happen if one cannot build an entire school—would it be sufficient to give something, at least? She answered, using traditional Arabic phrasing, that *Insha Allah* still would benefit, because "it is not how much you give, but your intention."

This class discussion had begun to circle away from the text of the Hadith, becoming an open discussion about moral issues. Mrs. Hillal called upon her students: "Students, think about it every day: if you know somebody is hungry, you take care of him! I have seen it with my own eyes. We're always thinking of the *Akhira* (afterlife)." As she spoke, I noticed many students nodding in recognition that this was a familiar concept for them. She also clarified for them that if a collection of food were taking place for *sadaka* and if one were hungry, then one's own needs could come first ahead of the needs of others." She taught them a Muslim moral maxim about modesty: "If you are giving with your right hand, your left hand should not know about it."

She assured the students that if they did something for religious reasons, the recognition did not matter. "Students, when you do something for *Allahu subhanahu wa ta'ala*, you will get the same reward, whether you get a response or not!" In other words, she explained, "A simple act of *salaam* [greeting] is *sadaqah*. A thank-you or a paycheck are not necessary." As if nodding to students who might wonder about rewards, she added, "Whether someone reciprocates or not, you did your part." The class ended on this high note with an acknowledgment that although the discussion had strayed from the Hadith and from the regular curriculum, the students had addressed some important issues in their lives.

When the 7th graders walked in for the next class period, I felt prepared for a fresh discussion about the day's Hadith. However, I noticed immediately that these 7th-grade students studied with a different tone. Some took notes, while others listened; she guided the students into a quick discussion about the Hadith and then set down the Hadith and turned to their textbooks, in which they read a story about the Prophet Muhammad and his wife. A positive role model of humility for the young people in the classroom, Mrs. Hillal reminded the students that Muhammad had been an orphan, while most of the students in the class lived with both parents. She also shared some of the history of the beginnings of Islam, when citizens of Mecca pledged to protect the weak and to assist oppressed people.

I was interested to know more about Mrs. Hillal's background, because she was an important role model for the students. She appreciated the intellectual flexibility of young people, and she was able to steer the discussion into new realms while remaining an authentic figure in traditional dress who could teach authoritatively about Muslim tradition.

When Mrs. Hillal and I had an opportunity to speak after class, I came to appreciate the authenticity of her moral voice: her grandparents were immigrants from Bombay, but she, herself, is a third-generation American. All along I had been impressed by the purity and excellence of her slightly accented English, thinking that she had been an immigrant; instead I felt that I shared a cultural connection to her, because I was reminded of Hasidic Jews I have met who were second- or third-generation American citizens, but who spoke slightly accented English because their first language was Yiddish. Mrs. Hillal understands her students and the perspectives that they bring, whether they immigrated from Africa or the Middle East, or whether they came from a nearby neighborhood in search of a private, faith-based education.

She cares deeply about her work, seeing the Hadith of the day as a way to enrich the curriculum with fresh moral content. Studying a new Hadith each of the 180 school days gives the students broad exposure to a wide range of Muslim moral concepts. She sees herself as a moral educator who understands that many of her students feel pulled between Muslim culture and mainstream American culture; she tries to relate the students' lives in America to Muslim values. As she put it, "It is important not only that they learn what the prophet [Muhammad] teaches, but also that they lead moral lives. That's the idea behind my teaching."

It was clear to me that the director, principal, teachers, and students whom I met at the school largely share the Authentic and Assured moral outlook. When I spoke with a few students after school at the Al-Quds playground, their respect for authority was immediately apparent. I shared with a few girls a scenario that I used in other interviews: I asked them what they would do if they were walking down the hallway at school and found a textbook with a $20 bill exposed, tucked into the middle of the book. A girl named Amilah replied quickly, "Honesty is the main thing in a personality. What if you took that $20 and they couldn't get a ride home? You just caused danger. That might happen to you, too. What goes around comes around." When her younger sister had in fact found $250 somewhere, her teacher had advised her not to keep the money for herself. She said that if she had found the person who had lost the money, she would have told the person not to bring so much money to school! The third girl whom I interviewed in that small group at Al-Quds, Leilah, shared that her family would tell her that it isn't right to keep the money. "It reflects on you," she said, "if you're not honest or trustworthy." She concluded, "You want to feel good about yourself." It was clear to me that these students saw the private act of finding the book and money as a public act of honesty. They had internalized the voices of their teachers and parents, and even if nobody had been looking, they said with assurance that they would have followed the values they had been taught.[5]

"WORSHIP BY USING YOUR GOD-GIVEN TALENTS!" THE ACADEMY OF THE SISTERS OF ST. THERESA

When I consulted with a colleague about contacting a Roman Catholic school to explore moral education in a Christian setting, he recommended that I visit the Academy of the Sisters of St. Theresa (ASST).[6] The Roman Catholic school could not have been more different in setting from the Muslim school. In contrast to the warehouses and boarded-up windows and doorways near Al-Quds, large houses with beautiful spreads of flowering plants provide a calm and affluent suburban setting for ASST. There is much less window diversity (relatively few students of color), though the school tries to encourage students from different backgrounds to apply. A number of students receive financial aid, and some students come from non-Catholic backgrounds, choosing the school for its clear values and moral mission.[7] The new and handsome gymnasium provides a setting for students to develop, in the words of the school's promotional brochure, "Christian attitudes of competition, cooperation, leadership, responsibility, sportsmanship, self-discipline, self-control, and self-confidence."

The school is one member of a network of several schools established by the order of the Sisters of St. Theresa. Thus it has a deep moral mission that pervades not only the athletic program but other areas as well. The promotional brochure conveys the school's strong commitment to community service, and the inside front cover describes four principles behind the school's philosophy: Mind, Heart, Body, Soul. It describes the school motto, "Actions, Not Words," in this way:

> At Academies of the Sisters of St. Theresa all over the world, this motto motivates students, teachers, families, and administrators to do more. Middle School students emerge from the Academy of the Sisters of St. Theresa's supportive and trusting Catholic environment—where faith, morals, and values are freely explored—equipped with character and principle, ready to act wisely in pursuit of peace and justice.[8]

While the school offers a strong secular academic program (and it proudly identifies the independent and Catholic schools that students attend following their graduation from the 8th grade), it also strives to play a role in each student's moral development.

With very direct language claiming authenticity with words like *Catholic nature,* the school seeks to provide its students with opportunities for leadership in a Catholic religious context. A section of the promotional brochure entitled "Building Moral Character and a Connection to God" reads in part:

> *Under the guidance of ASST's devoted teachers, students develop an awareness of their place in the world and their obligation to society. The lessons learned here are carried into adulthood, helping to shape a life of moral integrity. While we hold true to our Catholic nature, parents of many religious backgrounds value that a[n] ASST education transcends any single denomination.*[9]

I admired that the school publications convey a clear stance on moral values. At some independent schools I have visited, the enumeration of each Advanced Placement class and the statistics about average test scores make the academic life sound competitive, while community service and other kinds of moral education appear either as a lower priority or as a diversion from the pressures of the regular academic course work. This seemed less the case at ASST, possibly because students graduate after the 8th grade, so they do not have some of the pressures of college preparatory schools.

On one of my visits, it was raining so hard that I had to take a detour to avoid a flooded road, and I arrived a few minutes late. When I entered the school building, the kindly receptionist took my umbrella to keep it dry and out of the way, as a result of which I forgot to take it home with me; later I told my host Tim Hurley, the director of student life to consider it a gift to the school. After Mr. Hurley met me at the reception desk, we walked upstairs, and students greeted Mr. Hurley and me in the stairwell and halls. While he took me first to his office and then to his first class for the morning, he explained that the 8th graders had just visited the infirm older nuns at the home sponsored by the Sisters of St. Theresa across the street from the school. Since the students had just presented *Joseph and the Amazing Technicolor Dreamcoat* for the spring show, they performed excerpts for the Sisters.

If I had been a parent visiting the school for the first time, I would have been impressed by the warm and easy relationships between teachers and students. The school offers a warm and nurturing environment. Not unlike Ahmed Habib Kerry, the principal of Al-Quds Islamic Academy, who greets the students every day by reminding them that they are "exalted creatures of God," I heard a teacher in another classroom across the hall at ASST, trying to motivate his students by calling on them to summon the divine spirit to their prayers. He said in a booming voice in a classroom across the hall from where I was observing another class, "Worship by using your God-given talents!"

I identified with that teacher calling to his students across the hall. As a teacher in a middle school with daily prayer services, I try to inspire my students to take advantage of prayerful moments, and I often feel frustrated that the students are so reluctant to pause for reflection. And also like that teacher, exasperation sometimes leads me to put my theological cards on the table and I have been known to say something similar to the words from across the hall: if only the students could channel their innate energy, their ability to sing, and their interest in one another's welfare and offer genuine prayer, then there would be the possibility of a spiritually uplifting moment! With some spiritual focus, they have the capacity to be transported beyond the limited and fixed texts that are on the page!

While I was observing an 8th-grade review of topics they had taken up that year, I took a moment to observe my surroundings. Looking up from my notes to scan the classroom, my eyes landed on two photographs of President John F. Kennedy that hung on opposite walls in the classroom, and I remembered how many of my Roman Catholic friends had photographs of the first Catholic president on their walls in the 1970s. I could only imagine what Kennedy must have symbolized for Tim Hurley as he must have been entering his own adulthood in the 1960s, inspired by the president to live out his values and to be proud of his Catholic heritage, not hesitating to help students to see the intersections between political, moral, and religious issues, whether in a discussion about the death penalty or about redemption and hope for the poor.

When I spoke with Mr. Hurley in a private conversation, I was interested to know how the school handles some of the complicated issues in which theology, politics, and American values may come into conflict. In science classes, for example, he told me that the students discuss evolutionary theory and divine creation. He explained that the school seeks to help the students to see that whether the students feel more comfortable with evolutionary theory or with a more traditional biblical view of creation, "No matter what you subscribe to, in point of fact, humanity becomes something very special." I commented that the Academy seems to give students a wide berth, and he explained that the school is unlike the more traditional diocesan schools, which receive a different kind of supervision, so it has more latitude in the choice of curricular materials. As a mark of the school's success, Mr. Hurley told me about the involvement that many alumni continue to have in community service and in their own spiritual lives: "There's a lot to life to value that goes beyond the day to day and the physical." This seemed entirely consistent with his approach to his students as a moral educator: as much as he was eager for his students to review for their final exam in his Religious Studies classes, it was important that they integrate the year's discussions of values into their lives.

Roman Catholic schools may have a popular reputation for insisting on strict behavior, but this one looked like many independent schools I know: the atmosphere was relaxed, the facilities were well-maintained, and the students were well-groomed and polite. Students at ASST have opportunities to develop their faith through their classes in religious studies. I heard voices of authenticity in a 7th-grade class with Mr. Hurley on the Gospels in the New Testament. While conducting a review session, Mr. Hurley asked the students to reflect back on the different units and texts they had studied that year. When he asked for a volunteer to describe the role of the parables in the Gospels, a girl in the class replied, "The parables in the New Testament are similar to our lives and how we can use them." Had I been in the teacher's position, I would have cringed upon hearing her inarticulate response, but in my position in the back of the classroom as an observer and researcher, I could hear from her response that the students had been encouraged to find personal meaning in the parables. This was confirmed when another student explained his own view, "The parables helped people to relate to a story . . . and understand what [Jesus] was trying to teach."

The school cultivated a positive atmosphere not only through the curricular materials but also through affirmations of a sense of community and through what Philip Jackson and his colleagues would identify as informal "expressions of morality" in their book *The Moral Life of Schools*. About halfway through the class period, all eyes turned to the door as a young man entered the classroom; rather than chastise him or question him for his lateness, Mr. Hurley accepted the late note from the boy, turned to the class, and asked, "Did you say 'Hi!' to Brother Simon?" This spontaneous gesture felt familial; Mr. Hurley was a role model for courtesy and for a unique, safe, and trusting friendship, a kind of authentic friendship that can exist between adults and children who aren't peers, but who respect and enjoy each other.

Earlier in the year, the students had performed skits for one another, based on the parables in the Gospels, and I observed the students begin to recall some of what they had learned. One boy described the parable about the rich man and Lazarus; the poor man Lazarus is seated in heaven next to Abraham, while the rich man in the parable can see how Lazarus is rewarded for his humility. A boy shared the message he learned from the parable, which is to be happy with what one has. A few minutes later, a girl confidently described the lesson of the Good Samaritan: "No matter who you are, you can help anyone. You don't have to be the same religion, same ethnicity." When Mr. Hurley asked who might be a Good Samaritan if the tale were to be updated today, one student volunteered, "Maybe somebody from Iran." Given the sometimes tense relationship between the United States and Iran, her suggestion that an Iranian could be a modern day Good Samaritan did not seem so far-fetched. The assignment had led the students to distill the parables into short moral life lessons.

In an 8th-grade Religion class, also with Mr. Hurley, the students were reviewing their biblical studies, enjoying the tangents that led them to explore religious issues that lay outside of the text. One girl volunteered that her sister and she had agreed that religion classes shouldn't include final exams: "You shouldn't be tested on your personal beliefs." Another student joked, "If you get an 'A' on the Religion test, does that make you a better Catholic?" Mr. Hurley, ready to banter, jumped in, "I take it as a rhetorical question, is that right?" The student took the bait, "Yes and no." To which Mr. Hurley offered a point of clarification and a moral message: "I'll take it as rhetorical because the ultimate test is between God and you. The ultimate point of each Gospel is what?" To which a student responded, closing the discussion, "To tell the story of Jesus and to guide you."

On a fall day when I returned to the school, some of the 8th graders and I recognized each other because they had been in one of the 7th-grade classes I had observed during the previous spring. With the Phillies expecting to play that night for a World Series game, Mr. Hurley and many of the boys and girls were in red Phillies fan gear; some of the girls were in their field hockey uniforms in preparation for a school game later that day, and the rest of the students were in their regular school uniforms.

In the class with Mr. Hurley, the students received copies of that week's lectionary (established liturgical) readings from the Roman Catholic community, and the students were charged with finding connections between the scriptural readings from the Hebrew Bible and the Christian Bible. One of the readings, Exodus 22:20–26, was a reminder to the ancient people of Israel not to oppress foreigners and not to forget their past as slaves. The reading from the Gospels, Matthew 22:34–40, recounts a conversation in which a scholar asks Jesus to identify the two most important commandments in Jewish law. Jesus answers, drawing from the Torah that the first of these commandments is the commandment to love God, and the second is to love one's neighbor as oneself. Mr. Hurley asked the students to consider what it means to be a good neighbor and what distracts people from being good neighbors. In setting aside the text to focus on this set of moral issues, he introduced the students to a way of thinking about the traditional texts as a springboard for discussion. While he could have had the students do the internal work of dissecting each of the texts, figuring out why each of the lectionary readings had been chosen, he instead asked the students to work with the meaning of each text.

Although I have seen and have, myself, taught lessons with this kind of bridge from ancient society to present meanings, I continued to feel that I was in the presence of a man with an Authentic and Assured viewpoint because he commented with deep conviction at one point, "You are called to action. Not to do that would be to turn away from God's word." A few minutes later, when he asked the students to consider whether they believed that they were doomed to fail as human beings, a student said that no, he didn't believe so. Mr. Hurley replied, "Then how can we turn some of this into good?" After some student ideas about how communities can work together to bring to life some of the love and connection they are asked to feel for God, Mr. Hurley suggested that they start with their families and communities.

The boy who had walked me upstairs to the classroom spoke with great affection about Mr. Hurley, and I sensed that the teacher's sincerity and authenticity was immediately apparent to the students. In fact, Mr. Hurley was highlighted on the cover of the most recent fund-raising brochures in honor of his retirement from coaching generations of football teams. He is the first to acknowledge that the team wasn't always the strongest in the league, but it always had a great spirit.

Following the class with Mr. Hurley, I joined a 5th-grade Religious Studies class with a teacher named Sister Katherine. The class was high in energy, from an opening prayer of petition in which one of the girls led the students in a prayer for the students and their parents and teachers to the heart of the class, in which the students identified a number of holy concepts such as the sacraments and sacramental objects. The students discussed the meaning and purpose of different kinds of prayer, and, after opening up a textbook, they became interested in Sister Katherine's ring, which symbolized the vows she had taken when she became a nun. The students' ability to absorb so much information in such a short amount of time was a testament not only to the teacher's lively manner but also to the authenticity of the material they were studying. For Sister Katherine, as for the students, the sacraments are part of their lives, not merely as rituals, but as expressions of religious faith. When the students asked about the pope's ring in their textbooks, Sister Katherine explained that the pope uses the ring to seal important documents "like when he proclaims people into sainthood," or, she added, "for church documents about morality or about what we believe." Children at this school feel confidence about their faith, and they also see the strong connections emanating from the pope to their teachers between religious life and moral life.

Like the teacher at Al-Quds, Mr. Hurley speaks from an authentic position as a practitioner of the religious tradition he teaches, and his students speak with assurance that they see themselves as the tradition's inheritors. At the same time, his moralizing seemed different from the moralizing of Mrs. Hillal from Al-Quds. The banter between the Catholic teacher and students was indicative of a warm rapport in the school that shrinks the gap between adults and students. Al-Quds may be a place with enough credibility and authority to succeed in keeping the most marginal students in school and off the streets, while ASST is a school for more privileged students who already buy into the education and who are prepared to go out into the world with everything they will have learned. At Al-Quds, the principal and teachers hope that the students at Al-Quds will go on to college and then find success in American society. The school leadership team at ASST doesn't need to focus on college because the school graduates its students after the 8th grade, and the school offers opportunities for the students to put everything they have learned into action. It's fair to say that ASST would embrace the salad idea of American society: they want their students to grow up, confidently identified as Roman Catholics and as able representatives of their tradition.

The patience, permanence, and assuredness of Roman Catholic tradition spoke most clearly to me when, at the end of my visit, Mr. Hurley asked me to wait a moment while he got something for me. He handed me the umbrella that I had left behind after my first visit. He had faith that I would be back.[10]

VOICES OF AUTHORITY IN PUBLIC SCHOOLS

At John Adams High School in New York City, a selective public high school that admits students on the basis of a citywide entrance examination given in the 8th-grade year, the principal, Dr. Grossman, saw himself in the role of instilling moral character in the students. He made it a priority to induct students into a unique school culture by reviving an ancient oath that was recited by young people in ancient Greece. Each year at an annual ceremony at the beginning of the school year, students at John Adams High School recite the Ephebic Oath,[11] affirming their duties to the community and pledging to improve upon their world.

One of the Latin teachers at John Adams High School, Dr. Martinson, told me that when disciplinary issues arise, students involved are asked to remember the Oath. Dr. Martinson looks to the Oath, not only as an important expression of tradition but also as a framework within which he can use his classroom as a pulpit from which to promote moral decision making. As he told me,

> *We care about standards and we have to do a certain amount of preaching.*
> *Don't think we push it to the point where students become cynical. Unlike the*
> *Pledge of Allegiance to the flag, we don't say [the Ephebic Oath] every day.*

He shared with me that when problems occur, the faculty may discuss a student's moral growth and development. At the same time, he assured me that there are very few problems, and he proudly told me that the school is very safe; the teacher's lounge and classroom doors often are left unlocked. He summed up the safety he feels: "Fewer locked doors, cleaner walls." Conceding that young people may be tempted to commit vandalism on occasion, he noted that it is infrequent at John Adams High School.

I could see that Dr. Martinson thinks about moral issues a great deal in his teaching. On one occasion when I was shadowing a student named Jeffrey Schochet, Dr. Martinson made a comment that suggested a lack of trust in his students. Upon administering a quiz, he had said, casually in a sing-song voice, "No cheating!" He explained the thinking behind the comment:

> *I make a joke about cheating to suggest it's so unimaginable, to suggest I don't*
> *seriously think they would cheat. I turn around my back, and ask, 'How many*
> *of you are cheating now' and a hand goes up when I turn around quickly—*
> *returning the joke. Kids know I take it (cheating) very seriously. You can convey*
> *how strongly you feel without resorting to empty platitudes. . . . [T]hey know*
> *how seriously I take breaches of ethics and decency.*
>
> *I like to have laughter in the classroom; later someone may step over the line*
> *and this runs the risk of laughter impeding the lesson vs. laughter which helps.*
> *At times I encourage laughter; at times, I need to say that was in poor taste.*
> *I don't feel I have to be stern all of the time. The third year class is very relaxed.*

Dr. Martinson reflected out loud about the moral climate of the school while we sat together in a faculty workroom. He described the moral climate as strong with the exception of some cases of cheating or plagiarism, or as he put it somewhat sarcastically, some "points of similarities which could not have been incidental." He said that cheating is the "most obvious sign of integrity to a teacher," suggesting that the degree of cheating at a school is indicative of a school's moral climate. Cheating was relatively rare at John Adams High School, something he believed to be a good sign of the moral health of the school. Although he would have liked to know more about the students' moral lives outside of school, he conceded that he mainly knew about the students based on their behavior in school.

Dr. Martinson had strong opinions about his role as a moral exemplar, and he was not shy about drawing a comparison between himself and some of his peers who may have more informal relationships with the students.

> *I do a great deal of lecturing—sometimes I am criticized—they say that the presidency is a bully pulpit; so is the teacher's desk. Some students don't show enough respect for classroom decorum. I don't see myself as one of the kids, as some might. In class, I prefer a certain amount of control and I don't apologize for it. It is more pleasant to overlook distracted kids, etc., and the more popular you'll be as a teacher, but I don't feel inclined to overlook very much. This may lead to a certain amount of lecturing. If moral issues arise, I don't hesitate to raise moral or ethical questions—it makes class more interesting. In second year Latin class, we'll discuss crucifixion not in religious terms, but because it was a common Roman punishment. I take opportunities to discuss Roman civiliza-tion and culture—we can't avoid it so long as we respect people's private beliefs and not try to influence their private beliefs.*

I could see that Dr. Martinson used his persona as a teacher to cultivate a moral atmosphere and to nurture a moral life in his classroom.[12]

At Haym Solomon High School, a public high school located in one of the most violent neighborhoods in Philadelphia, the moral atmosphere is vastly different from John Adams High School. One of the teachers at Haym Solo-mon, Mr. Paschko, sees his role clearly as a moral role model and as a partner in the moral education of his students. To spark conversations with his stu-dents, he occasionally reveals his personal moral stance on a given issue and explains how he arrives at his conclusions. He seeks to teach students how to develop their own ideas "rather than build the structure for them."

In one of the chapters of his book *Educating for Character,* Thomas Lickona describes the teacher as a caregiver, model, and mentor, and in his essay "The Power of Modeling in Children's Character Development," he argues that teachers, like parents, are influential role models, not only when we model success, but also when we model effort, faith, love, thoughtful disagreement, reconciliation, and even failure.[13] Gary Fenstermacher, a professor at the Uni-versity of Michigan School of Education, describes the ways in which a chem-istry teacher, for example, functions as a role model and moral educator:

Chemistry can be taught in myriad ways, but however it is taught, the teacher will always be giving directions, explaining, demonstrating, checking, adjudicating, motivating, reprimanding, and in all these activities, displaying the manner that marks him or her as morally well developed or not. Teachers who understand their impact as moral educators take their manner quite seriously. They understand that they cannot expect honesty without being honest or generosity without being generous or diligence without themselves being diligent. Just as we understand that teachers must engage in critical thinking with students if they expect students to think critically in their presence, they must exemplify moral principles and virtues in order to elicit them from students.[14]

Just as an academic requirement to take chemistry puts students in the chemistry lab, the social studies requirement puts students in Mr. Paschko's classroom, and he becomes the kind of role model who tries to draw students out of their personal concerns toward more global concerns.

As an inner-city teacher with 9th- and 10th-grade students who find success elusive and who allow themselves to fail, Mr. Paschko has found success by engaging his students in personal and informal conversations outside of class and by sending them back to their parents. In an unusual statement coming from a teacher, he said that as much as he wants the young people to become independent adults, he also tells them to obey their parents: "You need to submit yourselves to authority." He is line with the findings of Professor William Damon of the Center on Adolescence at Stanford, who describes the moral dimensions of the primary relationship between parents and children: "The child's respect for parental authority sets the direction for civilized participation in society when the child later begins assuming the rights and responsibilities of full citizenship."[15] Another thinker in moral education, Marvin Berkowitz, writes that parents exert the "predominant influence on the child's character formation" through their affection and respect for the child, and a school influences a student's "self-concept (including self-esteem), social skills (especially peer social skills), values, moral reasoning maturity . . . and so on."[16]

Mr. Paschko believes that students ultimately benefit from an acceptance of parental authority; he also calls upon his students to accept the authority of the police in spite of their bad reputation for having roughed up some of his students without any apparent provocation. Shining a positive light on this, he shared a dream for a moment: "If we made our neighborhood the kind of neighborhood where cops wouldn't do that, then we could take responsibility instead of just complaining about the cops." He recognizes that he is not the primary parent, but he sees that he has succeeded at reaching students, so he has come to see himself as a moral role model. He shares love with his students, sometimes in the form of tough love and discipline: "If they see that you love them, they respond in kind."[17]

Students at Haym Solomon treat respect as a core moral value that cannot be violated. They love to speak about respect, and I heard the word so often and in so many interviews that I was tempted to write a separate chapter about the concept of respect. Instead, I decided to discuss respect in this chapter, because it is so important to the moral life of adolescents that I heard discussion about respect from students across the spectrum. Students often speak about it as if it is an authentic value that everyone already understands, something that hardly merits questioning. I have come to believe that it means different things at different times.

How do students speak about respect? For some, it means outward behavior: a polite attitude and even reverence toward others who have wisdom and authority. When I interviewed Darshona, a senior at Haym Solomon High School who had published a book of Christian poetry, she immediately related that her family had taught her to respect others around her so that she could get respect in return. Having seen her brother shot and killed when she was still a child, issues of respect are deeply important to her. In her book's first poem, "Year 1999," she concludes that religious faith can bring self-respect and the capacity to overcome the hard life on the streets, bringing fulfillment and a better life: ". . . listen and learn, look and discern, think about it in concern, your walk you can change, and your life you can turn."[18] For Darshona, respect involves piety and self-respect. For her and for her classmate Quanesha, whom I also met at Haym Solomon High School, self-respect appears to be necessary before facing God and before looking to the future with a sense of dignity. Quanesha related that from the time of her mother's death when she was just 12 years old, she did not know who would be taking care of her, and she felt disrespect coming from her grandmother: "I've had to think about what I'm going to do. . . . I'm 12 years old, worrying about getting a job. I had to get out of my grandmother's house because she didn't treat me as well." As one boy put it, "Respect is—you know how far you go. You listen to your elders; you watch your mouth. You shouldn't talk to someone like you wouldn't want them talking to you. How you represent yourself. Your appearance."

Another classmate, Qasim, spoke about respect in terms of integrity: "Be yourself. Don't let anyone persuade you to do stuff that don't fit your character, because if you do, you'll run into a brick wall that is not what you wanted to do!" Qasim said that a lot of the seniors and juniors respect the teachers, while the underclassmen are less respectful; they haven't heard yet about the importance of respecting the teachers. He said so, praising his teachers in some of the most colorful, enthusiastic, and resonant language that I have heard: "They bust they butts to make sure we're on point! I'm going to give the teachers 100 percent because they put out."

In the eyes of some of the students I met, respect really means the way in which they would like to be treated by others. When two girls at Haym Solomon High School were sent out of class into Mr. Wesley's classroom, they sat quietly, waiting for Mr. Wesley to talk to them about discipline. I was interested to hear their perspective on respect, and I wanted to know what kinds of values they believed the school taught. While they sat there in a sort of detention, one of the girls, Jeanelle, commented that in her younger years, "Teachers were like your parents, teaching you to do your best, never to give up on anything." The other, Khalida, added, "If you work at improving your vocabulary, some teachers treat you like you're their own kids! Some will know how to joke with you and some will be serious, and you know not to go over the limits." Respect involves these kinds of limits and personal boundaries between adults and students. I heard in Jeanelle's voice an eagerness to be taken seriously as a young adult:

> I would never disrespect Mr. Wes because of the kind of person he is. There are certain teachers that overdiscipline and kick you out. That's not discipline; that's just kicking out of class! Sometimes some teachers don't give respect right off the bat. Teachers get treated the way they act.

Khalida nodded in agreement as Jeanelle spoke. Respect, for these girls, makes it possible to have meaningful student-teacher relationships. Without showing respect for students "right off the bat," the teacher cannot expect to receive student attention and student respect. Authentic respect, they believe, has to come from the adult teacher first.[19]

OBLIGATIONS TO THE COMMUNITY

When I first began to study the moral outlooks of adolescents, I wanted to find out what it would take to persuade adolescents to set aside their own priorities in order to fulfill a duty to the community. I wasn't sure how easily teenagers could be moved in a moral direction that would involve giving to others and giving up their independence, so I constructed a scenario for the students to consider in their interviews with me.

First, I asked a series of questions focused on issues of charity and justice. I asked the students who participated in the study to consider the Jewish concept of charity, which is called in Hebrew *tzedaqa*. While the word *charity,* refers to "care," the Hebrew word, *tzedaqa* and the Arabic word *sadaqah* come from the root word for "justice," *tzedeq*. A desire for justice is thus embedded in a charitable act. I asked students to consider what they would do if they had experienced great financial success during their adulthood. As I expected, several students mentioned that they would give some of the surplus to charitable causes. A student at John Adams High School in New York City named Jeffrey, who took an Authentic and Assured view of Jewish tradition, insisting that women should not assume some of the ritual traditions that have been the domain of men, told me that he would want to apply Jewish principles of *tzedaqa* to address the problems of homeless people in New York. Jeffrey expressed his antipathy to welfare, but he said that he would approve of applying Maimonides's principles of *tzedaqa* by focusing on helping homeless people to help themselves. When I asked him directly if he had given money recently to *tzedaqa,* he answered, "Honestly? I have no money. . . . My family's not struggling at all, but, um, I don't have a job." If he had a job and he were to give a donation, he said that he would contribute to his synagogue and to cancer-related funds.

For Jeffrey, theology did not guide him the way that tradition and obligations did. "To me," he said, "Judaism is all about maintaining the tradition. . . . It's just about, you know, knowing who you are in the sense of that, following the moral codes." Speaking about the importance of affirming a positive ethnic and religious identity, he offered, "It's not about the way you observe them . . . It's more about knowing that you're Jewish . . . You know what I mean?"

Tamar, a student at Amesbury High School, also spoke with an Authentic and Assured voice. She spent a great deal of her weekend time with her synagogue youth group. Her answers about *tzedaqa* were more vague than Jeffrey's, but she remained focused on what she could offer the community. What would she do if she experienced great financial success in the future? "I'd probably share it with others who need it," she said. This concern about sharing has echoes in the work of Nel Noddings who writes about the importance of teaching children to develop both an ethic of justice and an ethic of care.[20]

The other scenario that I posed involved the fulfillment of a ritual obligation. In Jewish tradition, there are certain prayers in the morning, afternoon, and evening services that cannot be said or chanted unless there are 10 adult Jews present. The quorum of 10 is called a *minyan*. In the interviews, I asked the students to respond to a series of three scenarios in which they were asked to imagine themselves walking down the street and approached by an individual who asked them if they could please come to the afternoon religious services;

the *minyan* would only take 10 minutes, and, in the first case, God expects it of them; in the second case, they were assured that they would feel good about participating; and in the third case, they were told that their presence would make it possible for a mourner to recite a prayer that could only be offered in the presence of 10.

Those who share an Authentic and Assured outlook said that they would accept the invitation to attend the *minyan* immediately because it would offer an opportunity to observe a commandment and to fulfill a duty to God. Even if an individual were distracted or uninspired during the entire 10 minutes of the religious service, it still could be meaningful because participating in the *minyan* included the satisfaction of fulfilling a *mitzvah*. In fact, someone who holds Authentic and Assured values might even feel some embarrassment about having to be asked instead of knowing to come on his or her own!

It is not easy for adolescents to do what they are told to do. One boy named Jared confessed that he might have wanted to rebel against any individual who told him what to do, though he acknowledged that he nevertheless does feel a sense of obligation to the community. Tamar described the challenge of suppressing her own needs in order to participate in the community prayer. Jeffrey, however, felt no such conflict. He saw the communal obligation as more important than whatever plan he may have had. Two members of his family had died near the time of our interview session. He could answer this question from personal experience. For Jeffrey, one of the synagogue's most important functions is to host daily services for people in mourning so that they could say a ritual prayer known as the Mourner's *Qaddish*.[21]

"HONOR CODE? PRETENTIOUS NONSENSE"

When an Authentic and Assured voice seems false or forced, young people see through it and their eyes often glaze over in boredom. Many adolescents experience their Authentic and Assured schools with a measure of cynicism; I remember seeing students who attended a Roman Catholic school in a New York neighborhood light up cigarettes as soon as they left school at the end of the day, and I also remember many of the girls at an Orthodox Jewish day school in another New York neighborhood wearing jeans under their ankle-length skirts so that as soon as the school day ended, they could resume their lives as American teens. When I visit schools and a teacher speaks of obligations that *we* must follow, I often look around at the faces of the students for hints about whether the students hear those obligations as belonging to others, or whether they feel that they are part of that *we*.

In a particularly poignant scene in Tobias Wolff's novel *Old School*, the narrator has been expelled from his school on an honor code violation, and his teacher Mr. Ramsey tells the boy he doesn't believe in honor codes:

> *"You don't believe in the Honor Code?"*
>
> *'That's not what I said. But no, certainly not. Send a boy packing if he breaks the rules, by all means. Plant a boot on his backside, but do please leave the word honor out of it. It's disgusting, how we forever throw it out.*
>
> *". . . Make good rules and hold the boys to them. No need to be pawing at their souls. Honor Code? Pretentious nonsense."*[22]

Honor codes are supposed to be revered and held as guarantees that students will live up to a code of honesty and integrity. In this scene, it is rejected as "pretentious nonsense!" Where does the impetus come for such a strong critique? In Wolff's novel, the teacher Ramsey rejects the attempt to normalize and to institutionalize honesty because he prefers instead to hold each student to higher standards of accountability. It's as if an honor code sets a minimum level for compliance with the rules, while Ramsey seeks for his students to achieve higher than minimum levels of honor. The book's narrator surmises that perhaps Ramsey thinks that even the most dignified honor code cannot protect people from hurt and from human flaws, whether they are adolescents in school or adults in the community who are susceptible to all kinds of temptations. Or perhaps Ramsey thinks that by the time a young person gets to high school it is too late to influence their moral behavior with an honor code.

Is an honor code a solution to the decline of morality among today's adolescents? The fictional Ramsey may be right in his cynicism that honor codes do not raise the level of moral culture in a school. Many think otherwise. Arthur Schwartz, Executive Vice President at the John Templeton Foundation, sees honor codes as an important part of a school's culture. Honor codes affect both academic conduct and social conduct. They are not meant to be coercive, because nobody should be forced to believe something, but they are, in a way, countercultural because they are meant to shape school culture even when the school culture may go against prevailing culture outside of the school:

> *An honor system impels, prompts, and motivates students to reflect on what it means to live in a community that affirms and defends a set of ideals related to honor and integrity. . . . [T]he school's honor code is a powerful voice that counters society's prevailing perception that all of us are unencumbered, morally free agents.*[23]

Recent statistics on adolescent behavior indicate that our high school students don't always value positive moral behavior as much as they did a few decades ago. Is Ramsey right that honor codes are a form of indoctrination, or is he wrong?

Girls Preparatory School in Chattanooga, Tennessee, for example, requires girls to adhere to an honor code. Mrs. Rickie Pierce, associate head of school, said that the girls there sign a pledge that they have not given or received help each time they complete an assignment, test, or quiz. The girls take the honor code seriously, choosing representatives from each grade in the Upper School to serve on the school's Honor Council. The Council, in turn, raises moral issues from time to time so that "the girls themselves publicize the code. . . . It is very much respected and the girls are proud of it."[24] The Gilman School in Baltimore, a boys' school, requires students to sign a pledge that says, "As a gentleman I have acted honorably on this paper."[25] John Adams High School, discussed earlier in this book, requires students to affirm the Ephebic Oath, in which they pledge to uphold a sense of citizenship and loyalty.[26] The 10th grader Jeffrey Schochet spoke about the Ephebic Oath with a touch of disdain (in one interview, he called it the "*Pubic* Oath"); he acknowledged that this disdain came from his disappointment in himself after having violated the oath and after having faced serious consequences. Jeffrey felt a combination of resentment and respect for the Oath as a set of core values affirmed by the school.

Questions about honor codes are not limited to high schools. Bowdoin College in Maine has had an honor code since 1964, stating, "Integrity is essential in creating an academic environment dedicated to the development of independent modes of learning, analysis, judgment, and expression." College leaders there believe that the rate of cheating is 33 to 50 percent less on campuses where students uphold an honor code. The honor code succeeds not only because it has become a permanent part of the culture of the college but also because students themselves support it. Faculty members support it by providing guidance and guidelines for students so that they learn how to show their work honestly and so that they can avoid cheating and plagiarism.[27]

Some schools do not go so far as to create oaths or honor codes, but they establish rules for conduct and discipline, and then they give the rules a layer of moral significance. Guidelines for hair length may ensure greater safety in the wood shop or the metal shop. Blue blazers for the boys and navy blue skirts for the girls provide a uniform look, establish conformity, and have the practical benefit of making it easy for students to get dressed in the morning. Schools might provide a moral rationale for a dress code by saying that it instills a sense of self-respect and that it promotes a more democratic atmosphere because clothing labels matter less than the school coat of arms.

Dress codes also play a different function for boys and for girls. In traditional boys' schools with dress codes that require a coat and tie, the young men are dressing up in preparation for the kind of clothes they may be expected to wear in the adult world, especially in business and law. In traditional girls' schools with dress codes that require uniform skirts and tops, there may be an opposite purpose: the school may be trying to keep girls from growing up too quickly and from adopting the sometimes inappropriate fashion trends of the adult world. In these cases, schools have to define why they see it as a moral good for boys to dress in coats and ties and why they see it as a moral good for girls to dress in uniform skirts and tops.

Administrators in new schools have a special opportunity to create a unique curriculum, disciplinary code, student government, and moral culture. Very few education schools prepare teachers to develop the moral climate of their classes,[28] so teachers may need guidance from their principals and colleagues. When I served as an administrator of an after-school program for 7th–12th graders, and then again when I was an administrator in a full-time 9th- to 12th-grade setting, I worked to develop honor codes and learned firsthand that students quickly become cynical about any attempts to ennoble them with moral talk. I also found that teachers, however noble their own calling and sense of idealism, have reserves of skepticism that come out when they are asked to set aside class or preparation time in favor of discussions about the moral life of a school. As much as they might agree about the importance of morality, teachers and students often prefer and need to tackle more immediate and less vague concerns like scheduling, curricular changes, and plans for new activities.

WHOSE VALUES SHOULD WE TEACH?

Authentic and Assured schools are very clear about whose values they teach, whether they teach from a religious perspective or from a particular ideological perspective. Schools with religious affiliations (Jewish, Roman Catholic, Muslim, and Quaker, etc.) make it clear that they aspire to give students the vocabulary, ideas, and benefits of those traditions. A charter school with an environmental focus or a school for African Americans with an Afrocentric focus also might be Authentic and Assured. Authentic values are not limited to religious traditions.

Thomas Lickona describes two fundamental secular values: respect and responsibility. *Respect* includes the ethical treatment of others in everyday interactions, and *responsibility* means, as Lickona puts it, an ability to respond.[29] He identifies the components of good character in three broad areas:

1. Moral Knowing (moral awareness, knowing moral values, perspective taking, moral reasoning, decision making, and self-knowledge)
2. Moral Feeling (conscience, self-esteem, empathy, loving the good, self-control, and humility)
3. Moral Action (competence, will, and habit)[30]

While some of these elements in Lickona's understanding of character, such as loving the good and self-control, echo the Greek philosopher Aristotle,[31] others, such as moral awareness, humility, and justice, echo the early American patriot, entrepreneur, and philosopher Benjamin Franklin;[32] yet others, such as competence and moral action, echo more modern educational philosophers such as John Dewey.[33]

In answering a question such as Whose values should we teach? Joan Goodman and Howard Lesnick clarify the difference between conservative and liberal answers to the question. Conservatives have inherited the Aristotelian position, preferring action—habits and practices—to lengthy reflection and questions. Taking a relatively simple example of a teacher asking a child to follow the school rules and to remove his hat while in school, Goodman and Lesnick explain that a conservative stance would hold that the no-hat rule is not merely a convention: it is the practical outcome of an important principle about respect, group discipline, and self-discipline. They write,

> *The removed hat (like the act of standing for the national anthem) has symbolic significance, expressing respect for a teacher and a school, and for learning. Respect for proper authority is a major social good, indeed, a necessity for social harmony. . . . he will be a better personal as an adult if he learns, through the inculcation of habit, to take his private preferences less seriously, to take more seriously the adverse reactions of his peers.[34]*

For conservatives, it is a moral good to maintain tradition and to respect authority. Individuals are better citizens if they give up some of their own preferences in order to conform to some group norms, cultivating good practices and practices. Goodman and Lesnick add,

> *. . . [T]o a conservative the primary objective of moral education is to inculcate character in children through insistent and directive teaching, especially*

around the 'hard' virtues such as courage, temperance, honor, fortitude, and self-
discipline. Conservatives are more concerned with the child's actions than with
his or her reasoning, which, they suspect, easily falls prey to rationalization.[35]

Liberals, in contrast, tend to challenge authority in principle, so as Goodman and Lesnick go on to explain, a liberal may question whether the school authority that requires hat wearing may be looking for respect (a moral value) or coercive authority (a kind of power). For a liberal,

it is as important to moral development to teach children to question as to follow
the demands of those in power. . . . What children need to learn is how to think
about difficult moral questions: to subordinate their self-regarding impulses, to
be sure, but then to reflect on the process of moral decision making, to learn to
think for themselves, and to exercise moral judgment.[36]

Liberals feel morally threatened by unquestioning obedience to authority. Moral thinking comes about through a process of critical inquiry and deep reflection. An educator should not mistake obedience for moral behavior: Joan Goodman writes, "Obedience can enable goodness or evil; it can be character building or character defeating."[37] Goodman and Lesnick help to explain why conservatives and liberals hold strong positions in favor of moral education, but conservatives and liberals differ in their view of the role of teachers and schools in engaging students in moral questions, moral reasoning, moral decision making, and moral action.[38]

CHARTER SCHOOLS AND SINGLE-SEX SCHOOLS WITH A MORAL MISSION

As discussed in the introduction to this book, recent years have seen a proliferation of charter schools, many of which have an Authentic and Assured outlook. Charter schools are public schools that have been given a charter by the district to educate children according to an approved curriculum that is different from that of regular district schools. Many of the newer public charter schools have a moral mission based on a particular theme. One school in New York was developed for children from Arab families to learn the Arabic language together with children from other ethnic groups, but it came under severe criticism in the summer of 2007 because some perceived the school to be a threat or a front for anti-American terrorism. The school, called Khalil Gibran International Academy, was not established to be a religious school at all, but to promote linguistic pluralism and cross-cultural understanding.[39]

Because of some controversial issues, the school's founding principal, Debbie Almontaser, ultimately resigned before the school year began; in the intervening months, the school has succeeded in opening and launching a second year under different leadership.

Some schools, such as charter schools and faith-based schools, are founded with an explicit moral purpose.[40] The strong moral commitment to environmentalism in many new charter schools shows that moral education is not limited to faith-based schools.[41] A new school called "Urban Assembly New York Harbor School," based in Brooklyn, seeks to connect its students to the Hudson River. While that, in itself, can be seen as a moral mission, the school's founders also hope that students will gain confidence by developing new skills on the water. One student who came to understand that mission, wrote, "I feel so privileged to learn about the water. The Hudson River is like an ancestor of our past, and if we listen to it, it just might tell tales." Another student, who faced her fears about the water, wrote about conquering the fear, learning to swim, and coming to feel protective of maritime life.[42]

Many parents have become interested in single-sex schools because co-ed schools do not appear to serve some of the specific learning needs of boys and girls. Single-sex schools not only recognize and support learning differences between boys and girls but also nurture different moral and social sensibilities, promoting academic achievement, self-confidence, and good feelings of success. On the Web site for Boys' Latin of Philadelphia Charter School, the page entitled "Why All Boys?" explains that boys in a single-sex setting are more likely to find teachers responsive to boys' learning styles: "This allows a young man more ease in developing his full potential." The single-sex environment may strengthen the moral outlook of boys, because "boys tend to soften their competitive edge and become more collaborative in a single sex setting. They can just be themselves and not worry about the social stresses inherent in a co-educational environment."[43]

To look at differences in the experiences of boys and girls, the Center for the Study of Boys' and Girls' Lives, a think tank at the University of Pennsylvania Graduate School of Education, was established and it strives, in its own words, "to capture the dynamism and agency in students' development and to help schools promote the widest sense of possibility and greatest hope for integrity in their lives."[44] Researchers at the Center have looked at the ways in which both co-ed and single-sex schools cultivate the moral sensibilities of their students through workshops highlighting certain kinds of behavior, through virtue-based explicit curricula, through more subtle rituals and traditions, and often through combating negative behavior.[45] At an all-boys school in Philadelphia, for example, boys in the lower school all wear a uniform jersey (made of the same indestructible cloth that is used for baseball pants!) with five contrasting stripes that are highlighted on each forearm, symbolizing five core values at the school: courage, honesty, integrity, loyalty, and sportsmanship. The researchers worked with the school on identifying ways in which students in the middle and upper school divisions continue to affirm those values; the researchers also helped the school to face an educational challenge that was presented because the school's values tended to fade into the background for many students. The values came to seem like ideals that were somehow less relevant for the students.[46]

The leadership at the Center for the Study of Boys' and Girls' Lives believes that it can have a significant impact on improving the moral lives of young men. After interviewing students and teachers at schools to probe moral attitudes, programs can be developed that "expose" and address known behavior and not just hypothetical behavior. The researchers and leadership declare, "[I]f it is a goal to invite boys to justice and the cultivation of other social virtues, exposing the spaces and practices within our schools in which boys are learning to fear and to abuse is a necessary first step."[47] Ultimately this could help schools to become more successful at fulfilling their moral mission.

Girls' schools have a parallel devotion to fostering the moral development of girls. Just after my graduation from college, I taught at a school for girls in the mid-Atlantic states called the Carey School. It continues to articulate its mission in educational terms and in moral terms. In addition to providing a "nurturing environment" as the setting for a "rigorous" academic curriculum" that "inspires a passion for intellectual curiosity and emphasizes the delights and demands of learning," the school also aspires to cultivate "respect for diversity and engenders habits of moral and ethical leadership and a sense of responsibility to the broader community." Here the mission statement sounds Aristotelian in the commitment to cultivating habits. Like many schools, the Carey School also aspires to see its graduates become "responsible and confident participants in the world" who will go on to contribute to society and "lead considered and consequential lives."[48] The school appears to combine virtues and a commitment to character education with a commitment to the educational process itself. Graduates can expect to emerge with an authentic and confident voice that is true to themselves as young women.

Teachers at single-sex schools are in a position to support the different approaches to learning that work best for boys and girls. Boys and girls tend to develop their verbal abilities and their eye-hand coordination at different rates; their different physiologies also call for different kinds of kinesthetic and hands-on learning in a classroom. How the boys and girls learn (their respective learning styles) can be nurtured by different pedagogies. Boys may need more exercise, so a teacher might encourage the children to jump while reciting a passage, while girls may learn more successfully in small group work that responds to their needs for social interactions. In response to the skepticism that many share about single-sex schools, Elizabeth Weil, in a *New York Times Magazine* article wrote:

> Single-sex schools are indeed better at providing kids with a positive sense of themselves as students, to compete with the antiacademic influences of youth culture; the other is that in order to end up in a single-sex classroom, you need to have a parent who has made what educators call "a pro-academic choice." You need a parent who at least cares enough to read the notices sent home and go through the process of making a choice—any choice.[49]

While single-sex schools can be effective at maintaining traditional gender roles, they also can be effective at helping students to develop their identity.

For parents looking at a school, what are the advantages and what are the drawbacks of a school that promotes an Authentic and Assured voice? Authentic and Assured schools do not apologize for requiring students to wear a uniform and to develop a sense of duty. They may require students to experience social and religious forces larger than themselves by requiring participation in community service programs and in regular religious services. Children who tend to be nonconformist, with more of an individualistic sensibility may feel more comfortable outside of an Authentic and Assured school, attending instead a community-oriented school.

To a great extent, young people repeat the morals they have heard at home. Some of their responses to my questions about respect and duty sounded as if they had come verbatim from the mouth of another adult. Many young people do not speak with an Authentic and Assured voice, and they tend instead to express skepticism and occasional doubts. They are in the process of integrating things they have learned from their schools, homes, and faith traditions. In the following chapter, I will introduce voices expressing the second moral outlook, Bridging and Binding, a middle ground that allows for questions about when authentic and certain duties to the community may give way to individual interpretation, liberty, and preferences.

Bridging and Binding

Only connect.

—*E. M. Forster,* Howards End

There is comfort and wisdom to be found in the middle. A middle position allows one to look at both sides of an issue and then to arrive at a new set of connections and a new synthesis. In E. M. Forster's book *Howards End,* the brief epigraph, "Only connect," anticipates the complicated relationships among the characters in the book and the failure of some characters to come to comprehend that it is possible to overcome and then to rise above the confining entanglements of love and family and history.

It takes a flexible moral outlook to connect with others without giving up the integrity of traditions and ideas that come from home or from any other formative setting. To connect with others is to meet in the middle and to nurture a synthesis between tradition and modernity, between faith and practice. In the field of education, there are opportunities to connect theory and practice, adults and children, and policy and implementation. Those who speak with an Authentic and Assured moral voice may feel threatened by an outlook that sounds neutral or that acknowledges the possibility of multiple viewpoints. Yet, a strong connecting voice provides the framework within which diversity and pluralism can thrive. The middle ground could be described as a process of bridging different viewpoints, seeking authenticity and remaining connected—and even bound—to tradition while still seeking some ideological independence.

Great 20th-century abstract artists such as Picasso, Matisse, and Mondrian (and any great master from earlier centuries, for that matter) did not begin to paint abstract forms until they had mastered the art of representation. With this hindsight, it is fascinating to see the landscapes and the still-life paintings of these great abstract artists and to know how life and the pursuit of art brought these painters to abandon conventional forms and paint abstractions of line and color. While they could have continued to paint a landscape or fruit bowl with the natural colors and overall look of the objects, they chose abstract forms to make statements about the interplay of light and dark, about form and negative space, and about the interactions between painters and viewers. Like artists, teachers need to learn conventional teaching techniques to help their students to learn the skills and content necessary for success in class; once they master the art of coaching students to develop those skills (of listening, writing, and problem solving, to name just a few skills), teachers are in a unique position to depart from convention if necessary and to nurture each student's individual efforts at self-expression. A teacher can help students to represent their ideas on paper and then to help them to understand where their ideas fit into a continuum that includes others' ideas as well. Young people are not necessarily interested in overthrowing the traditions and precedents they have inherited; they often are, however, interested in making meaning and in finding relevance. The students who are Bridging and Binding are actively trying to make meaning, connecting with the past, often going in new directions.

To what extent is any of us bound by a strong connection to a tradition and to what extent do we negotiate the terms of that connection ourselves? We all live with many identities, and we are linked to many traditions: we are male, female, single, partnered, urban, suburban, members of a faith group, and members of a national group; sometimes our identity is hyphenated, and we describe ourselves with terms like African Americans, Afro-Caribbean Americans, Asian Americans, Irish Catholic Americans, Jewish Americans, Muslim Americans, and so forth. Our identity group and our origins may shape our response to a given situation or dilemma. To look at the ways in which young people bridge culture and identity with moral decision making, I revisited the founding mission of the high school I attended, I visited the classes of my colleagues at the Jewish school in which I teach, and I also visited a Chinese heritage school that meets on Sunday afternoons at a nearby community college.

GOODNESS AND KNOWLEDGE

When John Phillips wrote the founding deed that established Phillips Exeter Academy, he had a moral mission. He understood that it was not enough to nurture good character (or as my book title suggests, to sow "the seeds of character"). Good character had to be practiced and not just studied, and one would be judged on the basis of whether one's learning bears fruit in the form of moral behavior. John Phillips wrote,

> *It is expected that the attention of instructors to the disposition of the minds and morals of the youth under their charge will exceed every other care; well considering that though goodness without knowledge is weak and feeble, yet knowledge without goodness is dangerous, and that both united form the noblest character, and lay the surest foundation of usefulness to mankind.*[1]

John Phillips calls upon students and teachers not to stop at knowledge, but to set high expectations for goodness, because goodness and knowledge complement each other. This means that for contemporary adolescents and teachers, biological formulas need to be studied together with case studies about genetic testing, geometry needs to be studied together with urban planning, literature must be studied with philosophy, and history must be studied with an eye toward current events. When I was a student at the school in the early 1980s, my classmates and I often questioned whether the school was doing enough to teach goodness. In the years since my graduation, the school has not given up on its mission, and in my own work, I continue to use it as a prism through which to look at other schools' efforts to combine the teaching of knowledge with the teaching of moral reasoning.

SOMETIMES A TOY IS JUST A TOY

At John Adams High School in New York City, the Ephebic Oath, described earlier, provides a traditional framework that also is a point of departure for students in their membership in the school community. All students recite the Ephebic Oath as part of their acculturation to the school, and it stands as a framework for student moral conduct. When behavioral issues arise, students are held to the standards of the Oath. Jeffrey Schochet, a sophomore at the time I interviewed and shadowed him, had been reprimanded for poor and destructive behavior early in his career at the school, and he was told to write an essay in which he affirmed that he was capable of redirecting his energy to fall into line with the community-minded spirit of the Oath. Although the essay reminded him of his duties, his teachers at John Adams gave him a variety of opportunities to come to terms with his own values.

Features like the Ephebic Oath led me to place John Adams High School within the framework of schools that are Authentic and Assured, but some of the classes I observed seem more typical of the goals of Bridging and Binding. I observed a particularly colorful moment in which Jeffrey's values clashed with those of the teacher. His English class was studying Marge Piercy's poem "Barbie Doll" from Piercy's collection *Circles on the Water*,[2] and Jeffrey objected to what he felt was the voice in the poem of an unhappy woman, blaming society for her unhappiness. Piercy's poem describes a girl who "was born as usual," but who, in spite of her health and intelligence, was reduced to "a fat nose on thick legs." Having recently written a report for his history class about the evolution of the G. I. Joe doll, Jeffrey already had been thinking about dolls and about the ways in which they have an impact on the psychology and self-image of children. When he and his classmates were assigned to write their own poems in response to Piercy, he wrote a deeply cynical poem that concluded,

> *"Barbie makes girls have bad body-image"*
> *Is just another feminist ploy*
> *If you're fat and ugly and miserable,*
> *don't take it out on a toy.*

In her comments on the poem, the teacher wrote that Jeffrey had made a simplistic and somewhat dismissive argument in these final lines of his poem, and she suggested a less simplistic approach would sharpen his credibility: "You can be conservative but *know* what the opposition is saying, so you can debunk their ideas while recognizing their complexity." She commended him for his cleverness and wrote, "A great poem, anyway!" In an interview, Jeffrey told me that he believed the teacher to have a liberal bias, so if Jeffrey's hunch is correct, then these comments are coming from a teacher who is willing to set aside her own views to help her student to connect his more traditional views with the perspective of the poet.

It interested me that in my research, I had spoken with many boys and many girls, but it was a boy and not a girl who raised strong personal feelings about gender and identity. Jeffrey and his younger sister had disagreed quite deeply on new roles for women in Jewish ritual. His sister and his mother believed that women should be allowed to participate in certain Jewish rituals in an egalitarian manner alongside men, while Jeffrey said that he favors the separation of gender roles. His feelings were visceral, and he asserted with a voice that sounded like something coming from an older man, "When my sister suddenly now wants to wear *tallit* (the Jewish prayer shawl worn only by men in traditional Jewish communities), that to me was a visual attack on that tradition." He did not want to see others (especially his sister) challenge his traditional understanding of gender roles and boundaries in Jewish ritual. His sister's egalitarian approach to prayer garb had become a moral issue, and like the older men I knew who shared his feelings, Jeffrey felt embattled, as if he were in danger of losing a position of privilege.

I was interested that his attendance at the Cyrus Adler Jewish Day School, a Jewish day school near his home, had not inspired him to become a more pious Jew, nor did it inspire a love of the Bible or of other Jewish traditional texts such as the Talmud. It did, however, inspire him to come to enjoy Hebrew. As he put it, "[I got] a good understanding of, you know, the Jewish religion and the morals behind it, and also, you know, the more you learn, really, the more well-rounded you are. So in that way, it was a good experience. But I wasn't nuts." In other words, he did not feel especially enthusiastic about certain elements of his Jewish day school education, but overall, he felt that his attendance was important to his Jewish identity.[3]

John Adams High School holds its students to high standards. Since the entrance examination is so rigorous, the school attracts and enrolls students who thrive in classes with teachers who are willing to nurture their curiosity and their ability to express themselves. Not surprisingly, students who are such high achievers also feel a great deal of pressure to succeed in gaining acceptance to highly selective colleges. The school leadership also understood the responsibility of helping parents to manage the anxiety of the students around college. When I spoke with Jeffrey's guidance counselor, Mrs. Ruxton, she described the atmosphere of the school. She confided to me that some students could be so competitive about their work that they were tempted to cheat from time to time. There was an 11th-grade parents meeting one night that spring, and she told me that the meeting was likely to attract a number of anxious parents because of the high level of interest and concern about the college application process.

In spite of the anxiety, Mrs. Ruxton said that student good will at the school tended to run high. When a student committed suicide the previous year, the community recalled the student's positive ethic and deep involvement with community service. The student's death affected student morale adversely. The Ephebic Oath, she said, encourages young people to live by positive principles, and she felt that on the whole, the students take it seriously, especially because the school's principal believes in its importance. A consultative council met regularly with Dr. Grossman, and the ethic of service in the Oath translated into clubs that aspired to contribute to society, including Students for the Preservation of the Earth, who made dinosaurs out of aluminum cans to sell and to raise money for Amnesty International, which focuses on activism on behalf of political prisoners around the world. Other groups prepared Easter baskets for homeless people living in shelters. Mrs. Ruxton pointed out that the school had been renovated without bulletin boards and that many of the students not only created bulletin boards but also helped to decorate them with the photographs.[4] The teachers, the counselor, and the principal at John Adams High School seemed to me like true believers, looking for opportunities for students to wrestle with moral issues in the classrooms, holding students accountable for moral behavior, and not shying away from opportunities to mete out discipline to reinforce the school's moral code.

"THE BEST POPCORN IN MY LIFE!" HAYM SOLOMON HIGH SCHOOL

Is it possible to fit a large comprehensive high school into one of these three categories? Private faith-based schools draw their students from faith communities and from families looking for ways to give their children grounding in a particular religious tradition, and private secular independent schools draw their students from families who buy into a particular mission or who seek the resources of an independent school such as a low teacher-student ratio that fosters academic excellence and strong programs in the arts and athletics. Some public schools, such as John Adams High School and Templeton High School in New York City, choose their students as much as the students choose them. Students who wish to attend those schools must take a rigorous examination, and they are admitted only if their scores fall within an acceptable range. Most public schools, however, are more inclusive, enrolling their students from the neighborhood. Public schools I visited, such as Amesbury High School, a suburban high school in Rockland County, New York, and Haym Solomon High School in an inner-city Philadelphia neighborhood, must offer a program that meets the academic needs of their students, regardless of the students' ethnic or moral background. I came to admire these schools for their efforts to cultivate a moral environment that would equip the students for honesty and integrity in the school building and with a commitment to service in the community. For that reason, I have placed my discussions about comprehensive high schools within this chapter about the Bridging and Binding outlook for the ways in which these schools seek to help students to bridge childhood with the responsibilities of adulthood.

As much as I felt privileged to have been able to spend so much meaningful time in such a wide variety of schools, my visit to Haym Solomon High

School was especially profound. Because I am familiar with the culture of private schools, I am not surprised when I see a self-conscious moral mission at schools such as the Academy of the Sisters of St. Theresa, described in the previous chapter, and at the Fairhill Friends School, described in the following chapter. The Al-Quds Islamic Academy falls, in my mind, into its own category as a pioneering school in a transitional neighborhood that offers a personal safety net along with a Muslim education. Haym Solomon High School, or Solomon, as the students call it, has the means to keep students safe, but it looks foreboding with the locked front doors, the security guard station and metal detector at the front door, and with the disciplinary officials who walk through the halls, telling the students to hurry to their classes. The school's location in a neighborhood with a relatively high crime rate could be intimidating to newcomers. Many of the row houses nearby stand in disrepair; auto body shops and beauty salons line the main avenues; many of the side streets appear not to have been cleaned in some time.

Once I entered the school, my fears about security gave way to feelings of optimism: in spite of the tragedies that no doubt affected countless students at the school, and in spite of a lack of resources at the school, I became aware of many efforts to build a positive school culture. I noticed the students and the guards greeting one another cheerfully. When I walked through the halls, I heard teachers introducing new subjects to their students, and announcements over the loudspeaker promised a fun evening at the spring prom. Although I knew that most of the students live with only one of their parents or with a grandparent, and although graduation rates were low and dropout rates were high, I was nevertheless impressed by the ambition of some of the students I came to meet at the school who wanted to beat the odds and attend college.

My host at Solomon, Mr. Michael Wesley, had been a teacher in the school for several years prior to becoming the Academy leader of the Academy of Creative Arts and International Studies, serving as a lead teacher with administrative responsibilities. The Academy functions as a school within the larger high school. Students who enroll in the Academy gain more exposure to culture than students in other academies within Solomon or in typical high school programs; during their senior year, students produce a major project in which they bring together literature, arts, and history of another culture. One year, a number of students traveled with Mr. Wesley to London, fulfilling the international mission of the Academy.

Large comprehensive schools like Solomon have reputations for high dropout rates, for not helping students to raise their low test scores, and for keeping disenchanted teachers on staff. Mr. Wesley and his students defied all of those stereotypes, and he was a strong advocate for the school. I could see that Mr. Wesley (or "Mr. Wes" as his students affectionately call him) is passionate about his work and that he is like an air traffic controller, observing and directing at the same time. In one 10-minute period, he was on the phone, arranging for substitute teachers, glancing into the halls every few minutes, and sitting with some students who needed to be disciplined. I enjoyed the comic relief when commotion in the halls led him to step outside the classroom and to raise his voice to a group of students milling about in the halls. He said to them in a firm and strict voice, "Excuse me. You're interrupting this class." When he found that the loud sounds were coming from students selling popcorn for a fund-raiser, Mr. Wes eased up immediately, smiled, and asked, "Will it be the best popcorn I've had in my life?"

The school had weathered some negative publicity earlier in the year related to a violent incident in the city involving three of its students, and he expressed his frustration that in their coverage of the crime, the papers seemed to point a finger of blame at the school without naming some of the achievements like the trip to London that had expanded so many students' horizons. He lamented that newspapers rarely seem to cover the positive moments that take place during the course of a school day when high school boosters are raising money for the prom, as they do at any suburban school in the spring. Nor does the press seem to cover the moral development of these young people who want to improve the community through community service activities.

Mr. Wesley was not the only one disappointed with the press coverage. One of the students whom I met at Solomon, a 12th-grade student named Qasim, wanted the newspapers to do more: he said, "The paper didn't report on community service or awards! Solomon students do so much other than 'Solomon students leave school early to jump a man!'" Qasim would have been happier to have seen a the paper write up programs like the community service project that involved Mr. Wesley's class every week with a class of 2nd graders nearby.

Haym Solomon High School faces several challenges: how to provide moral education for inner-city adolescents who may disengage or, worse, drop out before crucial lessons in moral education even begin; and how to help students to feel a connection to their city, history, neighborhood, and culture so that the moral life feels like a natural extension of who they are. In light of the school's negative reputation, can any teacher succeed with direct attempts to convey moral values? I tend to believe that teachers are more successful when they are subtle, presenting moral issues through regular content and offering moral hints without moralizing or sermonizing. However, when I observed

Mr. Wesley in class, I saw that a direct approach could succeed. He holds his students to high standards, and they know he cares about them.

As part of the *Journey of a Champion* program, Mr. Wesley taught a class about how people balance basic biological and psychological needs. Guiding his students through a discussion about self-actualization as articulated by Abraham Maslow, he asked the students to envision their future and how they would balance their own needs. He encouraged his 18-year-old seniors to think about what it would mean to have children and to set aside some of their own needs for the needs of a new child. "If you had a child," he began as he gave the students a journal assignment, "what would your hopes and dreams be for the child?" One said that his own hopes and dreams helped him to survive. Another student added that without hopes and dreams, survival could be in jeopardy.

Mr. Wesley challenged the students to look ahead and not to dwell in the past: "I would argue that the family or the life we dream about may be more important than the past." I wondered if this was helpful for his students who have lost family members and friends in violence; in their 18 years, they have seen more violence and dysfunction than many may seen in a lifetime. The quiet in the room at that moment suggested to me that Mr. Wesley had been successful at moralizing; he was able to succeed at breaking through a typical student's passivity. "Whether or not you're going to have kids," he said, "if you don't have a hope or a dream, you stay focused on basic biological needs and if your safety needs are not met, then it prevents you from feeling comfort. We want every kid to feel safe and also to have a sense of belonging and love."

Only minutes later, after having offered this call to his students to offer safety to younger children in the next generation, the students left the classroom to walk together to visit the Joe Louis Elementary School for a weekly community service project in which Mr. Wesley's students would read aloud and serve as reading tutors to a class of 2nd graders. Mr. Wesley expressed pride in his students' commitment. At any moment, students could have left the group and decided not to participate in the community service project. The 15-minute walk to the elementary school offered opportunities for students to step away and even to disappear into the neighborhood for the rest of the day, but he had succeeded in instilling a sense of obligation to the younger children.

That commitment and sense of obligation was matched in the 2nd-grade classroom that the students visited. All of the students were dressed in light blue shirts with navy pants, and they sat with partners. The room could have won an award as a language-rich environment with banners hanging on the walls listing synonyms, antonyms, homophones, and sight words for the students to know. The 2nd-grade teacher's sense of purpose was clear from another set of posters listing expectations and rights:

As your teacher

1. I expect you to always do your best and be your best.
2. I expect you to respect and be kind and courteous to everyone.
3. I expect you to come to school prepared.

Rights

1. To learn something new each day.
2. To feel comfortable and safe in our classroom.
3. To be treated fairly with dignity and respect.

If one had to define a moral environment, these lists qualified. This was a room in which learning could flourish and in which everyone had a role to play and a set of responsibilities to fulfill. The high school students accepted those expectations and responsibilities, though Mr. Wesley did have to remind one of the students to remove his hat upon entering the elementary school building. Once inside, the high school students all spread out, sitting together with the younger students, one pair reading the Mercer Mayer book *Just Grandma and Me*,[5] and another pair beginning Roald Dahl's book *Fantastic Mr. Fox*.[6] Mr. Wesley pointed out one of his high school students who was reading with one of the 2nd-grade boys. He was dressed with a long T-shirt. Mr. Wesley explained to me that some of the younger boys fear the older boys who "want to live the hard life," and the younger boys also look up to the image of tough street-wise kid, and they aspire to be tough. "Here they show different qualities." One of the students had "hustled on the street" but was able to show a nurturing side to the 2nd graders. While the high school girls are expected to be nurturing, it is more unusual to see that quality in the boys. Mr. Wesley saw the reading sessions as one of the rare occasions when the second graders could interact with young men, since so many African American children are raised without the presence of their fathers.

This was a risky service project, because it required channels of communication between a high school and an elementary school, each one already facing concerns about student and faculty safety and about student achievement. This kind of community service required a deep commitment to moral education on the part of both teachers. It was worth it for Mr. Wesley, because his classes and service projects attempt to bridge the world of the neighborhood (crime, drugs, dead-end jobs) with the world of possibility (optimism, ideas, service to others). The reading program between the two schools fulfilled a moral goal of bridging several gaps: the gap between the two age groups was the most obvious gap to bridge first. One could say that the high school students faced a turning point: either they could bridge the gap between their own youth and adulthood by preparing for life on the streets or by preparing for an adulthood of responsibility that would involve mastering job skills and nurturing others. Their teachers hoped that service-learning programs and other programs through the Academy at Haym Solomon would enable them to bridge those gaps.[7]

"BRIDGING THE CULTURAL GAP"—MEIGUO CHINESE ACADEMY

Chinese culture, deeply influenced by ancient moral principles, continues to thrive in the overseas Chinese community in the United States. These overseas Chinese families are extending some of the same civic discussions that began in Mainland China about the importance of education and citizenship.[8] I studied Chinese when I was in college, and it wasn't until I visited Meiguo Chinese Academy that I found myself participating in a Chinese-language class and using my Chinese dictionary for the first time in many years. In spite of the difference in age between the students in the class and me, the material the students were studying was strikingly familiar because of the emphasis on moral behavior and folk wisdom.

The Academy meets at a community college in suburban Philadelphia. For two hours on Sunday afternoons, about 500 students fill classes offering several levels of Chinese. Some of the children are second-generation American and some are themselves first-generation immigrants. Some who attend the Academy were adopted by Caucasian parents, and they come to Meiguo Chinese Academy to learn about their culture of origin. The program's mission is to promote "understanding and appreciation of Chinese Language and Culture" through weekend classes, athletic and cultural programs.[9] While some of the classes focus on traditional stories and on written and spoken Chinese grammar, some students take classes in Chinese dance, and others learn to type in Chinese. The program is not limited to Chinese studies: on one floor, I also saw a classroom of Indian children studying together, and I wondered if they were studying Sanskrit or Hindi.

In the halls of the community college building during the break at 3:00 P.M., students gathered in two large clumps: One group huddled around a bank of computers that were available for public access. Their laughter and excitement filled the hall with energy. Another group of students spread themselves along a hallway to look at a series of posters created by each class. One poster celebrated the interests and talents of the members of the class, while another poster illustrated the places where the students had been during the summer.

Just after the break, I visited a class of fourth-year students who were studying an ancient and well-known story about a 16th-century folk hero called Master Dongguo who gets ensnared in mischief perpetrated by an ungrateful wolf. The story is so well known that when I was introduced to the teacher, she assumed that I was familiar with the story since I had studied Chinese for two years and then lived in China. A standard Chinese dictionary includes an entry about him:

> Dongguo: Master Dongguo, the foolish, softhearted scholar who narrowly escaped being eaten by a wolf which he had helped to hide from a hunter—a naive person who gets into trouble through being softhearted to evil people.[10]

In this classic story, Master Dongguo saves a wolf from some evil hunters by hiding the wolf in a scholar's bag. After the hunters go away, Master Dongguo lets the wolf out, and then the wolf tries to eat Master Dongguo. Ultimately, the wolf is outwitted and Master Dongguo's life is preserved, but not until after he nearly loses his life.

Although most of the class hour was devoted to the grammar and vocabulary that would enable the students to read the story, Teacher Chen, as the students call her (*Chen Laoshi* in Chinese), also engaged the students in a discussion about the naive character Master Dongguo. One student described him as *hutu*, a little silly. They agreed that the Master was too easy on the wolf. The conversation and the story were not unusual: the students have studied other moral tales, which are themselves part of a genre known as *gushi* (pronounced [goo-shur]). There had been another lesson on four significant Chinese inventions that have contributed to the development of technology, and in the coming year, the students will read *The Monkey King*, also known as *The Journey to the West,* about a popular figure in Chinese literature who makes mischief, gets into trouble, does battle with god-kings, and eventually makes it to India, the birthplace of Buddhism. Since the overall goal of the Academy is to reinforce a sense of pride and culture, the literature is meant to serve as a vehicle both to help students develop their proficiency with the language, and also to give students a sense of the moral values in their ancient culture.

In an interview with Teacher Chen a few days after I visited her class, she told me that she devotes a great deal of discussion to the morals of each story.

Some stories have a great deal of moral content, such as the story called "Yu-gongyishan," about a man who tried to move a mountain so that he could get a better view from his house. Teacher Chen tries to help the students to understand the implicit values in the stories, even if they are well known. Some lessons are about honesty, and others are about hard work and teamwork. She told me that students often find that they recall an expression or a story that they had studied years earlier. Even when the students are just learning vocabulary, she tries to give a sense of the origins of each Chinese character. The character or ideograph for *fetch,* for example, combines an image of an ear with an image of a hand, recalling a time when soldiers would fetch the ear of a dead enemy soldier to prove that they had been victorious. When learning new material, the students also learn some of the classical four character expressions known as *chengyu.*

I was introduced to three young men, Henry, Paul, and Li. Henry, a 9th grader, and Paul, a 10th grader, had been born in the United States. Li was a 10th grader who immigrated to the United States from China when he was younger. When I asked the boys what they thought the school was trying to teach, they agreed on the centrality of Chinese culture. Henry added that there might be a practical element as well: by learning Chinese and by reinforcing what the young people got at home, it could be good for job opportunities and for "future considerations." Culture is a broad term that can mean many things, so I asked the students to elaborate. Henry identified values of high self-esteem and hard work, to which Paul chimed in, "Underline that!" Henry added, "Being royal." The three boys bounced ideas back and forth, contrasting Chinese culture with Western ideals. Chinese ideals include family values, hard work, an appreciation for Chinese heritage and for old stories and myths, and, as Henry put it, imitating the voice of his elders: "Do what I say!"

Since these Chinese values stand in contrast to Western values, I asked the boys if they buy into those values. Henry said that he anticipates that when he is 18 or 20 years old, "we'll understand that hard work and self-esteem do pay off." Li, who said that he wished he didn't have to study so much, said that the values of diligence and hard work are so ingrained that "I can't think of doing badly even if I want to!" The boys also recognize the drawbacks to such a strong work ethic in American society. As Paul put it, with a constant focus on hard work, "there's an inherent disadvantage with social skills, so it's harder to get into top management, so the new trend is towards social skills." While Henry and Paul joked about Li's frequent use of his cell phone, Li quipped that he would rather see more of an emphasis on social skills and less of an emphasis on hard work!

The students don't always work so hard. "This is a safe space where Asian people can come and relax," Paul said. "We bond together. If someone moved, we would welcome them here." Coming to Meiguo Chinese Academy helps the students to figure out their identity: "Are we Chinese or American? This is just a place where we can get the middle ground. . . . This bridges the cultural gap." The students had a healthy sense of humor and Henry told me they often joke with each other about being Asian. They kidded about trying to avoid the stereotypical Chinese bowl haircut, and, still riffing on the subject of cell phones, they acknowledged that many Chinese are becoming more Americanized, the way they constantly send text messages on their wireless phones. Ironically, cellular telephone use is so widespread in China that Chinese who live in China tend to be far ahead of those who live in the United States. Li's cell phone use might have been completely normal in China, but his American friends saw it as a sign of his Americanization.[11]

Having heard the students speak at length about the atmosphere and moral values at Meiguo Chinese Academy, I was interested to know how the boys would respond to some of the moral dilemmas that I had posed to others in the study. Like most high school students, if they saw a little boy or girl in trouble, they would try to find a responsible adult, and they might even ignore the child if they thought somebody else were watching. Their answers were different from many of their peers, however, when I asked them how they would respond if they saw someone being bullied. Henry and Paul seemed especially attuned to issues around teasing. Henry said that if his friends are joking around at someone else's expense, he often tries to stop his friends and say, "Come on, guys!" if it gets "over the top." Paul said that he makes a special effort to befriend students who are not so popular. "I'll be friends with whoever," he said. He added that in spite of the different groups of students, including "nerds, jocks, and popular kids, I just try to talk to all people."[12]

"I MAKE IT MY OWN"—THE JERUSALEM SCHOOL

The 45 students in the 7th grade at the Jerusalem School gathered together on a mid-November afternoon in the chapel, not knowing what their spontaneous assembly was to be about. The principal, Mrs. Rose, stood at the podium and called attention to a breach of trust that had occurred as a result of an incident involving some students. She spoke sternly, but not in anger about the inappropriate behavior of the students. "Our school runs on trust," she said, telling the students that when trust is broken, the positive relations that she takes pride in can turn sour. After some initial giggling among those who knew what had happened, the mood gave way to seriousness, and I had the sense that the students were absorbing the solemn words coming from their principal.

Like several other K–8 schools discussed here, such as the Academy of the Sisters of St. Theresa and Al-Quds Islamic Academy, the Jerusalem School, has an opportunity to shape each student's moral outlook through the formal curriculum of Jewish and general studies classes and through the informal curriculum of activities, holiday celebrations, community service projects, and field trips. Although Mrs. Rose did not specifically use Jewish language about trust, the formal setting of the chapel with a sculpture of the Ten Commandments behind her conveyed the gravity of the situation.

Only a few days earlier, Mrs. Rose had sent an e-mail to the middle school parents with great pride, describing the wide range of election-related activities in the weeks leading up to the 2008 presidential election. While it probably did not surprise the parents to learn that social studies classes were discussing each candidate's opinions on major issues such as domestic health-care policy and the war in Iraq, the breadth of other activities probably did surprise the parents. Hebrew classes looked at Israeli Web sites to see how the Israeli press was reporting on the election. Science classes looked at the candidates' stands on scientific issues ranging from the environment to stem cell research. Math classes looked at data collection and statistics related to polling and voting. Jewish history classes compared the challenges leaders faced in ancient times with the challenges that leaders are facing in the contemporary era. Classes in Rabbinics—the study of the Mishnah and other ancient rabbinic texts of 2,000 years ago—drew parallels between the presidential candidates' and the ancient rabbis' perspectives on issues such as poverty and war.

As a teacher at the Jerusalem School, I know the students and faculty intimately. As a writer, I noticed the overall atmosphere and different elements in the curriculum with a fresh set of eyes, and my experience at the school gave me access to the students and classes that I might not have had otherwise.

The middle school Bible curriculum is taught entirely by one teacher, Mr. Goodson. A teacher in his late twenties who is known for his puns, projects, and charts, Mr. Goodson always uses an overhead projector to take his students through the day's texts and explanations. His 6th-grade Jewish history class was studying the Ten Commandments and the many interpretations about how God addresses the Israelites. By opening up so many different interpretations, he hoped that the students would understand that a pluralistic approach to Biblical study could enhance religious beliefs and not detract from them. One of the interpretations raised a moral issue for discussion: he asked the 11- and 12-year-olds if the way we treat others is shaped by a belief that we encounter God through the words of the Ten Commandments and that we are made in the image of God. These kinds of moral issues often come up in Mr. Goodson's classes, though he explained, "It's an overarching curricular goal, but not necessarily a stated purpose for each class." His main purpose as a teacher of Bible is to teach the skills of biblical study and to help students to develop an appreciation for the Bible. "Only in some ways is it studied as a moral guidebook," he explained.

Every Friday morning, the 8th graders gather in a large classroom with the school rabbi, whom the students know as Rabbi Michael, to prepare for the 8th-grade trip to Israel coming up in the spring. The students study poetry, news items, the geography of the land, and some of the institutions they will visit. On the November day that I visited the class, Rabbi Michael introduced the students to Yemin Orde, a multilingual, multinational, and multiracial boarding school in Israel for high school students who were orphaned or whose family members were unable to care for them. The Jerusalem School students will visit this unusual school and spend a Sabbath there during the course of their trip. Rabbi Michael took a group there in the past, and he pointed out to the 8th graders that the visit would be likely to raise the students' awareness that the privileges they were enjoying from their suburban Philadelphia homes and school were not universal. Some of the Jewish teenagers at the school had crossed the desert by foot from Ethiopia, and others had struggled with their families in the face of economic hardship in Brazil and Eastern Europe. Mrs. Rose framed the experience for the students, echoing the sentiment that the visit will give the students a wonderful chance to meet new people along with a new perspective on their own lives: "You will see that they are just like you are, but it will make you count your blessings 100 times."[13]

The language arts curriculum joins the Jewish studies curriculum in creating springboards for discussion that help students to bridge Jewish tradition with contemporary life. One of the language arts teachers, Mrs. Williams, has a commanding presence: students almost universally respect (and sometimes complain about) her high standards, strict discipline, and personal investment in the success of her students. During my visit, a class of 8th graders began to read a dramatization of *The Diary of Anne Frank*, taking turns reading each part aloud. In the class, questions naturally arose about the gradual losses in Anne Frank's experience: the loss of her schoolmates, her bicycle, movies, and access to streetcars. Students talked about the black market and about the moral issues around the Frank family's loss of dignity illuminated by the line, "I never thought I'd see the day when a man like Mr. Frank would have to go into hiding."[14] Mrs. Williams asked the students what kinds of risks they would be willing to take. Sharon, who had spoken thoughtfully in a group interview, said that she would want to take the risk because she "would at least be saving two whole families. . . . It's like a really big deal. They have the right to live, too." Oren, who also participated in a student interview, cautiously said that he would hide someone else if he only had to worry about himself, but "if I'd be risking my family, I might not." Having raised a number of questions, it was appropriate to the mission of the school that Mrs. Williams provoked moral thinking without necessarily offering answers.

The school shares a campus with several other Jewish institutions, including the lower school division of the Jerusalem School, a Jewish educational agency, a college and graduate school of Jewish studies, a day-care center, and other smaller organizations. The institutions touch, but rarely interact, so students in the middle school feel that they have full access to their building and to the outdoor space. In a lunchtime interview with four 8th-grade boys who usually spend their lunch and recess time tossing around a football, the young men spoke quite openly about the moral values that they have been taught by their parents and the school: one of the boys, Oren, credited his parents with guiding him and with pointing him in the right direction, but he also said that there are limits, because, "It's going to be my choice." Another boy, David, said that his parents instilled in them a strong sense of Jewish identity: "Stand up for your beliefs like Judaism, and always keep Judaism with you. Lots of laws in Judaism, like the Ten Commandments, help you to be a good person." A third boy, Alex, said that his parents "want to raise me to be a proud Jew and to marry someone Jewish and to treat the world and the environment and other people with respect and to try to use manners." The four 8th-grade girls I interviewed spoke about how their family values affected the kinds of things they do in school: one of the girls, Sharon, said that her family wants to see her "do the right thing, like hang out with people who don't have any friends." Adding to that, another girl, Orit, said that her parents "care about my school work, but they'd rather me be nicer than have really good grades."

The students spoke with clarity about the moral lessons that the school is trying to teach them; it is clear that they grasp the school's policies, mission, and priorities. The girls commented on certain policies and Jewish traditions in the school like required daily prayer that seem designed to shape the students' character as much as the classes. Orit described the way in which the school seems to teach respect for God while enforcing Jewish practice: "Sometimes when they enforce it too much, it turns us off and we lose interest, but when we can relate to it and see it's something we can do and we might like doing, then it turns us on."

There are ways in which the school touches the lives of students outside of their classes. The advisory program is based on *Second Step,* mentioned earlier in chapter 1. Orit spoke well of the program: "In advisory they teach us to stand up for ourselves in this program called *Second Step.*" Sharon criticized one of the ways in which students receive feedback for their contributions to the school community. Teachers are asked to fill out "*Nahat* Notes," certificates that commend students for cooperation, decency, and acts of kindness. The word *nahat,* also pronounced *nahas,* describes the feeling of deep satisfaction that an adult gets from the achievements of a young person. Sharon saw the *Nahat* Notes as a limited tool: "They use *Nahat* Notes to try to get us to do good things like behave in class—things we should be doing, anyway. They use the bait of a *Nahat* Note as a reward for our good deeds." Sharon is partly right; several students and parents have told me that as much as they may be embarrassed about receiving yellow *Nahat* Notes decorated with smiley faces, they always go up on the refrigerator.

Oren accepts that the school often needs to teach negative lessons as much as it teaches positive lessons. Taking an example from something that had occurred earlier that week, Oren said, "School is here to teach us about life, that life might not be fair sometimes. Like if a teacher gives you a different topic from what you wanted." Sharing a more positive lesson, Ari said that the school tries to teach students the perspectives of others. "Charity can be fun," he said; he had enjoyed and learned from a hunger-related project that the school had done a few weeks earlier with his classmates. He also spoke of absorbing the scholarly perspectives of others: "like in Bible, they teach us how to look at something differently."

I was not surprised to hear that each of these students, like the students I met in other settings, had strong feelings about respect. The Golden Rule was a theme for the boys and the girls. One of the 8th-grade girls, Talya, explained, "When you treat people the right away, you acknowledge they are a person like you and you wouldn't want to be treated badly." She added, "If someone drops their books, pick them up," to which Orit added, "When you walk by someone, acknowledge them." Oren spoke about respecting older people by treating them respectfully. David explained that he sees respect as listening to others' ideas, and Alex added, "Treat that person the way you would treat yourself, listening and being mannered to people." If they found themselves in a situation in which they were not experiencing respect, like if they saw someone painting a swastika on their school, David said that he believes that "some things are worth getting in fights for, like Judaism." Oren was more cautious and said that in a situation like that, "You should tell them it's no good, but if they're bigger than you, you're going to lose." It was clear that the boys had thought about what it means to experience anti-Semitism. Ari described a particularly disturbing incident that had occurred during his 6th-grade year at a baseball game when a parent from the other team began to shout anti-Semitic slurs. The boys were in the awkward position of not being able to do anything, so they were grateful that the Jerusalem School baseball coach (who, himself, was not Jewish) called attention to the unsportsmanlike conduct, defending the boys and their religion.

While I heard confident, authentic voices that might have led me to identify some of the students as Authentic and Assured, it was clear that these students are bridging their lives as American teenagers together with their commitments as Jews. Their teachers engage them in significant questions from Jewish culture and general culture, and the principal believes in preparing the students for the moments that occur in middle school, but also in their adult lives ahead. When they were asked if they buy into what the school is trying to teach, Elisabeth said, "I don't go by the teachings—if I find something and it relates to the text I just think of what I do and I do it. I don't feel I have to compare my life to the Bible or whatever." Sharon expressed a similar sentiment: "The rabbis aren't always right. I'm not going to go specifically to do what the rabbis do—I'm going to do what I think is right. No matter what, I should always show respect." Oren, addressing his experience of the daily prayer required by the school, showed his own efforts to bridge when he answered, "Sometimes I try to pray, but sometimes I make my own prayer, like I take the most important prayer and make it my own."[15]

"IT DEPENDS"—BRIDGING TRADITION AND THE MOMENT

For educators looking to see young people develop a language of morality that bridges home traditions with their own intuitions, commitments can hinge on phrases such as "it depends." Someone who is Authentic and Assured may feel no hesitation about giving to the poor, about sharing food, and about relinquishing some personal freedom. Someone seeking to bridge traditions is likely to undertake an internal negotiation that might go something like this: "I am a member of this extended community that shares an understanding of ethical practice; even if the moment may not be right for me, I am willing to stand with the community and relinquish some of my own desires because there may be meaning or some other personal gain from this experience." Or the internal negotiation might go something like this: "I would like to help this person, but my priorities don't quite feel aligned, so at the risk of offending someone, I'm going to say no to their request." To illustrate, when I posed the hypothetical question to the Jewish students about whether they would attend Jewish prayer services and become the 10th individual, completing the *minyan,* or the quorum, a suburban 10th grader named Tamar Minick told me that she was willing to respond to others' needs for the *minyan,* even though she, herself, might not have wanted to pray at that particular moment. Both she and an urban 10th grader named Felicia spoke conditionally in separate interviews, using the word "depends" to express their hesitation to commit to the *minyan.* This echoes Carol Gilligan's early research on female development and decision making: Gilligan found that women often find themselves traversing the transition from selfishness to responsibility that enables them to participate in society.[16]

While responding to the question, Tamar was willing to consider whether the expected social conventions would apply to her. She paused before answering the question: "It's hard to say," she offered, cautioning that just because someone might tell her that she would feel good about attending the *minyan,* that person could hardly know or judge her motivations and responses. She ultimately concluded that if she helped to make the *minyan,* then the invitation would have fulfilled its promise that she would feel good. She was the kind of student who knew what Jewish tradition would have told her to do, and she said that if someone had asked her to attend the *minyan* because God expected it, then she "wouldn't need convincing" because she already saw herself as connected to God. Some of her peers in my study said that it was of primary importance to fulfill a *mitzvah* (commandment from God), so they would have responded positively to the obligations imposed by the community. Tamar, however, was looking for room to negotiate whether the attendance would be obligatory or voluntary, and whether there might be meaning to be found in accepting the obligation. A 10th-grader named Jared said that he would attend the *minyan* because it would involve "actually helping somebody else." Jared and Tamar were looking for a way to make their attendance meaningful, and it is quite possible that they would not have attended the *minyan* without being prompted about an obligation. The internal decision making before choosing to attend meant that they were trying to determine the boundaries of obligation.[17]

"MORAL ERIC" DECIDES TO CHEAT

Everyone makes mistakes. Students expressing the Bridging and Binding moral outlook may struggle with a combination of a voice within and a voice from traditional expectations. Some students say that they never cheat, but statistics indicate that a high percentage of students do indeed cheat. Some personalize the experience of cheating, cheating only in certain classes and never in others. I had an opportunity to speak about a cheating incident with a student named Eric, who was known to his friends by the nickname "Moral Eric" because his friends knew that he was serious about issues of morality.

Although Eric was a successful student, he was not immune from peer pressure and from academic pressure. He found himself in an academic situation that challenged whether to fulfill or defy the moral code of his school. He decided to cheat. On the one hand, he felt guilty about it, and on the other hand, he felt deliciously wicked about finding his way out of a tight spot without being discovered.

He had a lot to say about morality. On the subject of respect, he said, "I try to respect others, and I try to earn it." He derided the students who called themselves Goths, dressing in trench coats and in black turtlenecks; their dark outlook made them seem sinister, and Eric was convinced that those students went through their school days without a set of moral lenses. Eric insisted on the importance of morality: "You have to have morals. They're unavoidable."

Eric took a strong stance against what he would consider immoral behavior, and he attributed his feelings in a simple way to "just the family I was raised in" and to the kind of morality he absorbed through Judaism. He expressed concern about the level of cheating at his school, and he wanted to maintain high standards that would keep him from being tempted to cheat. Eric was genuinely interested in exploring the connection between God and morality. He recalled a discussion that had electrified him at the after-school program of Jewish studies he attended: "And the question of . . . how this moral a God could annihilate a people, and declare war on God's children? The question is, does God dictate morals? I don't know. My response to it: Maybe God is morality. . . ." Eric no doubt is not alone: there are Erics in many different religious traditions who want to bridge an understanding of God and goodness with an explanation of war and other ills of the world.

Eric asked me to maintain confidentiality in one of our interviews because he had cheated on a test just a day or two earlier. If this information were to have come out at the time, it could have jeopardized his opportunities to get into college, he explained. I promised that I would use a pseudonym, as was the case with every student who participated in my study, but he insisted that the experience not be mentioned in my dissertation. I followed through with his wishes, but I have remembered the story, and now that he has graduated from high school and from college, I share the story because it illustrates the extent to which even students of high moral character cheat because of the pressure they feel.

Eric's response to pressure is consistent with James Davison Hunter's findings in *The Death of Character* that young people with strongly held religious beliefs are not immune to cheating. They are one-third as likely to cheat as students with a less rigorous moral compass.[18] Nobody told Eric to cheat, of course, and he knew that his family would have understood (though they may have been upset) if he had explained that a significantly large workload was preventing him from adequate preparation; yet he chose to cheat in the face of the pressure to perform and pressure from his particular peer group to maintain high grades to reinforce their sense of self-worth. Privately, I found myself asking if the public moral imperatives to succeed and to contribute to the world were trumping the private moral imperatives to act honestly and to persevere, even in the face of possible failure. From the tone of his voice as he described what he had done, I also found myself asking if he secretly had enjoyed getting away with cheating. During the course of his confession to me, he hadn't sounded remorseful; he sounded relieved and even a little pleased not to have been found out. Nevertheless, he had no plans to cheat again, and he spoke about not wanting to repeat the experience.[19]

At the time of my collaboration with Eric, I was serving professionally as the principal of a Jewish high school, where cheating incidents came before me from time to time. One of the cheating incidents that came across my desk ultimately led to a student's dismissal from the school because she had been cheating for the second time. It was a heart-wrenching decision for me as a principal, because I understand the desperation that many students feel when they give in, but as a school leader, I believed that the school could not afford to tolerate cheating. The institution had to fulfill its obligation to define and to uphold standards of honesty and integrity; the student's dismissal was a necessary consequence of those standards, though it was painful to explain that to a family, for whom my decision and the student's action set into motion a long search for a new high school. Sometimes students can cheat without being discovered, so they interpret it as a victimless crime. When they are discovered, however, they sever a bridge of trust, and they have to work especially hard to rebuild trust and to bind themselves back to their schools; when that is not possible, they have to find a new institution where they can earn the trust of a new group of adults.

COUNTERACTING DOWNWARD SPIRALS
IN PERSONAL MORALITY

Is it possible to measure the impact of moral education, and can educators use that information to intervene and to prevent students like Eric from cheating? In the 1920s Hugh Hartshorne and Mark May of Yale University conducted an experiment in which they attempted to gauge the moral impact of reciting the Ten Commandments in schools. One group of students recited the Ten Commandments every day and others did not; the experimenters wanted to see if they could predict whether those who did not recite the Ten Commandments would be more likely to cheat on a test of state capitals. At the conclusion of the experiment, they could not find a correlation between the recitation of the Ten Commandments and the degree to which the students behaved honestly.[20] Some recent studies have tracked trends related to moral behavior, such as the increase in student cheating. Researchers have found that students continue to use a variety of methods, including plagiarism, looking at a classmate's paper, and newer methods such as the electronic transmission of data through carefully hidden wireless phones. Frank Furedi of the University of Kent, Department of Sociology writes that cheating has become so prevalent that young people who plagiarize believe that it is an acceptable practice.[21]

Founded in 1992 to develop academic policies, educational programs, and procedures, the Center for Academic Integrity (CAI), based at Clemson University in South Carolina, includes 360 member schools. The CAI Web site serves as a resource for institutions wishing to develop their own honor codes and policies by providing links to relevant sections of college and high school Web sites. The CAI Web site even includes quotations on six values that are part of academic integrity: honesty, integrity, responsibility, trust and trustworthiness, respect and self-respect, fairness and justice.[22] A related report, published by CAI when it was based at Duke University, notes that 80 percent of college-bound high school students report having cheated and that half of the college-bound students do not believe it to be a serious transgression.[23]

James Davison Hunter participated in a 1989 study of 5,000 ethnically and sociologically diverse young people from grades 4 to 12 in rural and urban areas. He came to identify several moral outlooks that he calls Expressivists, Theists, Utilitarians, Humanists, and Conventionalists. The students were asked about lying, academic dishonesty, and altruism, and they also were asked about their attitudes toward sexual activity and drinking. The researchers found a wide range of responses, but they also found sufficient consistency to conclude that the students' moral and ethical systems "act very much like moral compasses, providing the bearings by which they navigate the complex moral terrain of their lives."[24] They also found that students with some moral dispositions were far more likely than their peers to engage in certain kinds of risky and morally dubious behavior. For example, among the Expressivists, who believe that moral authority comes from each individual in a moment of "emotional sensibility and felt need," nearly 20 percent said that they would cheat, and nearly 50 percent said that they would lie. In contrast, among the Civic Humanists, who tend to feel a sense of responsibility to the community and who are willing to subsume some of their own desires to the needs of the community, only about 10 percent would be likely to cheat, and a little more than 40 percent said that they would lie. In further contrast, among the Theists, who see religious law as authoritative, just over 5 percent say that they would cheat, and under 20 percent say that they would lie. Hunter and others found similar data in a 1996 study, confirming their data about moral outlooks.[25]

Hunter's findings led him to conclude that these moral dispositions do lead to different moral outcomes: the Theists and those with a conventional disposition show a tendency toward altruism and an ability to show restraint in sexual behavior and potential drug use, while the Expressivists and Utilitarians are more likely to experiment in sexual activity and drug use, showing less restraint.[26] Hunter's findings are supported by other recent research. A contemporary study conducted by psychologists from the University of Miami explored the degree to which religious belief and practice are factors in self-control. The psychologists, Michael McCullough and Brian Willoughby, found that prayer helps to promote "self-regulation and control of attention and emotion." McCullough adds, "The rituals that religions have been encouraging for thousands of years seem to be a kind of anaerobic workout for self-control."[27]

Hunter is a strong critic of moral education that leads to expressivist and utilitarian behavior, in which an individual's moral behavior is read as no different from a set of straightforward menu options selected in the moment. Hunter is an advocate for a new emphasis on character that should lead to the development of responsible and principled young people who feel the claim of the community acting on them to behave with a sense of obligation to society.[28]

This kind of critique that emphasizes commitments to others echoes the social philosophies and findings described in the 1980s by Robert Bellah and his coauthors in their book *Habits of the Heart*. Those with a communitarian outlook, or, as Bellah and his coauthors call it, a biblical or republican outlook, speak about duties, traditions, and how individuals are expected to assume responsibilities in society. Those whom he describes as utilitarian individualists and expressive individualists focus on their own self-expression, their desire to "get ahead," and on determining much of their own moral system.[29] Although Bellah and his coauthors were describing the adults they interviewed, they might just as easily have been describing adolescents whose views ranged from an acceptance to a renunciation of obligations to others.

Bridging and Binding is not merely an intermediate step between Authentic and Assured voices on one side and Constructing and Considering voices on the other. It is an outlook committed to a reasonable balance. In a philosophical study of moral education, Tim Sprod describes the goal of moral education as nurturing "reasonable children." He describes reasonableness as "critical, creative, committed, contextual and embodied." Reasonableness entails having an imagination; a capacity to be moved by emotion; an ability to calculate risks, benefits, and outcomes; and a sense of belonging in a community.[30] Adolescents are capable of this kind of reasonableness, and they naturally embrace pluralism in the sense described by the contemporary philosopher Charles Larmore, who writes in *The Morals of Modernity* that pluralism is a part of modern culture, and that reasonable disagreement is inevitable.[31] In the pluralistic settings and even in the less diverse settings described in this chapter, a range of opinions proliferate; reasonable disagreement takes place when rational people have different reasons behind their beliefs, whether they are adults in the workplace and at home, or whether they are teenagers at school and entering the world.

In E. M. Forster's book *Howards End*, Margaret delivers the words as in a sermon, "Only connect!" The narrator continues: "That was the whole of her sermon. Only connect the prose and the passion, and both will be exalted, and human love will be seen at its height. Live in fragments no longer. Only connect, and the beast and the monk, robbed of the isolation that is life to either, will die."[32] Adults have the capacity and, one might even say, obligation to connect with students, to connect students with knowledge, and to connect students with one another.

Constructing and Considering

"Daddy?" Harriet said after a while.
"Yes?" said Mr. Welsch.
"Are you religious?"
"No," said Mr. Welsch, looking up at the sky.
"That is, I don't follow any organized religion.
That is not to say I am not a religious man.
I don't know how I could look at those stars and not be a religious man.
I just mean that I have made up my own set of ethics
and don't take them from any organized religion."
—Louise Fitzhugh, The Long Secret

The first of the three outlooks in this book, Authentic and Assured, de-scribes moral certainty. In some cases, an Authentic and Assured outlook looks like religious or moral orthodoxy, especially when decision making ap-pears to be grounded in strictly held religious tenets. Those who are Authen-tic and Assured are not looking to be swayed by concerns of the moment, so their decision making is not especially flexible. The second outlook, Bridging and Binding, connects ideologies, community expectations, gender expecta-tions, and religious ideas with concerns of the moment in shaping a moral decision. Bridging and Binding thinkers do not necessarily seek complete in-dependence from their families or from their family religion, but they main-tain ties to shape their moral thinking. This third outlook, Constructing and Considering, allows for more independence. Like Mr. Welsch in the epigraph from *The Long Secret,* to be Constructing and Considering is to think expansively and not necessarily to limit one's moral thinking to a particular set of religious or community-oriented ideas.

Charter school and independent school teachers and leaders may be more likely to support the kind of thinking and creativity that is part of the Constructing and Considering outlook if it is part of their mission, and if they have the funding, a highly motivated faculty, a creative student body, and families who buy into that mission. If every classroom were to cultivate a Constructing and Considering outlook, some teachers might find it frustrating, not only because classes could get slowed down by an excess of the contemplative life, but also because students might not have enough time to prepare and learn the objective material that appears on standardized tests for college admissions and for state standards.

DRAMATIC LIGHTING AND ETHICAL FOUNDATIONS—HANFORD DAY SCHOOL

Hanford Day School is an independent school in Manhattan with no religious affiliation that prides itself on its nurturing atmosphere, the diversity of its student body, and on the academic and cultural accomplishments of its students. At the time of my research, the school's home page portrayed a boy posed casually, playing the trombone on a stool next to a girl standing with a backpack slung over one shoulder. The school's Web page conveys the sense that students come to discuss great ideas and to stretch themselves without feeling overly constrained by ideology or by others' expectations.

At Hanford Day School, I shadowed a boy named Gadiel Himmelfarb who was passionate about music. He began many of his mornings in the music room, playing piano. When we climbed the stairs for the first time during my visit, he noticed a new feature in the stairwell lighting right away. A student group was playing with the filters, covering the fluorescent lighting and changing the hues several times. Each time Gadiel and I had to go up or down the stairs, a new color cast a glow throughout the stairwell. It gleamed an unnaturally sunny yellow when we first went up the stairs. During another passing period while we headed to another class, the stairwell reflected calm when it was lit midnight blue. Gadiel did not like the devilish red very much.

School design and architecture helped to enhance the moral climate at Hanford Day School. On one of the floors that housed upper school classes, a large central area provided gathering space for students and faculty to plan together or to meet for quick extra help sessions. During unscheduled periods (free periods), students gathered for informal conversation, sometimes while standing and sometimes while seated with their feet up. This kind of inviting architecture has a deeply moral quality to it because it affirms the importance of community. While some schools have a hierarchy of gathering places (with places designated the Freshman Corner or the Senior Lounge), the open area with the presence of the teachers appeared to be a fulfillment of the school's statement of mission to be "an intellectual community dedicated to academic excellence that teaches traditional content, demands responsibility, and promotes the power of collaboration, creativity and critical thinking."

Because Gadiel was so passionate about music, I sought out his music teacher Mr. Douglass first for insight about the school. Mr. Douglass was forthright about the positive ways in which students participate in community service activities at a Habitat for Humanity project and a homeless shelter on the Lower East Side of Manhattan. He described the students as very productive and independent, and he felt that students seemed to be allowed to do much of what they wanted. He qualified his thoughts about respect at the school: he did not experience the students as particularly disrespectful, nor did he feel that he was on the receiving end of a deep respect for authority from the students either.

Gadiel's Constructing and Considering outlook was tested and confirmed in a 10th-grade class called Ethical Foundations, in which the students explored a series of hot issues from accommodations for students who are unable to complete standardized tests during the allotted time frame to sexual orientation and homophobia. The class, not unlike values clarification classes two decades earlier, offered an open forum for students to wrestle with contemporary issues and to develop their own perspectives. At the same time, it was clear that the teacher, Mr. Visconti, had an Authentic and Assured position already in his mind, and he wanted the students to accept the legitimacy of extra time given to students with learning differences.

Mr. Visconti also shared some of his own observations: he told the class that when he proctored SAT tests, he had noticed that many of the students who had arranged for untimed testing privileges also appeared to be wealthy and white. Gadiel was entitled to those accommodations, and he openly told the class, "It only helps. Everyone should have it." Gadiel's classmate Liam spoke cynically before the teacher could intervene. He said, mocking a student with learning issues, "I need more time for untimed testing, not because I need more time, but because I'm just stupid." It was a complicated moment, because Gadiel was naturally offended and he got up from his seat, clearly wanting to hit his friend Liam (or at least to tell him off!), but he restrained himself while Mr. Visconti tried to explain that accommodations in testing of course have nothing to do with stupidity.

During the discussions in Ethical Foundations about homophobia and homosexuality, the students were encouraged to share myths about gay and lesbian people. While a teacher with an Authentic and Assured outlook might have begun with a clear view of homosexuality that was either sympathetic or rejectionist, Mr. Visconti didn't offer any such boundaries. When students began with stereotypes such as "they all have AIDS," he taunted them to be more creative. Revealing that he, himself, was gay, he said, "Come on, you're not going to offend me." Among the stereotypes that students called out was one that I thought was particularly provocative: "All [gay] men have unprotected sex," to which Mr. Visconti added, ". . . Or are oversexed." Following this opening salvo of stereotypes, the students spoke about stereotyping in general, and then Mr. Visconti assigned the students to write a coming-out letter to their parents, as if they were planning to reveal to their parents that they had discovered that they were themselves gay or lesbian.

In spite of the teacher's superficial openness, the atmosphere in the classroom seemed weighted toward the teacher's perspective. When a student asked the teacher about the biblical prohibitions of homosexuality, Mr. Visconti dismissed the question. This was the kind of moment and the kind of class that had led critics in the 1960s and 1970s to dismiss the values clarification movement as a way to encourage a set of "preferences, inclinations and choices" that were part of a "style of life in a certain set of surroundings."[1]

When the students returned with their letters one week later, a number of them, including Gadiel, read aloud what they had written. His mother, he said, wanted Gadiel's school to be an accepting environment, but, at the same time, she was afraid that too many teachers were gay and that it was too easy to be gay. He related a story about his summer camp, where there had been a Bisexual Gay and Lesbian Awareness Day ("BGLAD Day"), and it felt excessive with a Capture the Rainbow Flag game. While he didn't mind it, he struck a nonchalant posture and said, "It's like, another day." He expressed intolerance toward the biblical view: "I think that anybody who takes the Bible too literally, you know, has got really serious problems."

Gadiel's moral life was not shaped by any single force, though it appeared to be influenced by a combination of Jewish ethics, family rules at home, and the ethic at his school. He admitted that occasionally he teased his sister, and he described a particularly tense relationship with his older brother that reached a stalemate when he grew to be larger than his brother. He surmised that this contentious relationship probably influenced him to see the Golden Rule as a frame of reference.

> *I'm not really sure if I have a world view. . . . Yeah, maybe I think it might*
> *be from the New Testament, but, um. . . : Treat others the way you want to be*
> *treated. Ah . . . I kind of live by that Golden Rule.*
>
> *Especially being in the city, you've got to be street smart. You've got to know,*
> *like, your boundaries and you've got to be nice when other people . . . are tough*
> *with you, you've got to show that you're tough back 'cause it's sort of a dog eat*
> *dog world, so I guess. . . . I live with, my brother, you know, and my brother and*
> *I fight a lot and have tons of family problems. . . . But you know, when he's nice*
> *to me, he gets something back. When he's an asshole to me, he gets it straight*
> *back in the face. So I guess that's the way my world view is . . . dog eat dog.*

It was clear that the Golden Rule did not always apply for him, especially when he felt threatened. As I took notes during the interview, I was surprised that after so many years of Jewish education, Gadiel attributed the Golden Rule to Jesus's words in the New Testament and not to its origins in the Hebrew Bible (Leviticus 19).

Did Gadiel ever intervene when he saw the Golden Rule threatened? Occasionally, he would intervene in a situation to stop someone from being mistreated. In his casual style of speech, he said, "So, sometimes, you know, I'll be doing . . . like, 'This is stupid,' and I'll just stop."

When I asked him if there were a particular value for which he would be willing to fight and even put his life at risk, he repeated his individualistic creed, saying that he would risk himself for one value: the value of being his own self. Gadiel's words called to mind the findings of contemporary thinkers Steven M. Cohen and Arnold M. Eisen, who described a trend among contemporary Jews to see themselves as "sovereign," and as above the authority of others.[2] In Gadiel's case, nothing could be more oppressive than peer pressure. He described a friend at another school who, he said, is not allowed by his friends to speak to kids in other groups. Gadiel was very clear about his feelings:

> *I think that really sucks. I hate when you feel pressure, something like that, that*
> *you have to like to wear the right clothing or stuff like that.*
>
> *I'm who I am. Like when I got my ear pierced, for example, I had this like*
> *charm on it of a G-clef and people were like ". . . That doesn't look too good."*
> *And I said, "You know what? Screw you, I don't really care." Whatever. It looks*
> *gay, whatever. I've heard it all. Say it . . . whatever. It doesn't bother me. I have*
> *people who would say things about my shoes. I'm like "Whatever. I don't care.*
> *You don't have to wear 'em." Or, "You don't think they're stylish? I don't care.*
> *Whatever." Everything that I do, I don't do because, like, I'm pressured to do it.*
> *If I want to do something, it's because I want to do it. I want to try it. I want to*
> *see if I like it. Nobody tells me what to do, really.*

TOURO COLLEGE LIBRARY

As a young man who loves music and improvisation, he was ready to Construct room for others to do their own thing so long as they would leave him alone.[3] When it came to music, Gadiel might have been Authentic and Assured because he knew that he could not progress without knowing his scales and arpeggios, but when it came to the rest of his class work, he put it well when he described his English class as "taking books and stuff and reading them and seeing what they really mean. You've got to read between the lines."

I observed a particularly spirited English class that illustrated for me the easy relationship that Gadiel had with his English teacher Mr. Neiderman and a way in which a student and a teacher can raise moral issues together. Gadiel brought the Billy Joel song "Goodnight Saigon" to complement a class discussion about Tim O'Brien's 1990 novel *The Things They Carried*, a poetic and fictional prose memoir about the Vietnam War. Launching a thoughtful moral discussion, Mr. Neiderman asked the students to respond to three direct quotations from the book:

> *The wounds of war (life) haven't been healed because we are just trying to ignore, not heal our pain.*
>
> *One must have a certain mentality to survive in war.*
>
> *War is more of a mental problem than a physical problem. There ain't no justice in war.*

The students were assigned to use the quotations in essays that would be written in class later on that week. Within the first five minutes of the class period, I could perceive the teacher's level of care for his students from his smile and direct eye contact with the students. The room was set up with several wooden chairs in a horseshoe shape to facilitate cross-classroom interactions.

Mr. Neiderman provoked nervous laughter by suggesting sarcastically that one way of dealing with dissent is to shoot everyone. The students avoided responding directly to the teacher's dark humor. His humor left room for students to accept that war leads to irrational decisions and to many mistakes. A student concluded, "I think the whole poem is about the mistakes we've made . . . [in spite of] My Lai and Hiroshima, we still haven't learned from it."

Mr. Neiderman turned the rest of the class period over to Gadiel, who had prepared a special presentation of the song "Goodnight Saigon," by Billy Joel, which related to the issues that they had been discussing in class. Gadiel had seen Billy Joel sing the song in concert with 20 American veterans of the army on stage. He highlighted these lyrics for the class, emphasizing the final line, "We said we'd all go down together, yes we would all go down together."[4]

After sharing these lyrics with the class, Gadiel played the song on his laptop CD player until the period ended. Everyone clapped in appreciation, and then they were dismissed. It had been a moral moment about heroism, life and death, and collective responsibility that could not have taken place without the teacher's involvement. In spite of the lack of discussion and processing time, the moment spoke for itself and quite possibly did not need further elaboration. By ceding class time to his student and by allowing Gadiel to play the music in the context of the Vietnam discussion, Mr. Neiderman brought to life one of the concepts that David T. Hansen describes in his book *Exploring the Moral Heart of Teaching: Toward a Teacher's Creed:* "teaching entails a moral, not just academic, relation between teacher and student. That relation surfaces in how teachers treat both subject matter and students."[5] In this case, the teacher's relationship with the student led the student to feel invited to bring the class discussion beyond the classroom text (*The Things They Carried*) toward a new text ("Goodnight Saigon") and toward a new level of meaning.

Gadiel's excitement about what he would discover on his own and his search for something that "has some relevance to it" makes him Constructing and Considering. Hanford Day School's open space, commitment to its class in ethics, and the willingness of its teachers to raise moral issues was a perfect institutional match.[6]

MORALITY IN A MEETING—FAIRHILL FRIENDS SCHOOL

The Fairhill Friends School is one of several independent Quaker schools in the Philadelphia area, but it is distinguished by its urban location and by its history as a venerable school that respects Quaker traditions and that welcomes students from all faiths. Like Hanford Day School, Fairhill Friends prides itself on its ethnic diversity and on its commitments to the arts. Its public literature includes photographs of Fairhill Friends students at work in their classrooms in partnership with their teachers, participating in sports and the arts, and even in a meeting with the current mayor of Philadelphia. While I don't think a school would want to photograph and publicize its students cramming for exams, rebelling against their teachers, or walking to the principal's office in shame, the easy relationships shown in the photographs between Fairhill Friends students and teachers brought to life an important dimension of moral education. On the way to becoming Constructing and Considering, students need to work as junior partners with their adults.

When I arranged to visit the Fairhill Friends School, I was told that the Meeting for Worship that morning was being held at a church just around the corner from the school, because the school's regular meeting place was under renovation. The elaborate church with its stained glass windows, banners, and carved wooden pews was markedly different from the school's modest Quaker meeting place with simple, straight wooden benches. The Considering nature of the school was palpable as the entire middle and upper school student body filed in together almost silently with their teachers. After a few moments, the coughing and brief conversations about the previous night's professional sports playoff game gave way to a settled feeling of silence. And then the Constructing nature of the school felt palpable.

By Constructing and Considering, I mean forgiving, empathic, and open to the chance that an unexpected voice might construct meaning for the group. As an authentic Quaker meeting, there was no formal liturgy, and the silence held until someone was moved to speak. The head of upper school was the first to speak, and he recalled having seen an Episcopalian Christian community and a Jewish community in Michigan sharing one or the other community's worship space. Comparing the elaborate space in which the community found itself that morning with the ideal Quaker space that the students overwhelmingly preferred, he offered an elegant and deeply moral soliloquy about finding one's place in a community while setting aside momentary discomfort in that particular sanctuary.

> For many, this space conjures up feelings of sacredness, and for others, it is not the case. Quaker tradition values simplicity of space. It's more about the space you find in yourself to reflect on who you are and how you fit in the community. In some ways, that can happen in any space. That's the hardest thing to do. I'm thinking in this space about who I am and how do I fit in the community, and that allows me not to think too much about the space.

His thoughtful remarks were followed by continuous silence until the silence was broken by another teacher who spoke about the beauty of sacred time and about the ways in which experiences of the sacred allow him to escape the particular confines of space and time. Both teachers empathized with their students' concerns. Although no student felt moved to speak during the remaining minutes of the meeting, the students filed out of the sanctuary appearing more calm than when they had arrived.

By Considering, I also mean tolerant with a generous spirit. Teacher Joan, the middle school division director (who also serves as the head of the Religious Studies Department) helped me in advance by coordinating a couple of small interview groups. As I went to find the students during one of the morning periods between the Meeting for Worship and lunch, I found them in the hallway by a table soccer game, so we sat down together and began a conversation right there. The students described the school as "open, free, accepting"; as a place in which they "don't push Quakerism on you if you're not Quaker"; and as a small school that "cares about what we think religiously, morally and academically." A boy named Jake said that the school demands academic honesty, not just by demanding no cheating and no plagiarism, but also by inviting students to try to be "honest about who you are, not a facade—everyone is their own individual person."

Teacher Joan had arranged for me to meet one other student, who came to her office during the lunch period. The student, an 11th-grader named Marcella, had been raised in a Roman Catholic family. She spoke enthusiastically about coming to school every day on public transportation, pursuing her passions for painting, photography, and guitar. When she first entered the school in the 7th grade after having attended a relatively large public school, the welcoming and accepting atmosphere surprised her. "I didn't really believe it," she told me, adding, "Quakers are very accepting, but at first I thought that nobody could really be *that* accepting!" In this accepting environment, she came to find her voice and a place in the political spectrum: "School brings out the more radical, liberal side of you."

She continued in this vein, speaking about her emotional satisfaction with her experience at Fairhill Friends. Although the Meetings for Worship and classes in Religious Thought have meaning for her, she felt more strongly about the psychological impact of being a member of the community: "You really learn these things from interacting with people. You won't learn from class until you meet people. . . . Things become more relevant when you know someone." Might she also have been rejecting some of her family's values at home, or was she at least trying to bridge the values at home with the values from school? She described herself as coming from a home that valued academic prowess and discipline, loyalty, etiquette, and respect for other people.

When I asked her the question I asked several other students about seeing graffiti painted on a neighborhood wall, I heard a clear Considering voice. "I kind of like it," she said, and if she saw someone painting graffiti on the school wall, she would be likely to question whether it was her place to tell someone what to do "to reinforce a policy." She decided that graffiti might constitute vandalism, but it was "not morally wrong" since it did not involving hurting anybody. When I asked her how she would respond if someone were writing graffiti on her home, "That would piss me off more," she declared. "That's really a violation there." One year, some vandals actually did vandalize her family's Christmas lights, cutting the electric lines, creating tension and sadness in the family. If she had seen the vandalism happening, she said that she would have stopped them.

Marcella's photo appears in the school literature, and she appears to be a free spirit, thriving in the academic structures that the school provides. Her upbeat and radical outlook could not have emerged in many settings, and the Constructing and Considering atmosphere at Fairhill Friends helped to make that possible. However, her lack of concern about graffiti, for example, probably made her more accepting of unusual behavior than most of the students, and her comments had a tinge of relativism.

In the school library, some younger students were chatting across a table (not about their class work!), and I asked them about their experiences in the school. Both of the students were 9th graders; Jackson, a boy, had been at Fairhill Friends since kindergarten, and Liz, a girl, crossed the Delaware River from New Jersey every day to come to Fairhill Friends. Liz credits the school with teaching her "to respect everyone's individualism." Although I'm not sure that her Quaker school would agree with her, she had concluded, "Quakerism is not really a religion. It's kind of like . . . everyone has their own values." Jackson spoke about the impact of the school on his appreciation for difference: When a student confessed to Jackson that he was an atheist, Jackson, a Quaker, found that uncomfortable. After much soul-searching about that student's atheism, he concluded that he could respect the boy after all, because, he said, "the school taught me it was his own choice."

Do classes teach this Constructing and Considering outlook, or does the outlook percolate from within the student body? I visited Teacher Amos's 9th- and 10th-grade classes in religious studies to learn more. Although less than 10 percent of the students come from Quaker families, everyone takes the 9th-grade class on Quakerism that introduces tenets of Quaker faith. I visited a class on a day in which the students were discussing the absence of creeds in Quaker faith. Early Quakers objected to creeds, I learned from one girl, because the meanings of words may change from one generation to another or from one community to another, and then a boy added that understandings of God change as well. A third student, ready with an idea about Quaker theology, offered the class, "A big idea behind Quakerism is that it focuses on looking at what is within," to which Teacher Amos added that Quakers believe in "continuing revelation—ongoing revelation of God." Then, as if he knew he were providing the theological backdrop to the interviews I was having with students that day, Teacher Amos explained some of Quaker theology that I realized the students had absorbed through the culture of the school. "God," he said, "continues to let us know more and more about God. As we gather in silence, we can hear more and more about God. It's not so much what you believe (not a creed) as much as what is the true test of whether you are a person of faith and conviction. How you live your life." This appreciation for the ongoing revelation of God through each individual helps to explain the appreciation that the students have for everyone, whether they see themselves as creative artists, accomplished athletes, outstanding scholars, or just as pretty good in any of those fields. The school and the religion together nurture empathy, appreciation for others, and an outlook that prizes time for silent reflection.[7]

"I LOVE DISCUSSIONS LIKE THAT"—TEMPLETON HIGH SCHOOL AND AMESBURY HIGH SCHOOL

At Templeton High School, a selective public high school in New York City, I observed moral leadership during a midmorning history class. Templeton High School established itself in the realm between top-tier competitive schools like John Adams High School that drew students from throughout the city and neighborhood schools that draw from a limited geographic area. Templeton High School fosters personal growth and expression through what is intended to be a strong advisory program and through a series of projects leading up to an academic portfolio that each student develops over the course of the high school years. The school values the personal search for meaning. At the same time, as a student named Felicia and her friends learned, effort and the search for meaning were not the only criteria for judgment: students were graded on their academic achievement as well. Teachers considered effort in the comments they wrote on students' papers, and students received positive forms of attention from advisors and teachers, but they still computed numerical grades for transcripts.

As a public school, there was no single tradition that the school espoused, and the two students whom I observed, Jared Greenberg-Wendt and Felicia Yanes, were different in temperament. Felicia had attended an Orthodox K–8 Jewish day school, expressing an Authentic and Assured outlook, but at Templeton, she expressed a Constructing and Considering outlook that is presented in the following chapter. Jared had attended a nondenominational K–8 Jewish school in Manhattan that I call the Rosenzweig School, and he regularly attended synagogue, sometimes even without his family. He credited the Rosenzweig School with raising his awareness and commitment to social justice. As someone who expressed a Bridging and Binding outlook, when I asked him what he would do if he had earned more money than he really needed, he said that he probably would "give it away to good causes." He did not identify any specific causes, nor did he use a language of religious values. It just seemed like a self-evident thing to do with a surplus, and having acknowledged his school's influence on him, perhaps there were religious values lurking behind his responses.

Felicia encountered sustained moral discussions in her history class with Mr. Phillips, who began a class with student responses to a provocative question about the human rights. The teacher, Mr. Phillips, had assigned the students to prepare an essay for homework in response to some provocative questions. He wrote the questions on the board and directed the students' attention to the front of the room as he read the questions aloud:

> *In your judgement [sic], what groups in today's Amer [sic] society are neglected, opressed [sic], or deprived of rights? What do you think would be the best method of correcting these wrongs through constitutional means?*

I was surprised to see the misspellings, and as he read the question out loud, he added the missing *p* in *oppressed*. Mr. Philips easily ignited a lively discussion with the assignment. One student spoke of certain racial and ethnic groups who are targeted for oppression, namely Hispanics and blacks; others mentioned Native Americans, gays, lesbians, and bisexuals. One student, identifying teenagers as a group subject to discrimination, pointed out that they don't get jobs because they lack experience; another, referring to the recent shooting at Columbine High School in Littleton, Colorado, added that teenagers cry out from oppression, "and that's why things like Colorado happen . . . I hear they're cutting after-school programs so kids have no place to go and everything." Felicia raised her hand to argue that kids should be given the right to vote: "I know lots of kids and some are really into politics," she declared. She also argued that the voting age should be lowered to age 15. When a classmate pointed out that some people make categorical decisions not to vote for someone because of the candidate's gender, or because the candidate is African American or Hispanic, Felicia pointed out that many adults do the same thing. There in Felicia's classroom, students were probing moral issues such as racism and responsibility, two topics with deep implications in the realms of dignity, the ethical treatment of others, and existential questions around the individual's role in society. Although there were no correct answers to the discussion question, the teacher had succeeded in triggering Constructing and Considering reflection.

Felicia's English class offered another opportunity for significant moral reflection emerging from the class's reading of Arthur Miller's play *The Crucible*. The teacher, Mr. McPherson, asked the students to consider the following issues that he wrote on the blackboard:

- Agree or disagree: The level of chaos and hysteria that occurred in Salem could never happen again.
- It's fair for the majority to decide what is right and acceptable.
- It is better to compromise than to suffer.
- Laws always uphold or restore justice.

Although the class met in a music room and not in a traditional classroom, Mr. McPherson used the space effectively, sending each team to a different corner of the room to formulate positions on each of the different issues. I was watching to see who agreed and who disagreed that the prejudices, superstitions, and cruelties of Salem could never happen again. In spite of her knowledge about the destruction of European Jews in World War II, Felicia, herself a Jew with an Orthodox educational background, spoke to her belief that what happened in Salem could not happen again, while many of her classmates of color strongly disagreed, saying that the hysteria and prejudice easily could happen again. I had expected Felicia's schooling to instill in her a sense that any kind of mass hysteria could be turned against the Jews, whether in Salem, ancient Persia or Egypt, in 20th-century Germany, or in some new and terrifying setting. In our interview later that day, she conceded that her position was not especially strong. In contrast, an African American girl in the class vigorously insisted that the experience of World War II shows that prejudice on a wide and violent scale can happen again, and that the hysteria of Salem could become the hysteria of an entire nation. When the subject turned to whether it is fair for the majority to decide, Felicia spoke with more passion. She was concerned that if everyone were allowed to make up his or her own rules, then chaos would prevail. Later, Felicia spoke enthusiastically about the discussion: "I love discussions like that."

Felicia enjoyed stretching the boundaries of moral discussion, and true to her Constructing and Considering outlook, she tended to prefer to stake positions that were not restrictive. She was less interested in abstract questions about morality and more interested in practical questions about how she, herself, might have responded in any particular situation. She said, for example, that she would prefer to compromise than to suffer, as she put it, "you know, go with the crowd and, like, privately do something else." This sounded remarkably like the participants in Brown and Gilligan's study of girls at the Laurel School who were afraid to risk exposing their feelings to others for fear of ostracism from the crowd. Brown and Gilligan describe the cynicism of these girls who learn quickly to read "subtle relational cues," and to be nice on the outside while thinking differently inside.[8] They learned to absorb messages about acceptable thoughts and feelings, and sharing those thoughts and feelings was done sparingly. Staying connected to other people seemed more important to Felicia than taking a stand that might be more pure, idealistic, and separate from the crowd.[9]

I got in touch with Felicia's teacher Mr. McPherson to learn more about how he uses his classroom as a forum for moral education; he struck me as an insightful practitioner who understood how important it was to raise moral issues. Although he did not moralize by taking a particular stand in front of the class, he did demand that students engage in thoughtful and logical discussion. He sounded like a man with a mission, eager to offer a forum for the students who, in his opinion, were lacking in opportunities for discussions about moral issues. Seeing students discuss whether the terror of Salem could occur again required a high level of moral engagement. He shared with me his conviction that we can't keep moral issues out of the classroom, adding his belief in the importance of offering community service experiences to provide a "real world connection."

Mr. McPherson expressed concern that in spite of his efforts to spark discussion, some students felt they couldn't raise their voices, and he feared that those voices were getting lost. In many of the large classes, it could be difficult for students to be heard. He felt that a stronger sense of community would lead to more listening and to more skills in negotiation. He also expressed concern that the rapid pace demanded by the curriculum limited discussion about moral issues. The curriculum included *Their Eyes Were Watching God*, *The Crucible*, and *Macbeth*. To complete each book in time, making sure that the students understand the plot and major characters, meant a brisk pace that often precluded time to linger and to "get caught" on an issue.

Mr. McPherson allowed for much back and forth among the students, letting the literature itself raise compelling moral issues for discussion. While he could have sought to influence the students' opinions, he tried instead to, as he put it, "introduce the topic, not broadcast my position." At one point, when his class had been reading *Macbeth,* they discussed the ways in which Lady Macbeth's criticizes her husband's lack of ambition. Before long, the students were talking about the ways in which people insult others and about the ways in which they express unrealistic ambitions and experience failure. In keeping with his own Constructing and Considering approach to teaching, he does not seek a single correct answer, but he does seek a high level of engagement from his students. He sees himself as a catalyst not only for the moral thinking of the entire class but also for the moral growth of each individual student.

We spoke about a girl named Lateesha whom I had observed in a few classes. She was a standout for her energy and her intellect, but her diction could be unclear at times. He was concerned that in spite of her sharp intellect, her relatively poor diction might be holding her back from further success. I was aware that if she had attended a suburban school with great resources and smaller classes, or, I surmised, if her parents had received a college education themselves, she might have been recognized for her intelligence and nurtured to develop raw areas of talent (in her case, perhaps debate or writing). She seemed the sort of student who should be directed toward extracurricular activities that could broaden her interests and talents.[10] In my conversation with Mr. McPherson, I asked if anybody was looking out for Lateesha and directing her toward a college guidance counselor. Mr. McPherson told me that teachers were trying to encourage her, but the small guidance staff and the lack of family knowledge about colleges meant that Lateesha might not receive the kind of guidance that would advance her toward higher education. She may even have gotten the message that she was between the cracks, not quite ready for a rigorous college education. He noticed that some students are labeled as strong at Templeton, but because Lateesha had not been turning in her work, she might have become labeled as weak and in danger of failing the course. While he did not have any solutions at that moment, his moral concern for the individual student appeared to match his concern for the moral content of the curriculum. Lateesha represented the kind of student he hoped to nurture further.

I had met another teacher at Templeton when I was shadowing Jared. Mr. Price, Jared's English teacher, struck me as someone who might be willing to talk about his experiences as a moral educator with me. While passing through the halls one day, I found Mr. Price and asked to sit with him so that we could talk about the overall moral climate at the school and about the range of moral issues that arise in curriculum and in the student body. Like his colleague Mr. McPherson, he agreed that moral issues belong in classrooms. He said, "I think it's pretty important to teachers to talk about the ethics of society." He also commented on the sense of partnership he feels with the parents of his students: "This is a school full of good people who have good luck not to be hemmed in by a metal detector."

Mr. Price had come to observe the powerful influence of parents on the moral outlook of their children. As an experienced teacher with many years of public school experience, he was able to declare without being condescending that "a lot of the parents are quite decent." There is "less neglect" for the children. "These are pretty concerned parents," he continued. "Those from Harlem, the Spanish parents, go to church. They do a good deal of good works, political works." As a good indicator of the positive influences of the parents, he added that there is almost no fighting in the school because they know that "this is a unique place, pretty diverse racially and economically."

Although his students did not make it to the most competitive examination schools, they had the intelligence and motivation to succeed in a school with rigorous academic standards. Mr. Price credited parents with socializing their children to succeed in school:

> Parents want their kids to be independent, and not just to get a diploma. There are lots of kids from progressive schools to whom we can say, "Go, get yourself to be an inquisitive person." Some parents say they work with their hands and don't want that for their kids. This [school] is a luxury. New York has a lot of rough edges in its schools. This school has a high-powered edge—it's a little competitive—sometimes there's a sense of forgetting to say, "Hi," to look someone in the eye, and to have a talk. Some may miss the chance to reflect a little.

He added that it was worth questioning whether the school was designed "for smart kids to get smarter," or in a more egalitarian way, as he put it, "for whoever is here to get a good education and feel welcome." Like Mr. McPherson, he could see how students come to achieve and build on their successes with the school's sanction. He saw this as a moral issue, because he could see how students sort themselves into groups based on their expectations for the future, some into groups of students who expected to share success, and some into groups of students who anticipated a more challenging high school experience that might involve not keeping up with the work and possibly sinking into academic difficulties. He concluded on this note, expressing his concern that the students who escape the attention of their teachers get "lost in the sauce." Reflecting out loud about the student I was working with, he confided to me, "I think Jared gets 'lost in the sauce' a little bit." Both Jared and Felicia had teachers who served as their advisors, and both had a number of teachers who knew them well and who sought to nurture their academic and social success.

Guidance counselors often play the role of advisor in public schools. They also function as moral role models for the students, and they stay attuned to changes in the moral climate of a school. More than 30 miles north of Templeton, Ms. Markson, Tamar Minick's guidance counselor at Amesbury High School, was quite open about the successes and shortcomings of moral education in that large suburban socioeconomically mixed setting. Although the school did not offer a specific class on character education, she said that the school administration believed that character education should permeate everything, so some of the course offerings touched upon public life and individual responsibility. A required 12th-grade course on community service and citizenship, called Participation in Government, brought students to attend community meetings and to perform voluntary service. A humanities course explored literature and history around topics such as the Kitty Genovese incident in the 1960s[11] and the destruction of the European Jewish community and other minorities perpetrated by the Nazi German government in World War II. About 60 students would enroll each year in this elective course.

Ms. Markson said that character education takes place in the context of the regular curriculum in each classroom. Some teachers promote cooperative learning as a teaching technique, requiring students to work together and not just toward their own goals. There are other opportunities for informal character education through the community service activities sponsored by the National Honor Society. The high school faculty does not necessarily discuss character education; she assumes that this is more likely to be found at the middle school level.

In spite of, or perhaps because of, the racial diversity, she told me that very few racial incidents arose each year at Amesbury. In the decade between the late 1980s and the late 1990s, the composition of the student body shifted from a balance of 80 percent white and 20 percent African American to a balance of 70 percent African American and 30 percent white. Upholding the school's commitment to moral education, Ms. Markson said that she worked with the Anti-Defamation League of B'nai B'rith each year to train group leaders to orient new 10th graders and to begin to build a sense of community among the students. The Cultural Diversity Club also convened periodic student workshops around prejudice. Thus the school provided several portals for moral education, but it could not take any particular position of advocacy.

While many of the teachers spoke with pride about the ways in which they set aside the curriculum, deviate from it, or reshape it to allow for discussion about moral issues, Tamar Minick's European history teacher, Ms. Leopold, felt under pressure to leave aside moral issues because there simply wasn't enough time. She appreciated students' moral questions about the nature of war or about Napoleon's use of power, but she could not assign those questions a high priority because she needed to keep focused on the core information that would be covered in standardized tests in the spring, including the College Board exams that would test the students' comprehensive knowledge. Upon further reflection, she offered that she tries to promote her students' character development by not being judgmental while they learn how to frame and then support a historical argument of their own.

Like Mr. Wesley at Solomon, Ms. Leopold said that she likes to lead her students to consider what they would have done during the time of the destruction of the Jews in World War II; she hopes that they learn to speak from their conscience against evil before "they come to get you," insinuating that at any time, there are evil forces that could take away liberty.

In some of her other classes, she said that she cannot help but raise moral issues. When students are studying comparative religions in her Humanities course, she asks students to consider the ways in which great sages have taught the Golden Rule: they come to see differences and similarities between the first-century Jewish sage Hillel, the Asian sage Buddha, and another first-century Jewish sage, Jesus. She asks if all religions say the same thing, and she asks why they also have the capacity to bring humans to act inhumanely. In the Advanced Placement History course, they discuss whether humanity is inherently evil. The Humanities course gives her more curricular freedom because there is no standardized test waiting at the end of the semester. In contrast, the Advanced Placement History course places rigorous demands on her, often restricting her ability to be flexible and to pursue different lines of moral thinking with her more than 25 students. It was clear that she had the capacity to ask provocative moral questions, but time did not always allow her to follow through and to wait for the answers. She left room for her students to weigh different viewpoints and then to come to their own historical and philosophical conclusions.[12]

LOST AND FOUND

While it was important for the students to experience the Authentic and Assured and the Bridging and Binding voices that often came from their teachers and school administrators, when they were left to respond to some moral dilemmas on their own, I often heard a more vague relationship to moral authority.

In an interview question that almost always got students to smile mischievously, I asked them what they would do if they were to find a science textbook on the floor with a classmate's name in it along with a visible $20 bill that was partially tucked inside the book. That particular dilemma generated some rich conversations as the students pondered their level of responsibility to their classmate and to the school. Most of the public school students assumed that the school had issued the book to the student-owner in the first place; independent school students tended to assume that the student actually had purchased the book. The dilemma usually generated further conversation about the extent to which any of us should take action when nobody is looking. When should we speak up and do a good deed? And when is it acceptable to keep on walking away from opportunities to act responsibly?

The students at Haym Solomon High School had the most to say about finding the lost book and money. A boy named Qasim said that some family members would tell him to give the book and the money back: "I should know what to do," he assured me, echoing the voice of his parents. His friends, however, would tell him to keep the money, and he claimed that his father would advise him to keep half of the found money. I wonder what he actually would have done, because in the heat of the moment, none of those influential people would have been around for a quick consultation.

A boy named Theodore had a practical solution that he believed would be supported by his mother: his mother, he surmised, would tell him to take the $20 but to return the book. She would reason that the student hadn't acted responsibly and that the student should not have left the book and the money there. Other students had similar conclusions, reasoning that if they kept the money and returned the book, then the money might represent a reward for turning in the textbook and for not increasing the cost of a lost book. Loshonda was cautious about seeing names in textbooks: she said that students do not write their names in textbooks, because if somebody finds a book with a name in it, "they might write profanity about you." Nevertheless, her family would have her give a teacher the money and the book. Rayanne, a 12th grader responded, "A real holy person might say 'return the book,' and I think that person doesn't have the responsibility to not retrace their steps. It would be nice if you got a blessing for returning it." Rayanne continued, "The teacher probably wouldn't tell me anything—they'd just look at you and go back into their room. Mr. Wes would tell me to return it. He would have told me to give it back because he's a religious man. He talks about God and blessings."

In asking this question, I felt as if I had touched upon some deeply held values. Although none of these young people at Haym Solomon High School were quite a Constructing and Considering student like Gadiel, they sounded Constructing and Considering as they weighed the possibilities, inventing their own solutions, keeping half of the $20 found in the textbook, or all of it, perhaps refusing to write their names into the textbooks in the first place.[13]

In contrast, when I asked this question to students at the Fairhill Friends School, the students whom I interviewed all answered that they would have returned the book and money immediately to the school office. This appealed to them as the most moral response to the dilemma; the office would no doubt have offered praise and a word of thanks. Nearly all of the students acknowledged that as the most appropriate response, though a few admitted that they would have liked to have seen the careless student held accountable somehow.

Would it matter if I could have found out how they would have responded in real life if I could have observed them finding a textbook with a $20 bill tucked inside? Would it matter if I could have seen if the students would follow through with their noble attitudes? Would they have caved into peer pressure and kept the money or even ignored the book on the floor by walking on by? In this first bystander question, most of the students expressed a willingness to stand out, separate from their friends, interested in seeing the textbook returned speedily to its rightful owner. Many of the students weighed their answers carefully, trying to imagine how their siblings, parents, grandparents, and teachers would have advised them. Some of the students who struck me as indifferent to their teachers, parents, and grandparents still tried to imagine what guidance they might have received from the adults they respect. It clarified for me that adults should not minimize their role as moral figures in the lives of young people. The young people hear adult voices, even if they don't always heed them and follow them. I suspect that even if one of the students had seen a textbook with a $20 bill tucked inside it, and even if that student had decided to keep the $20 bill, she still would have heard the moral voices of her adult parents and mentors. The challenge for educators is not just to have those voices heard, but also to be sure that they are followed, especially if the lost object were something of greater value like a ring or a treasured photograph or a laptop left on a train that had confidential medical information stored on the hard drive.

KEEPING VALUES CLARIFICATION OUT OF THE CLASSROOM

Teachers like Mr. Paschko, Mr. Wesley, Mrs. Williams, and Mr. McPherson are all successful at raising issues of integrity through the kinds of issues that arise in the secular studies curriculum. Mr. Hurley, Mrs. Hillal, Mr. Goodson, Rabbi Michael, and others raise moral issues through the religious studies curriculum. The class taught by Mr. Visconti at the Hanford Day School sparked discussions about values, and it was reminiscent of a program of moral education called values clarification that was widely used and then widely criticized in the United States and abroad. Values clarification was meant to provide a forum for open discussion among students in which they would be asked to respond to a variety of situations, gradually gaining an understanding of their own values. In a values clarification class, when students are given a scenario for discussion, they are asked to clarify their values by explaining what they stand for while the teacher encourages them without criticism.

Values clarification rebelled against traditional ethics instruction, which a teacher's guide and text about values clarification described as "moralizing," a process equivalent to "inculcation, imposition, indoctrination, and in its most extreme form, 'brainwashing.' "[14] As Thomas Lickona points out, many values clarification classes lacked substance. In an original manifesto of the values clarification movement, called *Values and Teaching* (1966), teachers are encouraged to accept their students' answers whether they succeed or fail at articulating a set of values.

Several Upstate New York families objected to this ambiguity when their children in high school were participating in a values clarification curriculum. The curriculum was designed to lead the young people to regard career choices such as engineering and farming as a matter of a personal choice between equal options. Even more upsetting, the curriculum seemed to hold cheating as a morally neutral choice, equivalent to other personal choices that anybody might make on an average day.[15]

In another instance from the study by Martin Eger, a girl and her teacher spoke about lying, and the girl said that lying was bad "because Jesus said so." The teacher, influenced by training in values clarification, seemed to accept her response, and the teacher also seemed to accept the option of lying on occasion, pointing out that "many people do lie."[16] Parents and academic critics could not feel enthusiastic about a movement that appeared to embrace a lack of morality and lying and that did not appear to uphold certain standards of behavior.

From halfway around the globe in New Zealand, one critic argued that teachers should be empowered to point out when some moral judgments that students offer in class may be misguided or mistaken.[17] In 1996, the Wellington, New Zealand, *Evening Post* published an editorial that easily could have been published in the United States because of the shared points of criticism. The author, Bruce Logan, explained the methodology of values clarification, in which teachers do not identify student values as right or wrong: "Instead, students are assigned the task of discerning their likes and dislikes, preferences and feelings." Logan objected that society no longer seems to affirm what he calls "Victorian" virtues "of family, fidelity, chastity, sobriety and personal responsibility." Logan blamed the adult world for failing to hold individuals as accountable for their own actions.[18] It is easy to blame the values clarification movement for leading young people to rationalize their beliefs, and here, Logan blames the adult world for failing to hold individuals as accountable for their own actions. Teachers cannot—and should not—always withhold judgment. As William Damon writes, "How can a teacher *not* take a position on honesty?"[19]

James Davison Hunter argues that values clarification and other forms of moral education seem more therapeutic than educational. When the teacher acts as a facilitator of moral discussion, helping students to clarify and develop their own morality in a completely nonjudgmental manner, the line between an academic exercise and a therapy session can become blurred.[20] Teachers have a unique ability to praise a child and to raise a child's self-esteem, but teachers should not think that praise for a child's artwork or praise for getting the right answer is the same as moral education. In a telling example, Philip Jackson and his coauthors describe a Mrs. Johnson who teaches in an inner-city school with marginal students; everyone receives lavish praise for his or her work, regardless of its quality. On the one hand, the observers write, Mrs. Johnson's students eagerly seek "to bask in the warmth of their teacher's admiration"; on the other hand, they question whether her praise is more of a desperate measure, "salvaging whatever interest is already there" and not going far enough to risk raising the intellectual demands of her class. Her caring, they believe, makes her a moral exemplar who shows genuine care for her students, but she also could be a greater moral exemplar who could challenge her students to go more deeply into intellectual realms.[21]

USING THE CLASSROOM AS A BULLY PULPIT

Teachers, more than parents, have the ability to prompt and to prod their students into taking a moral stand. As they grow up, children come to know what their parents expect of them, but in high school, young people come into contact with many more adults, each of whom may have his or her own moral expectations for students to learn. Some teachers are successful moral leaders by playing devil's advocate, provoking a discussion or putting students in a position in which they must make a decision. As William Damon writes, "Moral education must be a cooperative enterprise between adult and children."[22] At two different schools, I observed advisory periods during which students were expected to choose their courses for the next year. At both Hanford Day School and at Templeton High School in New York, I did not observe the advisor playing anything more than a minimal role, giving the forms to the students and collecting them when they were completed at the end of the period. As a teacher, I recognize the moments in a school day when students tend to need downtime without any official program, but it seemed like a missed opportunity that the students were not consulting with their adults about decisions for their junior year in high school that could affect their position in the college admissions process. To be fair, it is quite possible that the students had consulted with their teachers and advisors on other occasions and that I was observing the final, independent steps of the process.

Dr. Martinson at John Adams High School described the teacher's desk as "a bully pulpit" not unlike the American presidency. It is an intriguing comparison. While of course there are significant differences between Teddy Roosevelt's vision of the bully pulpit and Dr. Martinson's Latin classes up in Room 413, it was clear that the teacher saw his desk and classroom space as a platform from which to share a particular intellectual heritage, to transmit knowledge about Latin to a captive audience, and to shape the moral character of his students. Thomas Lickona and Matt Davidson articulate this idea in greater depth in their report *Smart and Good High Schools: Integrating Excellence and Ethics for Success in School, Work, and Beyond.* Teachers have an opportunity—and, some would argue, privilege—to cultivate both "Performance Character" (competence, effectiveness, skill, lifelong learner, follow-through) and "Moral Character" (commitment to principle, self-discipline, ethical thinking).[23]

Other thinkers agree with this principle: Larry Nucci argues cogently that moral education aims to socialize students into an understanding of right and wrong so that they can understand how personal choice, "prescriptivity and universality" combine to help one make decisions.[24] Choosing between chocolate and vanilla in the lunch line at the school cafeteria does not constitute a moral choice, but buying an ice cream for a hungry classmate, stopping a classmate from stealing, or telling a classmate not to be rude to the lunch ladies does. Nucci describes the many factors in moral character that can be nurtured by a skilled educator. He writes that traits do not constitute one's moral character so much as "the integration of moral and social understandings, affects, and skills." We can describe one's moral character as the way in which "one defines oneself in moral terms and in relation to the given social context." A teacher may be able to spark a student's thinking through good questions that ask students to define their moral beliefs. Nucci writes, "All teachers are engaged in at least some tacit form of moral and social normative education." A teacher's influence is extensive (the desk certainly *is* a bully pulpit for some teachers), but a teacher may not always (or ever) see results. A student's ability to reason may be more of an indicator of the teacher's success.[25]

In contrast to Dr. Martinson, with his classroom at the more exclusive John Adams High School in New York, where his moral leadership is mediated and enhanced by the curriculum and where his high-achieving students un-questioningly accept his authority, Mr. Wesley and Mr. Paschko from Haym Solomon High School in inner-city Philadelphia also use their desks as a bully pulpit, but sometimes they don't have a desk, and sometimes their audience drops out of school. As Mr. Paschko told me, he feels a responsibility to look for what he calls "core values" to share with the students: as a facilitator of discussion and as a mediator between the material from the social studies curriculum and the students, many of whom reject the enterprise of formal schooling, he tries to help the students to "provide them with tools to establish their own moral values" because they might not be getting it from home. As a public school teacher, he is not permitted "to build the structure for them" using any single particular ideology; students have to build it themselves.

When he speaks like this about encouraging students to arrive at their own conclusions about morality, Mr. Paschko sounds to some extent like he es-pouses the classic liberal view described by Goodman and Lesnick, that teach-ers are obliged to help young people to discover their inner values and to lead young people to question authority. At the same time, Mr. Paschko also seems to espouse the classic conservative view: he respects authority and calls upon his students to obey their parents. He recognizes impulsive behavior in his students that needs to be curbed. In a light moment during our interview, Mr. Paschko first mocked the same egocentrism of many of his students: "What I want is what I should have and you are wrong to try to stop me!" And then he decried that egocentrism, telling me that although he left the Chris-tian community in which he grew up, where he and his fellow community members revered religious truths, he continues to feel a sense of obligation to the community and wants his students to feel that sense of obligation as well. He wants his students to come to their own conclusions, but he also wants to be sure that they have a sense of right and wrong.

Mr. Wesley has a realistic view of his work as Academy leader at the Acad-emy of Creative Arts and International Studies at Haym Solomon High School. Although he and his students might not be able to raise the funds each year for an annual trip overseas, and although the school district might prevent a trip from going, he still finds that the international mission is a deeply moral mission "because it helps to overcome narrow-minded thinking about some-one else's differences that leads to immoral actions against others." He doesn't see moral education as a series of absolutes. Like Mr. Paschko, he expressed his hope that the students will come to develop a core set of values: "Respect is a core moral issue because [the students] feel so disrespected by society and by each other." He and his students talk about giving and getting respect both inside and outside the classroom when the students are at home or on the street; he presents ethical dilemmas, pitting the desire to be honest against a desire to be loyal to a friend, for example. Students come to identify their own ethical values, identify possible sources of conflict, and then attempt to resolve their conflicts. When they look at bystander issues, he encourages the students to "make a commitment not to sit and watch when right in front of their face someone is doing something awful."

Mr. Wesley told me that he is troubled that some of the parents in his school are teaching their two-year-old children to fight. Although he finds it "morally unacceptable," his students do not object, because they believe it necessary to fight to survive in the streets. While he understands the impulse not to let one's children be victims, he sees great danger in the love of violence that seems to prevail in the neighborhood, and he tries to point out to his students that their constant focus on violence and on self-preservation makes them victims of violence in a different way, exerting so much energy on self-defense instead of on positive values and experiences. They have to make the values their own: "I want them to *think* more than just accept some precept about moral values." By teaching about the Holocaust and about the experiences of African slaves in the United States, he tries to teach about the ways in which people "can twist any moral system. I almost want to create moral uncertainty for kids." If there is more uncertainty, then he hopes that there will be less violence in the world.

A critic might have difficulty with a teacher like Mr. Wesley or like Mr. Paschko. Mr. Wesley, himself, confessed that someone could accuse him of being a relativist for the way in which he wants his students to speak their minds in an open atmosphere, but he is not a relativist. He is very clear about teaching some topics like American slavery and the destruction of European Jews during World War II as morally wrong. When he teaches about honesty, for example, values stand in conflict with one another: honesty might lead one to hide an escaped slave or a fugitive Jew, and honesty might also lead one to confess it to the authorities. The choice is clear for him, as he hopes it might be for his students: "If I was hiding someone on the Underground Railroad or in World War II, I would lie."

With widespread cheating, some of his students rationalize that cheating will help them to pass a course, which will, in turn, enable them to get a diploma, which will, in turn, enable them to get a job, to grow in a career, and ultimately, to succeed in life. He points out to his students that cheating will not further their growth and that if they lie their way to a job, then the diploma will become meaningless if they turn out to be incompetent. At the risk of offending the parents of some of his students, he cautions his students so that they do not repeat their parents' mistakes, warning them that they could grow up to be unskilled workers, spending their lives between two jobs because they did not prepare for the working world: "You don't see them at home because they didn't do well when they were in school. . . . Is that what you want for yourself and your kids?"[26]

Mr. Wesley takes a stand with his students, addressing them directly about the choices they have ahead of them. For teachers in programs as varied as *Second Step* or *Journey of a Champion*, it is necessary to help students to make a connection between thinking about values and acting on them. These kinds of programs require teachers to be skilled discussion leaders and facilitators, not just experts who impart academic information. It is easy to find fault with efforts at moral education, because, as my students and my own children at home put it, sometimes it feels silly. I found very few published critics who hold that moral education does not belong in schools at all, though it is not difficult to picture a cranky local citizen saying something like, "Why spend time talking about abortion in school; leave that for the family to discuss while you focus on algebra!"

WHICH VALUES SHOULD WE TEACH?

The earlier chapter that highlights the Authentic and Assured outlook considers the question, *Whose* values should we teach? An Authentic and Assured school has no difficulty answering that question, because it teaches its own clearly defined values. The Constructing and Considering outlook takes a different approach, so it may be more apt to ask a Constructing and Considering school, *Which* values should we teach? The moral psychologist Lawrence Kohlberg established an open approach to teaching values. He argued against teaching specific values, preferring instead to introduce students to a wide range of values, which he called "a bag of virtues and vices."[27] Goodman and Lesnick paraphrase Kohlberg's argument that young people should learn to practice justice and resolve their conflicts. Rather than prescribe exactly which virtues to teach and practice (and which vices to avoid), Goodman and Lesnick describe Kohlberg as saying that young people should try to absorb the larger values of society and develop an ability to reason morally. Good moral reasoning skills will provide them with tools to consider their options when presented with dilemmas and then to construct thoughtful responses.[28] This is an important step in citizenship.

To offer a closing thought, the process of Constructing and Considering need not be limited to the classroom. Children become active citizens and develop virtues through service not only in their schools, but also in their communities. Entire communities can play important roles in the moral education of young people by providing coaching, counseling, and opportunities for young people that they wouldn't otherwise have. Children are in a position to reciprocate and to serve their communities as well, by providing babysitting, participating in service projects, and by looking for other opportunities to intervene in positive ways to improve their communities.[29] In the next chapter, we will explore ways in which experiences of play help young people to be flexible in their thinking, creative when they are looking for solutions, and skilled in moral decision-making. In the crux of a moment, when children do not have much time to think through issues of authenticity, bridging, or constructing, they need to be able to react quickly and to draw from a strong set of values. Play can create the conditions for children to construct and then to test their values.

Play: Getting into Character

The children made a list of peaceful games to play on the playground and discussed how to solve their problems.
　　　　　—Kindergarten newsletter, The Jerusalem School, May 16, 2008

As a relatively inexperienced parent, I remember thinking that the real work of parenting had begun not so much when I changed the first diaper or did the first nighttime feeding, but when I had to help my then 11-month-old work out issues of sharing with another child when they would play together on Fridays. The two boys wordlessly took toys from the other, and, most of the time, neither child was bothered. Somewhere around 15 months of age, once my child had begun to grasp the idea that some objects belonged to him and some to others, the stakes were higher and I had to become a more active referee. It was clear that sharing was quickly becoming a moral issue.

Moral issues around play become more complicated as children mature. From toy sharing to rule making to card trading, children begin to develop a sense of fairness and exchange. When children make teams on the playground, issues of inclusion and exclusion arise, and they begin to figure out one another's strengths, weaknesses, and abilities as emerging leaders. At the Jerusalem School, enough issues arose during the course of the spring that the kindergarten teachers sent home a note to parents (quoted above in the epigraph to this chapter), reassuring them that problems had been resolved. The teachers played active roles in helping the children to work out their differences and to develop skills to resolve future conflicts. As I described earlier in chapter 2, Jean Piaget writes that children at the third and fourth developmental stages have strong enough social skills that enable them to play together and claim a win without bragging, accept a loss without complaining, and to negotiate a rule when the game doesn't seem to be fair.

Middle and high school students often experience play through athletics. In *Kids of Character: A Guide to Promoting Moral Development*, David Shumaker and Robert Heckel identify 12 ways in which athletics can foster moral development:

1. Socialization
2. Teamwork
3. Commitment/motivation
4. Discipline
5. Skills training
6. Enjoyment/fun
7. Selflessness/sharing
8. Concern for others
9. Learning how to win
10. Learning how to lose
11. Obedience
12. Patience

Sports may have a negative impact on young people if there is too much attention on becoming a media star, if the coaching is poor, and if the play draws the student too far away from academic responsibilities.[1] Sports also can be demoralizing for young people who are not chosen for a team or do not feel valued by their coaches, or if other factors impede the potential pleasures of play.[2]

What is play? The 20th-century educational philosopher John Dewey described play as a psychological attitude, not as an external form. Play involves cultivating one's own interests and bringing together "all of the child's powers, thoughts, and physical moments, in embodying, in a satisfying form, his own images and interests."[3] We also might see play as a form of recreation; Stuart Brown, the director of the National Institute for Play, in an interview with Krista Tippett on the American Public Media radio show *Speaking of Faith*, defines play as "anything spontaneously done for its own sake." Play has an interesting evolutionary role; it does not necessarily produce food or any other immediate necessities that further human survival. Thus, it can be spontaneous or organized; it can be rough-and-tumble out of doors, or it can be safe and indoors. It can involve heady math problems, crossword puzzles that bend the mind, or word games that lead to clever rhymes. Play can be athletic or it can involve the arts—drama, music, sculpture, drawing, or painting. Although we often associate play with children and young adults who are not yet responsible for putting food on the family table, play is part of middle and later adult life as well. He emphasized that play is not limited to any one particular moment in life: "We really are designed to retain immature playful-like attributes throughout our life cycle. That's a fundamental part of our design. . . . " When he added, "Now take that into policy matters," it could be heard as a call to educators and other policy makers to continue to fund recreational leagues and playground equipment and not to give up valuable time for recess.[4] The decline of bowling leagues and other community activities (along with, interestingly, a counterintuitive increase in the number of people who are bowling) is discussed in the book, *Bowling Alone* by Robert Putnam, who offers a window into the economic changes that have affected middle-class families in the United States; this also reveals a decline in the ability of adults to set aside time for group and individual play unrelated to work.[5]

Young people love to play, but many begin to lose their sense of play around adolescence. Play becomes more serious and less fun when it also becomes more competitive. Joel Fish, a psychologist specializing in sport psychology who directs the Center for Sport Psychology in Philadelphia, identified several trends that have changed the experience of play: there are more organized sports than ever before, capturing the interest of the youngest children with standings and trophies; there are more elite teams than before for older children; and children are specializing at an earlier age (in contrast to the past, when the all-around three-season kid was the model). With these changes, there is a risk that the competition will, as Joel Fish put it, "will squeeze out some of the natural character building dimensions of play." When children play without adult supervision, the coaching is not likely to be as good, but the moral development is significant. Fish added,

> *It's not a myth to say that a lot has been lost by the loss of spontaneous play: kids having fun; kids learning through sport to work out disagreement and take sides and deal with all the decisions that come along with just playing a game; or even holding a place on a playground.*[6]

Could a more positive attitude toward play in schools help to restore the sense of spontaneity that is so fundamental for human moral development? Joel Fish believes that schools can help students to compete in healthy ways by encouraging a variety of markers for success. Athletics have the benefit of teaching many life skills, such as goal setting, cooperation, teamwork, perseverance, and the lesson that "you can't always get what you want." Young athletes should mark their success with improvements in their performance, with better teamwork, and with better sportsmanship. Just as teachers begin and end a class with questions that warm up the class and bring things to a conclusion, coaches can ask their players to envision the game ahead and the ways in which they can promote the success of the team; at the end, they can ask the same questions and measure their success. As serious as they are about playing, coaches should ask, Did you enjoy yourself?[7]

There are times when physical play and sport appear to be the same thing, especially when children throw a ball to each other with great laughter, or when they chase one another in a game of tag or in a race to the end of the street. These kinds of spontaneous play offer opportunities for children to be creative and to develop their character as leaders among their peers. When athletes follow planned strategies and drills and participate in organized competition, they become more skilled, more agile, and more competitive at a particular sport. They often develop a new sense of belonging and citizenship, and participation on a team may foster social development and discipline.[8]

Arthur Wellesley, the Duke of Wellington, is said to have given one of the greatest tributes to alertness, fitness, discipline, and play when he declared, "The battle of Waterloo was won on the playing fields of Eton." Although those words appear to be misquoted, attributable to the biographer William Fraser instead of the Duke of Wellington, the idea is an important one: that a healthy approach to play builds camaraderie, thoughtful approaches to risk, and a strong character that may accompany an individual into battle.[9]

Research on the moral development of players on a New England private-school basketball team found that the relationship between coaches and players went far beyond basketball: the coaches developed strong relationships with the students that extended beyond practices and beyond the gym. The students came to appreciate that the coaches cared about them "as people" and that the coaches themselves "valued a life marked by consistency and integrity."[10] The coaches and the players were put under significant strain after experiencing several losses, and the coaches spoke to the team not only about strategy but also about "teamwork, communication, hard work, and support for one another."[11] These values, together with hard work, proper behavior, respect, and a positive attitude would enhance the team's performance, but would the values also turn the players into individuals with a heightened sense of morality? The authors of the study conclude, "Sports do not necessarily build character; but coaches can if they have knowledge, commitment, and skills to create environments that challenge kids to put values in action."[12]

Play advocates have founded organizations that provide opportunities for children who lack the resources and time for play and competition. Children with significant physical differences can compete in the Special Olympics, which sponsors regional and worldwide athletic competition in events as varied as speed skating in the winter and swimming in the summer. Countless children who experience economic deprivation and dislocation benefit from the activities of an international organization called Right to Play, which operates in Africa, the Middle East, South America, and Asia. Right to Play programs benefit refugees in Azerbaijan by providing opportunities for free supervised play, coaching in conflict resolution, and health education. Right to Play programs in Tanzania provide HIV/AIDS education while also providing coaching in volleyball, football and other sports.[13] Young people benefit from the presence of adults who help them to develop their skills, and they also benefit from coaches and referees who guide them in the etiquette of their sports while also managing the inevitable conflicts that occur during play. Whether they are privileged children on "the playing fields of Eton," high school students on a basketball team, schoolmates playing hopscotch, or neighborhood kids in an old-fashioned pick-up game of stickball, play does not need to be guided by heavy-handed adults to be meaningful. School and neighborhood fields and courts and sidewalks are fertile grounds for moral growth.

In Stuart Brown's research on different kinds of play and on the role of play in personality development, he found that a lack of play is detrimental both to personality development and physical development in human beings and in animals:

> [W]hen you see animals and humans who are deprived of [play], they are fixed and rigid in their responses to complex stimuli. They don't have a repertoire of choices that are as broad as their intelligence should allow them to have. And they don't seek out novelty and newness, which is an essential aspect of play, both in animals and humans. So if you look at the human situation, at least for the last 200,000 years or so, our capacity as a species to adapt, whether we're in the Arctic or the tropics, the desert or a rain forest, appears to me to be related significantly to our capacity and, as developing creatures, to play.
>
> The human being really is designed biologically to play throughout the life cycle. And that, and from my standpoint as a clinician, when one doesn't really ____ at all or very little in adulthood, there are consequences: rigidities, depression, lack of adaptability, no irony—you know things that are pretty important, that enable us to cope in a world of many demands.[14]

Brown makes the case for rough-and-tumble play, calling it essential in both boys' and girls' development:

> *If you are to observe kids, like in a preschool, that are involved with all the exu-*
> *berance that preschool kids have age—3, 4, 5, and you watch them at play, it's*
> *chaotic, anarchic, looks violent on the surface. They're diving. They're hitting.*
> *They're squealing. They're screaming. But if you look at them, they're smiling*
> *at each other. It's not a contest of who's going to win. And a lot of well-meaning*
> *parents and a lot of, certainly, a lot of preschool teachers put the lid on that.*

Brown justifies this kind of play because it is "driven from within by the child's own personality and temperament in mixing with others." Children learn about their own physical limits, and they also learn about empathy. He added:

> *But think about this. If . . . you are in a rough-and-tumble situation, somebody*
> *hits you too hard, you know what that feels like. And that's the roots [sic], for*
> *example, of an emphatic response. . . . And I think there has to be reasonable*
> *protection by adults, but not the kind of helicopter parent hovering over the situ-*
> *ation, which prevents the spontaneity from occurring and the kids from solving*
> *their own problems that are age appropriate for them.*
>
> *. . . . In general, the kids solve their own problems. And that's one of the most*
> *important things they learn about themselves. They learn whether they're strong*
> *or not so strong, fast or cagey, verbal or nonverbal, imaginative or something*
> *else.*

His comments remind me of the play I have observed among both girls and boys at my school. When I am outside at lunch duty in my role as a teacher, I observe my students at play, which is a surprisingly interesting part of my job. As the teacher on duty, I am obliged to keep everyone safe, so I have broken up fights, I have helped injured students to find help inside the building, and I have watched many pairs of students tumble around each other outside in various games. As with my own children at home, I try not to intervene in my students' play at school unless they are likely to get hurt or overly wet or muddy. Schools must take additional caution so that the school does not become liable for a bad injury during the school day.

From conversations with my colleagues, I know I am not the only one observing the ways in which our students play. On days with poor weather when we might rather be indoors, there are some groups of boys who often ask us to come outside so that they can play their daily game of football in all kinds of weather, from cold autumn days to frigid winter days and hot spring days.

Every few minutes, play stops while the players argue passionately about a broken rule or about a successful interception, and then play resumes again because the clock is ticking and recess will be over all too soon. While it seems that the majority of the boys often follow a set of rules that are understood by the group, the majority of the girls seem to spend their recess time gathered in small groups, walking around, circumnavigating the fields together, deep in giggles and plans. Sometimes mixed groups of girls and boys roll on the ground, sit in one another's laps, and engage in antics, jumping on each other and then chasing each other. This kind of irregular, less predictable play can be disconcerting for a supervising teacher because there are no rules, and the boys and girls often cross personal boundaries and often test school boundaries. As a supervising teacher, I often wish that these mixed groups could be as predictable in their play as the football players so that I wouldn't have to spend so much time setting limits, but I also understand that they are improvising, posturing, bantering, and establishing a social hierarchy that has a moral purpose as well: each child's identity is affirmed as part of the group, and the group also comes to identify its leaders and priorities.

However children go about their play, recess plays an important role in their academic performance. According to a longitudinal study based on children who entered kindergarten in 1998–1999, by the time they were about 8 or 9 years old and in third grade, children with at least one daily recess period lasting at least 15 minutes tended to perform better in their classes. They were more focused on their school work and they were better behaved. The authors of the study point out that American children have experienced "a 25% decrease in play and a 50% decrease in unstructured outdoor activities" since the 1970s. They add that this decline is accompanied by a decline in class time in the arts and in physical education and they attribute the decline in part to the demands of the public testing requirements of the No Child Left Behind Act of 2001. The American Academy of Pediatrics, which published this study in the journal *Pediatrics,* regards free and unstructured play as a moral good, not only for healthy physical development, but also for "important social, emotional, and cognitive developmental milestones."[15] Dr. Romina M. Barros, the primary author of the study, concluded, "For [kids] to be able to acquire all the academic skills we want them to learn, they need a break to go out and release the energy and play and be social."[16]

Play is not limited to sports, and as Stuart Brown pointed out in his interview, an absence of play could have detrimental effects on human development. How can play extend to young people who may be social outliers? The high school years represent a formidable challenge for any young person on the social margins, especially for the many gay and lesbian youths who are coming to terms with their identity in what may be a hostile atmosphere. Gay and lesbian students have a reputation for finding their way to the drama club, where they play at having different voices, different identities, and even, in some productions, different genders. In today's schools, many gay and lesbian students participate in a full range of extracurricular activities from athletics to the performing arts, uncertain about whether to identify themselves publicly as gay or lesbian. With the thoughtful title, *When the Drama Club Is Not Enough: Lessons from the Safe Schools Program for Gay and Lesbian Students,* Jeff Perrotti and Kim Westheimer describe the success of school organizations called Gay/Straight Alliances, in which gay, lesbian, and straight students can speak about who they are and about what they face as young people who don't always fit conventional expectations. Gay/Straight Alliances may provide information for school communities by explaining issues of identity. This is a moral imperative, not only because gay and lesbian students often face teasing, making them struggle harder than most of their peers to feel a sense of dignity, but also because successful mixed Gay/Straight Alliance groups may help lower the risk for teen suicide.[17] The Safe Schools Project in Massachusetts that led to the creation of Gay/Straight Alliances in many schools also encourages bicycle trips and overnights that "level the playing field," providing ways for students to break down cliques and to develop friendships in informal settings outside of the rigors of classes and organized sports.[18] Gay and lesbian high school students benefit from faculty support and from having a wide range of options and safe places in which they can meet and feel affirmed in their identity.

My research allowed me to see play in a variety of forms as it shaped the moral outlook of students. Gadiel, whom I observed at the Hanford Day School, an independent school in New York, played piano in a jazz band at school. During practice, he made musical jokes at the electric piano, breaking into different modes by pressing the sitar button to get the sound of Indian music or the guitar button to evoke a folk-music sound. He and the trumpeter played with a few call-and-response musical phrases that brought them both to laughter. He often began his day downstairs in the music room, and he felt he belonged there. Gadiel found a core element of his identity through playing music; his classmates and teachers respected him and admired him for his passion and for his skill.

Jeffrey at John Adams High School in New York played the center position in a soccer game in gym class, and he loved to play with ideas. When I visited John Adams High School in New York to shadow him, it was soon after the

Littleton, Colorado, shootings at Columbine High School. At the time, many pundits were blaming the media for encouraging children to play with dangerous toys; they reasoned that the high school students had ready access to weapons and that the media had influenced their violent behavior. When I asked Jeffrey about the extent to which he thought that toys were to blame for the excessive violence, he expressed his own conservative leanings, and he began to mock overprotective parents who place excessive blame on toys and media images. He took the position that critics cannot simply dismiss musicians or video games like Super Nintendo that seem to promote destructive and violent messages, though those kinds of messages don't exactly promote peace and good will, either.

> *Marilyn Manson t-shirts who say like, "kill you parents" on it . . . These are not*
> *messages we should be giving out to the 16-year-olds. Of course, I'm sounding*
> *like I'm 50 but, whatever. Uh . . . I don't blame toys. . . . I don't really blame*
> *rock music. I don't blame Marilyn Manson but I don't think they help. Um . . .*
> *I think that these things just happen. There are crazed people out there and they*
> *take action. People want to blame things like toys or . . . or rock music just be-*
> *cause they already have predispositions against it. Like people hate toys so they*
> *say, "Oh, look these two kids killed, um, killed sixteen kids." "Oh really? They*
> *used to play with SuperNintendo." "Oh, really? Well, you know, maybe it's Su-*
> *perNintendo." It's not. It has nothing to do with toys or games, you know?*[19]

While Jeffrey agreed that some messages from popular culture might encourage young people toward violence, he also dismissed their potential influence and the potential influence of games like Super Nintendo. In the poem about Barbie dolls that he wrote for an English class (described in an earlier chapter), he dismissed the impact of the dolls on girls' self-image. He felt conflicted: he saw these games as just for play, but he also saw in his own life that play also could function as a rehearsal for life. He could take center in a gym class soccer game and dominate the game, and then, one period later when gym class was over, he could take center stage in a class and dominate it. After time in college, it was likely that he would find a way to the center again through politics or through another field.[20]

As much as parents are responsible for helping their children to focus on school when they would rather play, with high-achieving students, the parents can encourage their children to maintain a sense of play. While watching a group of young people playing Guitar Hero, a video game involving mock musical instruments, I noticed that when they made a mistake and got penalized for a wrong note, they laughed and kept playing. Surrounded by friends with the sounds of a rock band in the background, they weren't threatened by their mistakes. The next day, while watching my son and daughter practicing saxophone and flute, I could sense their frustration immediately when they made mistakes. "Playing" an instrument was not as playful as "playing" a game. To try to restore a sense of play, I encouraged them to make up their own tunes, to find fun ways to distort the dull exercises while still developing their technique, and to play along with a recording, but it wasn't easy to compete with the electronic feedback of points and bright video lights from the video game.

While young people play at being members of a rock band, imagining themselves basking in the cheers of their fans, Tom Stoppard's play *Rock 'n' Roll* lionizes an actual rock band called The Plastic People of the Universe that was suppressed by the Czech Communist government for trumped-up charges of subversion and for allegedly causing disturbances of the peace. Young people were arrested at a concert in 1974 and the band was unable to play in public until 1989 when the Communist government fell. Stoppard's drama chronicles the government's steps to shut down the rock band through characters who had believed in the Czech revolution, but who were sent to prison because they could not conform to the official restrictions on freedom.

In a scene set in autumn 1975, two of the characters, Ferdinand and Jan, assess the state of things in their country and the future for the band and its ideals. One of the musicians who had played in The Plastics, as the group was known, went to prison for defending his right to play music. In the scene, Ferdinand and Jan feel themselves at a turning point. They had wanted to act against the repression by doing something heroic, but they were not sure what exactly to do. Assessing what steps to take next, Jan says, "Heroic acts don't spring from your beliefs. I believe the same as you. They spring from your character." In the scene, Jan is clear about his beliefs and he knows that his and Ferdinand's belief system is right and that it stands on a strong moral foundation, but he is stuck. It requires strength of character to take action. It is easier to hold strong beliefs while accepting and complying with authority than it is to defy authority. In response to Jan, Ferdinand speaks admiringly about the musician Ivan Jirous, who does defy the authorities and resists the temptation to give up on his ideals:

> *The tempter says, "Cut your hair just a little, and we'll let you play." Then the tempter says, "Just change the name of the band and you can play." And after that, "Just leave out this one song" . . . It is better not to start by cutting your hair, Jirous said—no, it is necessary. Then nothing you can do can possibly give support to the idea that everything is in order in this country.*[21]

Play can be the ultimate expression of individual freedom, especially when it is safe and not meant to cause hurt. When it takes place under duress, it can be poignant and have lasting meaning, like the theatrical production of *Brundebar* that took place in the Nazi concentration camp known as Terezin. When it is not allowed to take place and when it is denied, restricted, or otherwise controlled, it becomes a tragic symbol of moral failure. When a government denies musicians or athletes the ability to play, an entire society suffers. Educators and parents have the opportunity to encourage young people to use play to learn, to develop skills, to build friendships and to practice how to build society.

BACK TO THE BASEBALL FIELD

At the beginning of this book, I referred to the moral success of Jackie Robinson in breaking the color barrier in baseball. In spite of the political significance of giving this kind of opportunity to an African American man, and in spite of the emotional challenges he faced in being the first African American on any Major League Baseball team, Jackie Robinson continued to remember that his purpose was to play, and it was the ability to play that furthered the cause of integration. Early in his athletic life (in the late 1930s), when he was playing for the Pasadena California Junior College football team, he played quarterback on a team with fellow students from Oklahoma who expressed discomfort playing with a black man. To make things more comfortable, Robinson would pass the ball to his teammates often, extending himself in friendship. His biographer Arnold Rampersad says that this strategy created allies who blocked for Robinson, protecting him. Robinson said, "That convinced me that it was smart to share the glory . . . that in the final analysis white people were no worse than Negroes, for we are all afflicted by the same pride, jealousy, envy and ambition."[22] Robinson succeeded in this rough-and-tumble play because he was able to identify a goal he could share with his teammates: winning games. While some might have treated the competition as "just a game," he treated it as a moral opportunity to develop friendships and a strong character.

At the time that Robinson played on a minor league team that was part of the Brooklyn Dodgers organization, he knew that each play helped to build his credibility and the credibility of his race. In 1946, his wife, Rachel, said, "We began to see ourselves in terms of a social and historical problem, to know that the issue wasn't simply baseball but life and death, freedom and bondage, for an awful lot of people who didn't have the rewards that came to us."[23]

Robinson's experience of play offers an instructive lesson for all educators who teach young people from different backgrounds, and who are charged with creating a classroom community in which differences are understood and celebrated without impeding students' ability to work together and to learn together. In 1947, a 15-year-old African American high school student named Roger Wilkins was struck by the drama of the moment, and he reminisced many years later,

> *In 1947, Jackie Robinson was as important to me and other blacks, especially young blacks, as a parent would have been, I think. Because he brought pride and the certain knowledge that on a fair playing field, when there were rules and whites could not cheat and lie and steal, not only were they not supermen but we could beat 'em. And he knew what he was doing. He knew what the stakes were every time he danced off a base. If he failed, we failed. . . . He knew what he was trying to do. And this man, in a very personal sense, became a permanent part of my spirit and the spirit of a generation of black kids like me because of the way he faced his ordeal.[24]*

Jackie Robinson's tremendous success earned him the respect and affection of his teammates and fans, and he did indeed become a role model. Jackie Robinson succeeded in working within the system, and with his sense of play, he continued to see his participation as a successful and permanent experiment. A boy named Jimmie wrote to the baseball player about how much he resented his black skin and his black heritage; Robinson wrote back, "I am so proud to be Negro that I feel really good. . . . God put us here on earth and gave us a color that is distinctive, and then put problems before us to see what would happen." Robinson saw the obstacles as great opportunities that built character: "Because of some handicaps, we are better off."[25]

Jackie Robinson's life and work changed history. The average adolescent is not likely to grow up to be a Jackie Robinson, but moral challenges continue to arise. When players earn such large multimillion dollar salaries, do they have moral obligations to society? Are athletes obligated to be moral role models, or are they entertainers? If they are moral role models, then drug use and legal infractions are especially outrageous in light of the high public profiles that they maintain; if they are entertainers, then performance-enhancing drugs might not be seen as so objectionable. With such large salaries and with the moral and legal dilemmas around drug use, a larger question looms beyond the scope of this book: is it still play? Or is it just another well-paying job? There are great lessons from Robinson's ability to take what he saw as a handicap of race and to use it to advance the moral life of his sport, the moral life of his community, and the moral life of his country.

As people may have a disposition to certain character traits, schools also play a crucial role in encouraging those character traits to flourish by advancing the moral lives of their students. Schools sow the seeds of character through numerous avenues, drawing from each of the three moral outlooks:

Authentic and Assured: Hold Students Accountable

Whether their outlook is Authentic and Assured, Bridging and Binding, or Constructing and Considering, teachers can hold students accountable for their behavior. Whether a school has an honor code that students sign, an oath like the Ephebic Oath, or simply a set of rules or guidelines, students should be expected to behave with decency and integrity.

Adults can help students work through their moral dilemmas: when "Moral Eric" decided to cheat, he knew that he was doing something wrong, and he responded honestly to a reminder of how his integrity slips when he cheats. When students are caught cheating, they need to be punished, but schools should not stop with the punishment: they should use it as an opportunity to discuss academic honesty, the cost of cheating to society, and the potential costs of restoring trust.[26] Teachers should seize opportunities in the regular curriculum to raise moral questions and to point out opportunities for moral action.

Bridging and Binding: Introduce Students to the Wider World

Schools can help students to bridge their own culture with the rest of the world, raising the level of moral discourse by bringing in diverse guest speakers such as political figures, community leaders, writers, representatives from summer programs, and representatives from volunteer organizations, all of whom can raise awareness of opportunities in the world beyond their home communities.

By discussing the moral dimensions of knowledge, students will create bridges between the knowledge they acquire in school and issues they will face in the adult world. In spite of the pressures of standardized tests, students should take time—even 15 minutes—to go beyond the academic knowledge into related fields. Biology classes can spend time discussing genetic testing; history classes can discuss the uses and abuses of power; teachers can raise moral issues through current events and through issues raised by students.

Constructing and Considering: Provide Safe Space

In the rough and tumble of childhood, good schools offer places for students of all kinds to grow intellectually while wrestling with great moral dilemmas that foster a thoughtful moral outlook. Academic excellence does not need to exclude moral development. Young people, whether they are social outliers, alpha males, or queen bees, need and benefit from opportunities to construct their own friendships, to experiment with ideas, and to take leadership roles. The Templeton School allowed Felicia and her friends to go to the spring prom in a group without a date without feeling socially awkward. Teachers at Hanford Day School encouraged Gadiel and his classmates to go out on a limb and discuss hot topics such as homosexuality without sacrificing their social standing. Mr. Wesley at Haym Solomon High School encouraged students to perform community service, giving opportunities for his high school students to have meaningful roles and relationships each time they sat together with a second grader. The moral mission and the Ephebic Oath at John Adams High School demanded that students determine what is meant by integrity after considering and debating the inhumanity of the boys in *Lord of the Flies*.

Cynical students often complain about having too many classes that expect them to show personal growth and to share their values. However, the success of programs like *Second Step* at the Jerusalem School and *Journey of a Champion* at Haym Solomon High School shows that students often want to open up, and they want and need safe places in which they can make sense of the social and physical changes that are part of adolescence. A good advisory session on cheating with a positive adult role model might have prevented Eric from cheating. Good advisors understand their role in helping students to shape their outlook.

SOW THE SEEDS OF CHARACTER: PLAY

Even at one of the toughest high schools in Philadelphia, Mr. Wesley joked with students about the popcorn they were selling. Moral education at home, at school, in the classroom, and out at recess, doesn't always have to be serious. Parents and teachers can be playful while also encouraging play. In school, teachers may be tempted to defer opportunities for play because they are busy teaching good behavior or because they are obliged to deliver information to students that will help them on a test.

Not only is it important for teachers to call students to account for displays of poor character, for foul language and for dangerous behavior, but it is equally important for teachers to identify moments of good character in their students, to ask them to hold the door for one another, to look out for a new student and to push students to play. Moral education is not limited to the formal curriculum or to the classroom. I have noticed during my own recess duty that even though it may seem intrusive, and even though I may prefer not to intervene, as a teacher, I have the responsibility as an educator to ask a group of children to accept another child onto their team. Teachers have the responsibility and authority to put a game on pause, to call attention to the moment, and to speak with students about correcting or elevating their behavior toward a more moral direction.[27]

One afternoon, a student challenged me to a one-on-one basketball game; he and I had had several conflicts earlier in the year. We played for about 15 minutes until I was rescued by the bell. I lost the game. Conceding defeat allowed us to laugh together, and I suspect that it increased the student's respect for me, not as a basketball player, but as a three-dimensional person with a love of play who could take a loss. Far from compromising myself by losing, I sensed that he respected me more for losing than if I had won. Some teachers go on walks with students, while others talk about music and art and movies. By playing—by being spontaneous—adults can have an impact on a young person's moral growth.

It is a privilege and it sometimes feels like a risk to be a parent, a teacher, and a moral role model. Moral education is more art than science: we can explain how to plant the seeds of character, and we can't always predict how they will turn out. With each new crop of students, we hope for the richest harvest yet.

Appendix: Interview Protocols

NEW YORK–BASED INTERVIEWS

In the first phase of this study, I shadowed and interviewed five students in an ethnographic study of Jewish adolescents who had attended full-time Jewish schools through the 8th grade and who, at the time of the research, were attending public or independent schools. One student, whom I refer to as "Moral Eric" in this book, had attended New York City public schools throughout his life, but like the rest of the students in the study, he was in 10th grade and he was a student at an after-school program of Jewish studies for high school students. I hoped that the interviews and observations would provide opportunities for me to learn about the moral language that they used in their everyday lives: I designed the interview and shadowing experiences to provide opportunities to observe the student wrestling with large and abstract issues, such as justice and the student's Jewish identity, while also seeing how the student weighed a range of moral choices, how the student expressed himself or herself in school friendships, and how the student faced moments of truth. In that study, which led to my 2002 dissertation, I conducted free-form interviews with one or more of the collaborating student's teachers, with the student's guidance counselor, and, if possible, with a school administrator at each school. This appendix includes only excerpts from the lengthy interview protocol that relate to this book.

Interview Protocol

A. Questions that provide an opportunity to hear the student participant discuss her or his moral stance.

    1. Do you think it is better to do something because you choose to do it or because it is expected it of you?

        a. If you were walking down the street and someone said to you, "Please come to our afternoon services—they'll only take five minutes and besides, God expects it of you," What would you do? Why?

        b. If you were walking down the street and someone said to you, "Please come to our afternoon services—they'll only take five minutes and you'll feel good about participating in the life of the community," What would you do? Why?

        c. If you were walking down the street and someone said to you, "Please come to our afternoon services—they'll only take five minutes, and someone is saying Mourner's *Qaddish*." What would you do? Why?

    2. Reconstruct a moment when you felt that you knew what you stood for. What value was at stake? Are there other values you've/you'd stand up for? What do you think it means to live a moral life? Is there a difference between being good and being moral?

B. Questions about adult role models and heroes.

Have you ever turned to an adult for help with a dilemma? Who was the adult? What did the adult say or offer?

Would you care to identify an adult you admire?

Is there someone that you know personally, that you've read about, or that you've seen in the media who is a hero for you?

PHILADELPHIA-BASED INTERVIEWS

In Philadelphia, I prepared for this book by visiting several schools and by interviewing students at each school. In the New York–based study, I interviewed and shadowed only one student at a time. In Philadelphia, I conducted initial interviews with one student at a time, and as the research went on, I found that interviews with two or three students at a time yielded greater success. Students seemed more at ease when they were with a peer, and they also checked one another; when one student said something that seemed out of character, a peer often would call attention to a comment if it seemed false or exaggerated. Each interview lasted from 15 to 20 minutes. I began each interview by assuring the students of confidentiality and explaining that I would change descriptive details about the school and about them to protect their identity. When possible, I also interviewed teachers to learn how they view their own role as moral educators. Those interviews, like the New York teacher interviews, tended to be more free-form; each interview would begin with the first questions and then evolve into a longer conversation about how each teacher used the formal curriculum as a launching pad for moral education. Because of the unique nature of Haym Solomon High School, I developed a separate set of interview questions for Mr. Wesley at that school.

Interview Protocol—Students

A. Basic information.

    1. Name, age, grade, how long at the school.

    2. Sports, church, other interests, siblings, with whom do they live?

B. What do you think your family tries to teach you about being a good person?

   . . . Does it succeed? How or why not?

C. What do you think your school tries to teach you about being a good person?

   . . . Does it succeed? How or why not?

D. What kinds of rules do you think kids need in society to get along in school?

   . . . to get along on the street?

E. What kinds of values do you think kids need to get going each day?

F. If you do community service:

Why do you think community service is part of your school day?
What do you think it accomplishes?

G. What do you think are the *school's* responsibilities to *you*? (What do you think you can expect from the school?)

Safety
Education
Moral education—nurturing, and so forth.

H. What do you think are *your* responsibilities to the *school*? (What do you think the school can expect from you?)

I. How do you understand respect? Respect from adults toward young people; respect from young people toward adults; among peers?

J. Bystander questions.

    1. Sympathetic bystander.

        a. If a 5-year-old hurt himself in front of you (skinned knee, cried, etc.), what would you do or how would you react?

        b. If a 10-year-old (4th grader) tripped and cut himself on some glass on the street on his way to return a library book (he fell onto the sidewalk and tried to break his fall with his hands, his hands landed on pieces of glass, and then he cried, etc.), what would you do or how would you react?

        c. If a 15-year-old (10th grader) hurt herself (she cut herself while using a kitchen knife to cut vegetables, or she slipped on the sidewalk and drew blood, etc.) in front of you, what would you do or how would you react?

    2. Less reason for sympathy.

        a. If that same 5-year-old were playing ball with a friend and a ball toss hit him in the head, what would you do or how would you react?

        b. If that same 10-year-old (4th grader) were running away from the wrong neighborhood or a fight he had been in, and he twisted his ankle on the sidewalk while he was running, what would you do or how would you react?

        c. If that 15-year-old (10th grader) were trying to paint graffiti on an outside wall of your school or the wall of a store in your neighborhood, what would you do or how would you react?

Interview Protocol—Teachers

A. What values does the school try to teach?

B. What values do you try to teach as individual teachers in a classroom?

C. Why spend class time on community service in the face of No Child Left Behind, state-mandated curricula, and other pressures?

D. Additional questions for Michael Wesley.

    1. How long has he been at Haym Solomon?

    2. How did he come to be the Academy leader?

    3. Describe the Academy curriculum and mission and how it promotes moral education.

4. Describe highlights and limitations for him as a moral educator, especially with pressure to prepare students for standardized tests.
5. How does he know if he and students succeed in moral education?
6. Does he think the kids buy into the moral values of the school? How can he tell?

Notes

INTRODUCTION

1. Alan Axelrod, *Profiles in Audacity* (New York: Sterling, 2006), 176.

2. Harry S. Truman Library, *Desegregation of the Armed Forces* (Independence, MO: Harry S. Truman Library and Museum) http://www.trumanlibrary.org/whistlestop/study_collections/desegregation/large/index.php?action=chronology.

3. Alan Alexrod, *Profiles in Audacity*, 174–79; and Arnold Rampersad, *Jackie Robinson: A Biography* (New York: Alfred A. Knopf, 1997), 121–23.

4. Rampersad, *Jackie Robinson*, 52.

5. Richard D. Kahlenberg, "Americanization 101," *New York Times*, August 19, 2007, The City, 9.

6. About banking and business: Thomas L. Friedman, "Why How Matters," *New York Times*, October 15, 2008, A35; about foreign policy: Mark Mellman, "Another Country," *New York Times*, September 17, 2008, A27; about religion in the United States: Ronald J. Sider, "Religion in America Is Open, Tolerant," *Philadelphia Inquirer*, July 6, 2008, C1, C3; about professional sports: Jere Longman, "The Deafening Roar of the Shrug," *New York Times*, July 29, 2007, Section 4 (The Week in Review), 1, 4.

7. Amy Brundage, "Obama, Durbin, Hare Introduce Bill to Improve Student Behavior in Schools," Barack Obama senatorial Web site, 2007, http://obama.senate.gov/press/071002-obama_durbin_ha/ (accessed August 31, 2008).

8. Sam Dillon, "Obama Looks to Lessons from Chicago in His National Education Plan," *New York Times* September 10, 2008, A21. Paul Tough, "24/7 School Reform," *New York Times Magazine*, September 7, 2008, 17–20.

9. Democratic National Convention Committee, *The 2008 Democratic Party National Platform: Renewing America's Promise* (Denver, CO: Democratic National Convention

Committee, 2008), p. 18, http://s3.amazonaws.com/apache.3cdn.net/8a738445026 d1d5f0f_bcm6b5l7a.pdf (accessed December 18, 2008).

10. Mark Helprin, "Full Text of McCain's Alexandria Speech, April 10, 2008," http://thepage.time.com/excerpts-from-mccains-alexandria-speech/ (accessed August 31, 2008).

11. Republican National Committee, *2008 Republican Platform* (Washington, D.C.: Republican National Committee) http://www.gop.com/2008Platform/Education.htm (accessed December 18, 2008).

12. Sam Dillon, "McCain Calls for Limited U.S. Role in Schools," *New York Times*, September 10, 2008, A21.

13. "Testing the Joy Out of Education," *American Teacher* 93, no. 2 (October 2008): 11, 16.

14. "Fighting the Web Bullying That Led to a Suicide," *New York Times*, June 1, 2008, 25; Gabriel Sherman, "Testing Horace Mann," *New York*, April 7, 2008, 22–27, 107–8; Tamar Lewin, "Study Finds Teenagers' Internet Socializing Isn't such a Bad Thing," *New York Times*, November 20, 2008, A20, A26; and Jennifer Steinhauer, "Arguments in Case Involving Net and Suicide," *New York Times*, A26.

15. Melanie Burney, "Time's Up; Put Down Your iPods," *Philadelphia Inquirer*, December 5, 2005, A1, A15; Winnie Hu, "Seeing No Progress, Some Schools Drop Laptops," *New York Times*, May 4, 2007, A1, B4.

16. Nicholas Bakalar, "Teenagers Changing Sexual Behavior," *New York Times*, August 26, 2008, F7.

17. Shelby Knox, "*Seventeen* Tackles New Teen (Pregnancy) Trend," *Huffington Post*, January 29, 2008, http://www.huffingtonpost.com/shelby-knox/seventeen-tackle_b_83886.html (accessed March 3, 2009).

For statistics about pregnancies between 1990–2002, see Stephanie J. Ventura, et al., *Recent Trends in Teenage Pregnancies in the United States, 1990–2002* (Hyattsville, MD: National Center for Health Statistics of the Center for Disease Control and Prevention, U.S. Department of Health and Human Services, 2007), http://www.cdc.gov/nchs/products/pubs/pubd/hestats/teenpreg1990-2002/teenpreg1990-2002.htm (accessed March 3, 2009).

18. UNICEF, "A League Table of Teenage Births in Rich Nations," Innocenti Report Card, July 2001, reported in Charles M. Blow, "Let's Talk About Sex," *New York Times*, September 6, 2008, A17.

19. Paris S. Strom and Robert D. Strom, "Cheating in Middle School and High School," *Educational Forum* 71, no. 2 (Winter 2007): 104–16. Matt Villano, "Fighting Plagiarism: Taking the Work out of Homework," *T.H.E. Journal* 33, no. 15 (October 2006): 24–30.

20. Maura J. Casey, "Editorial Observer: Digging Out Roots of Cheating in High School," *New York Times*, October 12, 2008, A28, http://www.nytimes.com/2008/10/13/opinion/13mon4.html?ref=opinion (accessed October 23, 2008). "Do Our Schools Invite Cheating?" Letters to the Editor, *New York Times*, October 20, 2008, A30.

21. Executive Office of the President, Office of National Drug Control Policy, 2002, "Drug Use Trends" (Washington, DC: Executive Office of the President, Office

of National Drug Control Policy, 2006), http://www.whitehousedrugpolicy.gov/public ations/factsht/druguse/. Also: National Institute on Drug Abuse, "NIDA InfoFacts: High School and Youth Trends, " rev. ed., (December 2007), http://www.nida.nih.gov/ infofacts/HSYouthtrends.html.

22. Stories my father told me about seeing his teacher's stick come down on his knuckles set me in a childhood fear of strict teachers who would teach that children "should be seen but not heard;" in those teachers' eyes, obedient children are part of the moral order of the world. Corporal punishment continues to be legal in 21 states and an August 2008 CNN report indicates that children are spanked at schools on a frequent basis in 13 states for disciplinary reasons ("More than 20,000 Kids Spanked At School," August 20, 2008, http://www.cnn.com/2008/US/08/20/corporal.punish ment/ (accessed February 5, 2009).

23. National Alliance for Public Charter Schools, "Fact Sheet" (Washington, DC: The National Alliance for Public Charter Schools, 2008), http://www.publiccharters. org/aboutschools/factsheet.

24. National Heritage Academies, "Moral Focus" (Grand Rapids, MI: National Her-itage Academies, 2008), http://heritageacademies.com/our_schools/moral_focus/.

25. For a piece on home schooling among Muslim families, see Neil MacFarquhar, "Resolute or Fearful, Many Muslims Turn to Home Schooling," *The New York Times,* March 26, 2008, A14. For trends in the Jewish community, see Jared Shelley, "To Be or Not to Be in the Classroom? Discussing the Pros and Cons of the Homeschool Trend" *Jewish Exponent* (November 29, 2007), http://www.jewishexponent.com/article/14718/. For national trends, see National Center for Education Statistics, "1.1 Million Home-schooled Students in the United States in 2003" (Washington, DC: U.S. Department of Education, Institute of Education Sciences, National Center for Education Statistics, 2003), http://nces.ed.gov/nhes/homeschool.

26. Confucius, *Analects* 15:24, ed., trans. by James R. Ware, "The Sayings of Con-fucius" (New York: Mentor/New American Library, 1955), 101; Luke 6:31, (Revised Stan-dard Version); Babylonian Talmud *Shabbat* 31a, trans. by the author.

27. By limiting myself to student observations inside schools, I may be capturing the spirit of Emile Durkheim who wrote that moral education is more effective in schools than at home because there are more opportunities for children to experience discipline, to learn the norms of the group. See Elliot Turiel's introduction to Larry P. Nucci, *Education in the Moral Domain* (Cambridge: Cambridge University Press, 2001), ix.

28. Thomas Lickona and Matthew Davidson, *Smart and Good High Schools: In-tegrating Excellence and Ethics for Success in School, Work, and Beyond* (Cortland, NY: Center for the 4th and 5th Rs (Respect & Responsibility)/Washington, DC: Charac-ter Education Partnership, 2005), 2; and Joan F. Goodman and Howard Lesnick, *The Moral Stake in Education: Contested Premises and Practices* (New York: Addison Wesley Longman, 2001), 33.

29. Katherine Simon describes these kinds of questions in greater length in her book *Moral Questions in the Classroom: How to Get Kids to Think Deeply about Real Life and Their Schoolwork* (New Haven, CT: Yale University Press, 2001).

30. Judd Kruger Levingston, "Startlingly Moral: The Moral Outlooks of Jewish Adolescents" (PhD diss., Jewish Theological Seminary, 2002). Judd Kruger Levingston, "Tamar Minick: A Moral Portrait of a Conservative Jewish Teenager" *Conservative Judaism* 56, no. 1 (Fall 2003): 90–106; Judd Kruger Levingston, "Three Moral Outlooks" *Journal of Thought* 39, no. 2 (Spring 2004): 61–76; Judd Kruger Levingston, "Jeffrey Schochet, Taking Center: A Moral Portrait" *Religious Education* 99, no. 4 (Fall 2004): 385–403.

31. This research method is described in greater length in Margaret D. LeCompte and Judith Preissle, *Ethnography and Qualitative Design in Educational Research*, 2nd ed. (San Diego, CA: Academic Press, 1993), 195–200; and in H. Russell Bernard, *Research Methods in Anthropology: Qualitative and Quantitative Approaches*, 2nd ed. (Walnut Creek, CA: AltaMira Press, 1995), 140–43.

32. LeCompte and Preissle, *Ethnography and Qualitative Design in Educational Research*, 166–67.

33. Sara Lawrence-Lightfoot, *The Good High School: Portraits of Character and Culture* (New York: Basic Books, 1983); and Sara Lawrence-Lightfoot and Jessica Hoffman Davis, *The Art and Science of Portraiture* (San Francisco, CA: Jossey-Bass, 1997).

34. Neil Gillman, *Sacred Fragments: Recovering Theology for the Modern Jew* (Philadelphia, Jewish Publication Society, 1990), p. 48.

35. Susan Gilbert, "Scientists Explore the Molding of Children's Morals," *New York Times*, March 18, 2003, F5.

CHAPTER 1

1. These areas of moral education are identified in Katherine G. Simon, *Moral Questions in the Classroom* (New Haven, CT: Yale University Press, 2001), 37–38.

2. William Golding, *Lord of the Flies* (New York: Perigree, 1954).

3. Larry Nucci, *Education in the Moral Domain* (Cambridge: Cambridge University Press, 2001), 168.

4. Simon, *Moral Questions in the Classroom*, 98.

5. Philip W. Jackson, Robert E. Boostrom, and David T. Hansen, *The Moral Life of Schools* (San Francisco, CA: Jossey-Bass, 1993), 42.

6. Thomas Lickona, *Educating for Character: How Our Schools Can Teach Respect and Responsibility* (New York: Bantam, 1991), 20, 62–63. Alternatively, Carol Ingall suggests that immigrant families in urban ghettoes at the beginning of the 20th century may have spent even less time with their children than working families do today! (Carol K. Ingall, personal correspondence, January 2009).

7. Nucci, *Education in the Moral Domain*, 51.

8. Personal communication with Beverly Anderson, Head of Middle School, Trinity Episcopal School, New York City, May 2002.

9. Kevin Ryan and Karen E. Bohlin, *Building Character in Schools: Practical Ways to Bring Moral Instruction to Life* (San Francisco, CA: Jossey-Bass, 1999), 105.

10. William Damon, *The Moral Child: Nurturing Children's Natural Moral Growth* (New York: The Free Press, 1988), 149–50.

11. Robert Coles, *The Moral Life of Children* (Boston: Atlantic Monthly Press, 1986), 149.

12. Joan F. Goodman and Howard Lesnick, *The Moral Stake in Education: Contested Premises and Practices* (New York: Addison Wesley Longman, 2001), 41.

13. John Dewey, *Human Nature and Conflict* (New York: Henry Holt & Co, 1922), 318, quoted in Goodman and Lesnick, *The Moral Stake in Education*, 43.

14. Nucci, *Education in the Moral Domain*, 137.

15. Thomas Lickona, Personal e-mail correspondence to the author, July 8, 2008.

16. Lickona, *Educating for Character*, 50.

17. Ibid., 20–22.

18. Kevin Ryan and Karen E. Bohlin, *Building Character in Schools*, 43, 58.

19. Nucci, *Education in the Moral Domain*, xx, 6.

20. Professor Nucci's Web site expands on these ideas in the section titled, "Domain Theory: Distinguishing Morality and Convention." http://tigger.uic.edu/~lnucci/MoralEd/overview.html.

21. Nucci, *Education in the Moral Domain*, 41.

22. Harry K. Wong and Rosemary T. Wong, *The First Days of School: How to be an Effective Teacher* (Mountain View, CA: Harry K. Wong Publications, 2004).

23. In 1997, Ruby Bridges Hall participated in an interview with Charlayne Hunter Gault on *PBS Newshour* where she recalled the events of that day in November, 1960. She spoke about the moral and spiritual implications for her of being alone in desegregating her school. In spite of the boycott from the families of the white students that left Ruby Bridges the sole student in her class, she continued to attend school every day. http://www.pbs.org/newshour/bb/race_relations/jan-june97/bridges_2-18.html (accessed September 8, 2008). See also Robert Coles, *The Moral Life of Children*, 22–27 and Coles's book for children, *The Story of Ruby Bridges* (New York: Scholastic, 1995).

24. Robert Coles, *The Spiritual Life of Children* (Boston: Houghton Mifflin, 1990), 260.

25. Coles, *The Spiritual Life of Children*, 235.

26. Here I have paraphrased and abbreviated the five concepts described by James M. Gustafson in his essay, "Education for Moral Responsibility" in *Moral Education; Five Lectures*, ed. James M. Gustafson, et al. (Cambridge, MA: Harvard University Press, 1970), 26–27. The five concepts are:

1. Moral training does not necessarily require religious training. There are other justifications for morality than religion; there are other experiences than religious ones which evoke commendable attitudes, intentions, and actions.
2. Religious training does not guarantee morally commendable conduct.
3. Religious training, trust, and belief have an intention distinct from moral education, namely, faith in, or orientation of life toward, God.
4. Religious training, trust, and belief have implications for morality. There are dispositions and attitudes, sensibilities, motives, and intentions which can be and ought to be evoked and nourished by religious life and faith.

There are moral dispositions, motives, etc., that religious men ought to have if their actions are to be consonant, congruent, or consistent with their trust and beliefs.

5. Religious moral training is not confined to authoritative rules of conduct and to sanctions of punishment and reward in eternity.

27. William Damon, *The Moral Child,* 52.

28. Jan Darsa, "Teaching the Holocaust" *Sh'ma* 36/630 (2006), 1.

29. Committee for Children, *Second Step: Student Success through Prevention* (Seattle, WA: Committee for Children, 2008), http://www.cfchildren.org/programs/ssp/overview/.

30. Debra Viadero, "Nice Work: The Growing Research Base for Character Education Programs Shows Benefits for Students' Social and Academic Skills," *Education Week,* April 20, 2004, 38–41.

31. Kevin Ryan, "Character Education: Our High Schools' Missing Link," *Education Week,* January 29, 2003, 35.

32. Barbara Greenspan Shaiman, *Journey of a Champion: Teacher's Guide* (Villanova, PA: Champions of Caring, 2002), 1–2, and student workbook.

33. Viadero, "Nice Work," 41.

34. Lickona, *Educating for Character,* 369.

35. Damon, *The Moral Child,* 146.

CHAPTER 2

1. David Hansen, *The Moral Heart of Teaching: Toward a Teacher's Creed* (New York: Teachers College Press, 2001), 38.

2. Mihaly Csikszentmihalyi and Reed Larson, *Being Adolescent: Conflict and Growth in the Teenage Years* (New York: Basic Books, 1986).

3. Space is insufficient here to do justice to this fascinating work of American social philosophy that continues to describe society more than 20 years since it was published. See Robert N. Bellah, Richard Madsen, William M. Sullivan, Ann Swidler, and Steven M. Tipton, *Habits of the Heart* (New York: Harper & Row, 1985), 28–35.

4. I have written about these three outlooks elsewhere, first in my doctoral dissertation from 2002, *Startlingly Moral: The Moral Outlooks of Jewish Adolescents* (PhD diss., Jewish Theological Seminary), and then in an article entitled "Three Moral Outlooks," published in *The Journal of Thought* (Summer 2004), 61–76. The material in this chapter is adapted and much abbreviated from chapter 10 in my dissertation, "Three Moral Outlooks." In that chapter, as in the article from *The Journal of Thought,* I called the three outlooks by different names: "Standard-bearing," "Connected," and "Permissive." I have changed those categories from "Standard-bearing" to "Authentic and Assured," from "Connected" to "Bridging and Binding," and from "Permissive" to "Constructing and Considering" in an effort to clarify my understanding and also to provide a more easily remembered designations.

5. Robert Bellah et al., *Habits of the Heart*, 8–13.

6. Henry Sidgwick, 1906, *The Methods of Ethics*, 7th ed. (Indianapolis, IN: Hackett Publishing Company, 1981), 105–6.

7. John Rawls, *A Theory of Justice* (Cambridge, MA: Harvard University Press, 1971), 114–17.

8. Immanuel Kant, 1785, *Grounding for the Metaphysics of Morals*, 2nd. trans. J. W. Ellington (Indianapolis, IN: Hackett Publishing Company, 1981), 29–30, §420–21.

9. James M. Frabutt, "Peer Influence," in *Moral Education: A Handbook*, ed. F. Clark Power, Ronald J. Nuzzi, Darcia Narvaez, Daniel K. Lapsley, and Thomas C. Hunt (Westport, CT: Praeger, 2008), 332–33.

10. Kohlberg and others describe Kohlberg's stages of moral development in a number of sources. One particularly straightforward chart and description can be found in Lawrence Kohlberg, "Education for Justice: A Modern Statement of the Platonic View" in James M. Gustafson et al., *Moral Education: Five Lectures* (Cambridge, MA: Harvard University Press, 1970), 71–72. A more complex and developed explanation appears in Lawrence Kohlberg, *The Psychology of Moral Development*, Vol. II of *Essays on Moral Development* (Cambridge, MA: Harper & Row, 1984), Appendix A, "The Six Stages of Justice Judgment."

11. Darshona, Interview with the author, May 5, 2008.

12. Charles Taylor, *Sources of the Self: The Making of Modern Identity* (Cambridge, MA: Harvard University Press, 1989), 36.

13. Carol Gilligan, *In a Different Voice: Psychological Theory and Women's Development* (Cambridge, MA: Harvard University Press, 1982), 64.

14. Charles Larmore, *The Morals of Modernity* (Cambridge: Cambridge University Press, 1996), 155.

15. This was part of a delightful conversation with a girl named A. S., who attended a high school program where I served as principal in the mid-1990s.

16. *The Breakfast Club*, DVD, Directed by John Hughes (1985; reissue, Universal City, CA: Universal Studios, 2003).

17. I observed classes at Templeton over the course of several visits from February to May 1999.

18. James Davison Hunter, *The Death of Character: Moral Education in an Age Without Good or Evil* (New York: Basic Books, 2000), 187.

19. Hunter, *The Death of Character*, 201.

20. Michael Sandel, *Liberalism and the Limits of Justice* (Cambridge: Cambridge University Press, 1982).

21. Taylor, *Sources of the Self*, 82.

22. This concept, that utilitarianism involves intuition, comes from Henry Sidgwick, *The Methods of Ethics*, 7th ed., 105–6.

23. Barry Chazan describes Jewish day schools as emphasizing ethnic identification over formal religious practices. He also describes some Jewish educational efforts as an effort to stem intermarriage, "guaranteeing the perpetuation of the Jewish group." Barry Chazan, "Jewish Education and Moral Development," in Brenda Munsey, ed.,

Moral Development, Moral Education, and Kohlberg: Basic Issues in Philosophy, Psychology, Religion, and Education, 298–325 (Birmingham, AL: Religious Education Press, 1980), 313.

24. Jean Piaget, *The Moral Judgment of the Child,* trans. M. Gabain (New York: The Free Press, 1965).

25. Piaget, *The Moral Judgment of the Child,* 28, 50.

26. Piaget, *The Moral Judgment of the Child,* 71.

27. Piaget, *The Moral Judgment of the Child,* 74.

28. Larry P. Nucci and Elliot Turiel, "The Moral and the Personal: Sources of Social Conflicts" in *Culture, Thought, and Development,* ed. Larry P. Nucci, Geoffrey B. Saxe, and Elliot Turiel, 115–37 (Mahwah, NJ: Lawrence Erlbaum Associates, Publishers, 2000), 119. The example from Hindu culture comes from Richard A. Schweder, Manamohan Mahaptra, and Joan G. Miller, "Culture and Moral Development," in *The Emergence of Morality in Young Children,* ed. Jerome Kagan and Sharon Lamb, 1–83 (Chicago: University of Chicago Press, 1987), 41, 50.

29. William Damon, *The Moral Child: Nurturing Children's Natural Moral Growth* (New York: The Free Press, 1988), 69–70.

30. David M. Shumaker and Robert V. Heckel cite the work of Cecilia Winryb in this area in *Kids of Character: A Guide to Promoting Moral Development* (Westport, CT: Praeger, 2007), 29–31.

31. Elizabeth Weil, "Teaching to the Testosterone," *New York Times Magazine,* March 2, 2008, 42–43.

32. "Give Single-Sex Schools a Try," *Boston Sunday Globe,* Editorial page, D8.

33. Michael Meyers, letter to the editor, *New York Times Magazine,* March 23, 2008, http://www.nytimes.com/2008/03/23/magazine/23letters-t-002.html?ref=magazine.

34. Nona Lyons, "Listening to Voices We Have Not Heard: Emma Willard Girls' Ideas about Self, Relationships, and Morality," in *Making Connections: The Relational Worlds of Adolescent Girls at Emma Willard School,* ed. Carol Gilligan, Nona P. Lyons, and Trudy J. Hanmer ed., 30–72 (Cambridge, MA: Harvard University Press, 1989), 34.

35. Mary Pipher, *Reviving Ophelia: Saving the Selves of Adolescent Girls* (New York: Putnam, 1994), 103.

36. Lyn Mikel Brown, *Raising Their Voices: The Politics of Girls' Anger* (Cambridge, MA: Harvard University Press, 1998): inability to relate to teachers and their teachers' inability to relate to them, 180–89 class prejudices and expectations, 165–67, 202–9; gender differences, 83–84, 98, 158–61.

37. Harbour Fraser Hodder, "Girl Power," *Harvard Magazine* 110:3 (January–February 2008): 34–43.

38. Christina Hoff Sommers, "How Moral Education Is Finding Its Way Back into America's Schools," in *Bringing in a New Era in Character Education,* ed. William Damon, ed. 23–41 (Stanford, CA: Hoover Institution Press, Stanford University Press, 2002).

39. Joselle Farrell and John Sullivan, "School Challenge: Transgender Student Is Age 9," *Philadelphia Inquirer,* May 3, 2008, http://www.philly.com/inquirer/local/pa/

chester/20080503_School_challenge__Transgender_student_is_age_9.html (accessed October 21, 2008).

40. Gloria Hochman, "Teens in Transition," *Philadelphia Inquirer*, October 21, 2008, C1–2. For further discussions on this topic, see Bob Meadows, "From Girl to Boy," *People* 66:18 (October 30, 2006), http://www.people.com/people/archive/article/0,,20060883,00.html (accessed October 21, 2008). Also see the following article about young women who enter college as females, but who see themselves in transition and who ultimately become male: Alissa Quart, "When Girls Will Be Boys," *New York Times Magazine*, March 16, 2008, 32–37. See also Talia Kennedy, "Gender Answers," review of *The Transgender Child: A Handbook for Parents*, by Stephanie Brill and Rachel Pepper, in *San Francisco Chronicle*, September 18, 2008, http://www.sfgate.com/cgi-bin/article.cgi?f=/c/a/2008/09/17/NSQR125MBC.DTL&hw (accessed October 21, 2008).

41. Taylor, *Sources of the Self*, p. 28.

42. Ibid., p. 29.

CHAPTER 3

1. Personal e-mail correspondence from Ahmed Habib Kerry to the author, November 2, 2008.

2. In a personal e-mail correspondence on November 10, 2008 with the author, Muhammad abdul Lateef Hayden helped to clarify some of the overall goals of the school leadership.

3. Abidullah Ghazi and Tasneema Khatoon Ghazi, *Teachings of the Qur'an for Children: Islamic Morals and Manners, Vol. 2* (Chicago: IQRA' International Educational Foundation, 1995).

4. Mrs. Hillal used a number of Arabic expressions, including *in sha' Allah* ("God willing"), *Allah subhanahu wa ta'ala*, which she abbreviated as SWT, meaning "Allah, Glorified and Exalted is He," and other more specific terms, which I will translate in the text. I am grateful to Muhammad abdul Lateef Hayden for assistance with translation.

5. Interviews with Salim Farhat and with Ahmed Habib Kerry, and class observation with Salim Farhat, Tuesday, March 25. Interviews with students, classroom visits and interview with Mrs. Hillal, May 13, 2008, at the Al-Quds Islamic Academy.

6. I wish to express my thanks here to Michael Baber of the Convent of the Sacred Heart School, Greenwich, Connecticut. Interview and conversation, April 22, 2008.

7. The Academy of the Sisters of St. Theresa Office of Admissions promotional booklet (which, in admissions parlance, is called a viewbook) is called "The Academy of the Sisters of Saint Theresa. Education in Action."

8. "Academy of the Sisters of St. Theresa," *Education in Action* [admissions brochure].

9. The Academy of the Sisters of St. Theresa, "Education in Action," admissions promotional booklet, 2.

10. This information and other information about the school primarily came from my first set of classroom observations and student interviews at the school on May 16,

2008; from an interview with Mr. Hurley on June 19, 2008; and from classroom observations on October 27, 2008.

11. The text of the Ephebic Oath can be found at John Adams High School's Web site and is as follows:

> The Ephebic Oath
> I shall never bring disgrace to my city, nor shall I ever desert my comrades in the ranks; but I, both alone and with my many comrades, shall fight for the ideals and sacred things of the city. I shall willingly pay heed to whoever renders judgment with wisdom and shall obey both the laws already established and whatever laws the people in their wisdom shall establish. I, alone and with my comrades, shall resist anyone who destroys the laws or disobeys them. I shall not leave my city any less but rather greater than I found it.

12. Dr. Grossman, Interview with the author, April 22, 1999; Dr. Martinson, Classroom observations, April 22, 1999, and April 27, 1999; Dr. Martinson, Interview with the author, May 17, 1999.

13. Thomas Lickona, "The Power of Modeling in Children's Character Development," in *Parenting for Character: Five Experts, Five Practices,* ed. David Streight, (Portland, OR: Council for Spiritual and Ethical Education, 2007.), http://www.csee.org.

14. Gary D. Fenstermacher, "Some Moral Considerations on Teaching as a Profession," in *The Moral Dimensions of Teaching,* ed. John I. Goodlad (San Francisco, CA: Jossey-Bass, 1990), 134–35, quoted in Joan F. Goodman and Howard Lesnick, *The Moral Stake in Education* (New York: Longman Addison Wesley, 2001), 160.

15. William Damon, *The Moral Child: Nurturing Children's Natural Moral Growth* (New York: The Free Press, 1988), 52.

16. Marvin Berkowitz, "The Science of Character Education," in *Bringing in a New Era in Character Education,* ed. William Damon (Stanford, CA: Hoover Institution Press, Stanford University Press, 2002).

17. Mr. Paschko, Interview with the author, July 15, 2008.

18. [Darshona], "Year 1999," in *Ask Me Why I Write* (Columbus, GA: Zion Publishing Company, 2008), 11.

19. Interviews with students on May 5, 2008, and on May 12, 2008.

20. Nel Noddings, *The Challenge to Care in School: An Alternative Approach to Education* (New York: Teachers College Press, 1992).

21. Jeffrey Schochet, Interviews with the author, April 22, 1999, May 17, 1999, and May 24, 1999; Tamar Minnick, Interviews with the author, February 18, 1999, February 24, 1999, and March 2, 1999; Jared Greenberg-Wendt, Interviews with the author, March 16, 1999, March 29, 1999, May 4, 1999.

22. Tobias Wolff, *Old School* (New York: Vintage, 2003), 149.

23. Arthur Schwartz, "Transmitting Moral Wisdom in an Age of the Autonomous Self," in *Bringing in a New Era in Character Education,* ed. William Damon (Stanford: Hoover Institution Press, Stanford University Press, 2002), 12, 17.

24. Rickie Pierce, 2008 (Associate Head of School, Girls Preparatory School, Chattanooga, TN), telephone conversation with the author, August 6, 2008.

25. http://www.gilman.edu/parents/fornewparents.asp. Because no students were involved, I do not use pseudonyms here or in the preceding example from Girls Preparatory School.

26. The text of the Ephebic Oath can be found at the John Adams high school Website: http://staff.thhs.qc.edu/thhs/oath.php.

27. Lisa Wesel, "Where 'Credit' is Due," *Bowdoin* (Winter 2003), 12–19.

28. Merle J. Schwartz, "Obligations in Character Education," in F. Clark Power, et al., *Moral Education: A Handbook* (Westport, CT: Praeger, 2008), 322–23.

29. Lickona, *Educating for Character: How Our Schools Can Teach Respect and Responsibility* (New York: Bantam, 1991), 44–45.

30. Lickona, *Educating for Character,* 53–62.

31. Aristotle, *Ethics,* trans. J.A.K. Thomson (London: Penguin, 1976), 104.

32. John Hardin Best, ed., *Benjamin Franklin On Education. Classics of Education,14* (New York: Teachers College Press, 1962), 28–30.

33. John Dewey, *Moral Principles in Education* (New York: Philosophical Library, 1959), 2–3.

34. Goodman and Lesnick, *The Moral Stake in Education,* 18.

35. Ibid., 19.

36. Ibid., 18.

37. Joan Goodman, "Obedience," in *Moral Education: A Handbook,* 320–21.

38. Joan F. Goodman and Howard Lesnick, *The Moral Stake in Education* (New York: Longman, 2001), 18–19.

39. Nathaniel Popper, "Chartering a New Course: Do Culture-Themed Public Schools Cross a Legal Line?" *Wall Street Journal,*(August 31, http://www.campus-watch.org/article/id/4018 and http://www.opinionjournal.com/taste/?id=110010547.

40. School mission statements often speak about academic excellence, about service to others, and about preparing students for positions of leadership. Two simple online searches using keywords "mission statement leadership" and "mission statement service to others" produced a number of Web sites promoting schools and places of higher education that seek to further those goals.

41. A quick Internet search led me to environmentally oriented charter schools around the country from the Environmental Charter School in Los Angeles County (http://www.echsonline.org/) to Green Woods Charter School in Philadelphia (http://www.greenwoodscharter.org/) and about 40 others that are listed together at a Wisconsin Charter School Association Web site (http://www.wicharterschools.org/news.main.cfm?id=55).

42. Sara Rimer, "Taking Lessons, and Confidence, from a Classroom on the Water," *New York Times,* June 26, 2008, B1, B6.

43. This topic of single-sex schools is explored in Elizabeth Weil, "Teaching to the Testosterone," *New York Times Magazine,* March 2, 2008, 38–45, 84–87. For information about Boys' Latin of Philadelphia Charter School, see http://www.boyslatin.org/page.php?pid=3.

44. Center for the Study of Boys' and Girls' Lives, http://www.csbl.org/pages/index.php.

45. This is discussed in depth in a research paper written by Michael C. Reichert, Peter Kuriloff, and Brett Stoudt, "What Can We Expect of Boys? A Strategy to Help Schools Hoping for Virtue" (Philadelphia, PA: The Center for the Study of Boys' and Girls' Lives, the University of Pennsylvania, 2008), http://csbgl.org/articles/expectof boys.php.

46. The home page for the Center for the Study of Boys' Lives (http://www.csbl. org/pages/index.php) provides links to a wide variety of girls' and boys' school Web sites, many of which include expressions of commitment to the moral lives of young men and women. The article "What Can We Expect of Boys" also describes some aspects of the moral life of boys at an all boys' school. (http://csbgl.org/articles/expectof boys.php).

47. Reichert, Kuriloff, and Stoudt, "What Can We Expect of Boys," http://csbgl.org/ articles/expectof boys.php.

48. These quotations from the Statement of Mission come from the school's Web site, http://www.[careyschool].org/about/statements.aspx#mission.

49. Elizabeth Weil, "Teaching to the Testosterone," *New York Times Magazine*, March 2, 2008, 87.

CHAPTER 4

1. John Phillips, *Deed of Gift to Phillips Exeter Academy* (Exeter, NH: Phillips Exeter Academy), 1781. See "Academy Mission Statement" at http://www.exeter.edu/about_ us/about_us_286.aspx.

2. Marge Piercy, "Barbie Doll," *Circles on the Water* (New York: Alfred E. Knopf, 1982).

3. English classroom observation at John Adams High School, May 17, 1999; Jeffrey Schochet, interview with the author, May 17, 1999.

4. Mrs. Ruxton, interview with the author, April 22, 1999; English classroom observation at John Adams High School, May 17, 1999; Jeffrey Schochet, interview with the author, May 17, 1999.

5. Mercer Mayer, *Just Grandma and Me* (New York: Random House, 2001).

6. Roald Dahl, 2002, *Fantastic Mr. Fox*, rev. ed. (New York: Alfred A. Knopf, 1970).

7. Observations of Mr. Wesley's classes and observations of community service project, Haym Solomon High School, May 5, 2008, and May 12, 2008; Mr. Wesley, Interview with the author, July 30, 2008.

8. Annping Chin, "The Newest Mandarins," *New York Times Magazine*, December 16, 2007, 34–6; and interview with Sydney White, April 7, 2008.

9. A more complete description of the program can be found at its extensive Web site: www.[meiguo]chinese.org.

10. *A Chinese-English Dictionary*, (Beijing: Shangwuyin Shuguan, 1982), 160. A brief synopsis of the story also can be found in Tian Yuan Tan, "The Wolf of Zhongshan

and Ingrates: Problematic Literary Contexts in Sixteenth-Century China," *Asia Major, Third Series* 20 (1): 105–131 (2007), 105, http://www.ihp.sinica.edu.tw/~asiamajor/pdf/2007a/05%20chenwolf.pdf (accessed October 23, 2008).

11. Sydney White, e-mail correspondence with the author, November 28, 2008.

12. Classroom observation with Teacher Chen and student interviews with the author, October 19, 2008; interview with Teacher Chen, October 27, 2008.

13. Classroom observation with Rabbi Michael and with Mrs. Rose, November 14, 2008.

14. Frances Goodrich and Albert Hackett, "The Diary of Anne Frank," in *Prentice Hall Literature* (Upper Saddle River, NJ: Pearson Prentice Hall, 2007), 783.

15. Jerusalem School observation of Mr. Goodson, November 10, 2008; interview with Mr. Goodson, November 14, 2008; observation of Rabbi Michael, November 14, 2008; observations of Mrs. Rose, November 21, 2008; observation of Mrs. Williams, November 12, 2008; interviews with the author, November 11, 2008 (girls), November 18, 2008 (boys).

16. Carol Gilligan, *In a Different Voice* (Cambridge, MA: Harvard University Press, 1982), 79.

17. Tamar Minick, interview with the author, February 24, 1999; Jared Greenberg-Wendt, interviews with the author, March 16, 1999, March 29, 1999; Felicia Yanes, interview with the author, May 3, 1999.

18. James Davison Hunter, *The Death of Character: Moral Education in an Age Without Good or Evil* (New York: Basic Books, 2000), 164–65.

19. Interviews with Eric, March 16, 2000, March 23, 2000, March 29, 2000, and April 13, 2000.

20. Hugh Hartshorne and Mark May, *Studies in the Nature of Character* (New York: Macmillan, 1928–30), described in William Damon, *The Moral Child: Nurturing Children's Natural Moral Growth* (New York: The Free Press, 1988), 6–7.

21. "Cheating Trends," in Gary K. Clabaugh and Edward G. Rozycki, *Preventing Cheating and Plagiarism*, 2nd ed. (Oreland, PA: New Foundations Press, 2003), http://www.newfoundations.com/PREVPLAGWEB/CheatingTrends1.html. According to a report from Nottingham Trent University in England, 70 percent of undergraduates in the United States admit to cheating at some point during their college careers. In contrast, about 20 percent of English university students admit to cheating. Frank Furedi, "Education: Higher: We Have to Start Young If We Want to Stamp Out Cheating: Comment," *The Guardian*, January 9, 2007, Education pages, 10.

22. Center for Academic Integrity, Clemson, North Carolina, http://www.academicintegrity.org/fundamental_values_project/quotes_on_honesty.php.

23. Nannerl Keohane, "Invitation," in *The Fundamental Values of Academic Integrity* (Durham, NC: Duke University, The Center for Academic Integrity, n.d.), 2. The Center for Academic Integrity was based at Duke University before moving to its present home at Clemson University.

24. Hunter, *The Death of Character*, 163. For more on Hunter's five moral cultures, see 158–59.

25. Findings from the 1989 study is presented in Hunter, *The Death of Character,* 157–69. The 1996 study, "The 1996 Survey of American Public Culture," is described on 169 and in note 31, 282.

26. Hunter, *The Death of Character,* 174–75.

27. John Tierney, "For Good Self-Control, Try Getting Religious About It," *New York Times* December 30, 2008, D2.

28. In his conclusions, Hunter writes that Americans have lost their moral habits, "undermin[ing] the social and cultural conditions necessary for the cultivation of good character" (Hunter, *The Death of Character,* 225). He writes with a grim prognosis that public institutions are no longer able to provide support for the moral habits that they did in the past, leaving that job in the hands of individuals and their families: "This is not to say that we have seen the last of character or the moral qualities of which it is made. It will be found, here and there, in pockets of social life—within families and communities that still, somehow, embody a moral vision." Later he writes, "The task of educating children means teaching them the larger designs that could give form and focus to their individual aspirations, so that they come to understand not only how to be good but why" (Hunter, *The Death of Character,* 227).

29. Space is insufficient here to do justice to this fascinating work of American social philosophy that continues to describe society more than 20 years since it was published. At the very least, see Robert N. Bellah et al., *Habits of the Heart* (New York: Harper & Row, 1985), 28–35.

30. Tim Sprod, *Philosophical Discussion in Moral Education: The Community of Ethical Inquiry* (London: Routledge, 2001), 14.

31. Charles Larmore, *The Morals of Modernity* (Cambridge: Cambridge University Press, 1996), 168.

32. E. M. Forster, *Howards End* (New York: Vintage, 1921), 308.

CHAPTER 5

1. James Davison Hunter, *The Death of Character* (New York: Basic Books, 2000), 76.

2. Steven M. Cohen and Arnold M. Eisen, *The Jew Within: Self, Family and Community in America,* (Bloomington: University of Indiana Press, 2000), 2.

3. Much of this material on Gadiel Himmelfarb has been adapted and edited from chapter 4 of my Ph.D. dissertation, *Startlingly Moral,* "Gadiel Himmelfarb. The Piano Man: Music and Leadership," 120–64.

4. Billy Joel, "Goodnight Saigon," *The Nylon Curtain,* Sony compact disc, September, 1982. Lyrics online at http://www.seeklyrics.com/lyrics/Billy-Joel/Goodnight-Saigon.html (accessed July 28, 2008).

5. David T. Hansen, *Exploring the Moral Heart of Teaching: Toward a Teacher's Creed* (New York: Teachers College Press, 2001), 10.

6. Classroom observations at Hanford Day School, and Gadiel Himmelfarb, interviews with the author, January 12, 1999, January 20, 1999, and January 27, 1999.

7. Teacher Joan and Teacher Doug, interviews with the author at Fairhill Friends School, May 6, 2008; Meeting for Worship, student interviews and classroom observations at Fairhill Friends School, October 8, 2008.

8. Lyn Mikel Brown and Carol Gilligan, *Meeting at the Crossroads: Womens' Psychology and Girls' Development* (New York: Ballantine Books, 1992), 25, 65.

9. Lyn Mikel Brown and Carol Gilligan, *Meeting at the Crossroads: Women's Psychology and Girls' Development* (New York: Ballantine Books, 1992), 217.

10. Mentors play an important role in steering young people toward activities and intellectual pursuits that encourage their emotional, intellectual, and moral growth. For further discussions on the roles of mentors, see Mihaly Csikszentmihaly, Kevin Rathunde, and Samuel Whalen, *Talented Teenagers: The Roots of Success and Failure* (Cambridge: Cambridge University Press, 1993), 23.

11. In a tragic incident in 1964 that has come to stand for the shortcomings of society, Kitty Genovese was stabbed to death in Queens, New York, in sight of a number of witnesses. Not only was the murder itself worthy of discussion, but one report indicated that over 30 witnesses observed or heard the stabbing, but they did not stop the violence out of their own passivity and fear. The incident continues to be used in discussions about the responsibilities of a bystander and the dangers of inaction.

12. Conversation between Ms. Markson and the author, February 24, 1999 and Ms. Leopold and the author, February 24, 1999. Observations of Ms. Leopold's class, February 18, 1999, February 24, 1999.

13. Student interviews with the author, May 5, 2008.

14. Sidney Simon and Howard Kirschenbaum, *Readings in Values Clarification* (Minneapolis, MN: Winston Press, 1973), 18, quoted in Christina Hoff Sommers, "How Moral Education Is Finding Its Way Back into America's Schools," in *Bringing in a New Era in Character Education*, ed. William Damon (Stanford, CA: Hoover Institution Press, Stanford University Press, 2002), 31.

15. Thomas Lickona, quoting Louis Edward Raths, Merrill Harman, and Sidney B. Simon, *Values and Teaching: Working with Values in the Classroom* (Columbus, OH: C.E. Merrill Books, 1966) and Martin Eger, "The Conflict in Moral Education: An Informal Case Study," *Public Interest* 63 (Spring 1981): 66–67.

16. Eger, "The Conflict in Moral Education," 67.

17. Thomas Lickona, *Educating for Character: How Our Schools Can Teach Respect and Responsibility* (New York: Bantam, 1991), 238.

18. Bruce Logan, "The Fanaticism of the New Moralists," *The Evening Post* (Wellington, New Zealand), February 23, 1996, 4.

19. William Damon, *The Moral Child: Nurturing Children's Natural Moral Growth* (New York: Free Press, 1988), 136.

20. Later I will look more closely at different strains in American moral education. For highly critical views, see Hunter, *The Death of Character*.

21. Philip W. Jackson, Robert E. Boostrom, and David T. Hansen, *The Moral Life of Schools* (San Francisco, CA: Jossey-Bass, 1993), 155–56.

22. Damon, *The Moral Child*, 119.

23. Thomas Lickona and Matthew Davidson, *Smart and Good High Schools: Integrating Excellence and Ethics for Success in School, Work, and Beyond* (Cortland, NY: Center for the 4th and 5th Rs (Respect & Responsibility)/Washington, DC: Character Education Partnership, 2005), chap. 2, 16–31.

24. Larry P. Nucci, *Education in the Moral Domain* (Cambridge: Cambridge University Press, 2001), 6.

25. Nucci, *Education in the Moral Domain*, 138, 167, 191.

26. Personal conversations between "Mr. Paschko" and the author (July 15, 2008) and between "Mr. Wesley" and the author (July 30, 2008).

27. Lawrence Kohlberg, "Education for Justice: A Modern Statement of the Platonic View" in James M. Gustafson et al., *Moral Education: Five Lectures* (Cambridge, MA: Harvard University Press, 1970), 59, 66, 69.

28. Joan F. Goodman and Howard Lesnick, *The Moral Stake in Education* (New York: Longman, 2001), 135–36.

29. David M. Shumaker and Robert V. Heckel, "The Community's Role in Character Development" in *Kids of Character: A Guide to Promoting Moral Development* (Westport, CT: Praeger, 2007), 81–111.

CHAPTER 6

1. David M. Shumaker and Robert V. Heckel, *Kids of Character: A Guide to Promoting Moral Development* (Westport, CT: Praeger, 2007), 174–90.

2. Nicole M. LaVoi and Erin Becker, "Sports and Character," in F. Clark Power et al., *Moral Education: A Handbook* (Westport, CT: Praeger, 2008), 428–30.

3. John Dewey, *The School and Society* and *The Child and the Curriculum*, Introduction by Philip W. Jackson (Chicago: The University of Chicago Press, 1990), 118.

4. Stuart Brown, interview by Krista Tippett, *Speaking of Faith*, American Public Media, July 24, 2008.

5. Robert Putnam, *Bowling Alone* (New York: Simon and Schuster, 2000).

6. Joel Fish, conversation with the author, November 24, 2008.

7. Ibid.

8. Matthew L. Davidson and Kelli E. Moran-Miller, "Character Development in Sport: An Ethnographic Study of Character Development in an Elite Prep-School Basketball Program," *Journal of Research in Character Education* 3(2), 2005, 121–22.

9. Arthur Wellesley, Duke of Wellington, quotation in John Bartlett, *Familiar Quotations*, 14th ed., Emily Morison Beck (Boston: Little, Brown and Company, 1968), 506a. See also Paul F. Boller and John H. George, *They Never Said It: A Book of Fake Quotes, Misquotes and Misleading Attributions* (New York: Oxford University Press), 1989, 130–31 and Googlebooks http://books.google.com/books?id=NCOEYJoq-DUC&pg=PR3&source=gbs_selected_pages&cad=0_1 (accessed February 15, 2009).

10. Davidson and Moran-Miller, "Character Development in Sport," 128.

11. Ibid., 132.

12. Ibid., 137.

13. For more information about these organizations, see http://www.specialolym pics.org/ and the home page for Right to Play: http://www.righttoplay.com/site/Page Server (both sites accessed February 16, 2009).

14. Stuart Brown, interview on *Speaking of Faith* from American Public Media, July 24, 2008. Transcript online at http://speakingoffaith.publicradio.org/programs/play/ transcript.shtml (accessed November 4, 2008).

15. Romina M. Barros, Ellen J. Silver, and Ruth Stein, "School Recess and Group Classroom Behavior," *Pediatrics* 123 (2009): 434–35.

16. Tara Parker-Pope, "Recess Found to Improve Behavior," *The New York Times,* February 3, 2009, D6.

17. Web sites have been established for gay and lesbian teens and for adults who care about them to learn more and to find a safe space where their identity is not questioned. See Laurie Lindop, "Gay, Lesbian, Bisexual, Transgender Youth Suicide," http://www.healthyplace.com/Communities/gender/gayisok/glbt_suicide_study.htm (accessed November 28, 2008). See also the Trevor Project: http://www.thetrevorproj ect.org/home2.aspx.

18. Jeff Perrotti, Kim Westheimer, *When the Drama Club Is Not Enough: Lessons from the Safe Schools Program for Gay and Lesbian Students* (Boston, Beacon Press, 2001), chap. 4, "Sports, Sexual Orientation, and School Climate," 73–97, and 138, on the ways in which the Safe Schools Project came about in part to address the reported high suicide rate among gay and lesbian teenagers.

19. Jeffrey Schochet, Interview with the author, May 24, 1999.

20. It may interest the reader that I have had some contact with "Jeffrey" because he has written and published several political opinion pieces in major American daily newspapers.

21. Tom Stoppard, *Rock 'n' Roll,* rev. ed. (New York, Grove Press, 2007), 38.

22. Arnold Rampersad, *Jackie Robinson: A Biography* (New York: Alfred A. Knopf, 1997), 49.

23. Rampersad, *Jackie Robinson,* 144.

24. Ibid., 179.

25. Ibid., 222.

26. Ann Marie R. Power, "Cheating," in Power et al., *Moral Education,* 72–3; also Steven D. Levitt and Stephen J. Dubner, *Freakonomics: A Rogue Economist Explores the Hidden Side of Everything* (New York: William Morrow, 2005), 35.

27. Joan F. Goodman and Howard Lesnick, *The Moral Stake in Education: Contested Premises and Practices* (New York: Addison Wesley Longman, 2001), 251.

Bibliography

Aristotle. *Ethics*. Translated by J.A.K. Thomson. London: Penguin, 1976.

Axelrod, Alan. *Profiles in Audacity*. New York: Sterling, 2006.

Bakalar, Nicholas. "Teenagers Changing Sexual Behavior." *New York Times,* August 26, 2008, F7.

Bellah, Robert N., Richard Madsen, William M. Sullivan, Ann Swidler, and Steven M. Tipton. *Habits of the Heart*. New York: Harper & Row, 1985.

Berkowitz, Marvin. "The Science of Character Education." In *Bringing in a New Era in Character Education*, ed. by William Damon, 43–63. Stanford, CA: Hoover Institution Press, Stanford University Press, 2002.

Bernard, H. Russell. *Research Methods in Anthropology: Qualitative and Quantitative Approaches*. 2nd ed. Walnut Creek, CA: AltaMira Press, 1995.

Best, John Hardin, ed. *Benjamin Franklin On Education*. Vol. 14, *Classics of Education*. New York: Teachers College Press, 1962.

Bettelheim, Bruno, James M. Gustafon, Kenneth Kenniston, Lawrence Kohlberg, Richard S. Peters, and Theodore R. Sizer. *Moral Education: Five Lectures*. ed. Nancy F. Sizer. Cambridge, MA: Harvard University Press, 1970.

Bolt, Robert. *A Man for All Seasons*. New York: Vintage International, 1962.

Boys' Latin of Philadelphia Charter School. Home page. http://www.boyslatin.org/page.php?pid=3.

The Breakfast Club. DVD. Directed by John Hughes. Universal City, CA: Universal Studios, 2003.

Brown, Lyn Mikel. *Raising Their Voices: The Politics of Girls' Anger*. Cambridge: Harvard University Press, 1998.

Brown, Lyn Mikel, and Carol Gilligan. *Meeting at the Crossroads: Women's Psychology and Girls' Development*. New York: Ballantine Books, 1992.

Brown, Stuart. Interview by Krista Tippett. *Speaking of Faith*. American Public Media, July 24, 2008. Transcript: http://speakingoffaith.publicradio.org/programs/play/tran script.shtml (accessed November 4, 2008).

Brundage, Amy. "Obama, Durbin, Hare Introduce Bill to Improve Student Behavior in Schools." 2007. http://obama.senate.gov/press/071002-obama_durbin_ha/ (accessed August 31, 2008).

"The Carey School." Home page. http://www.[careyschool].org/about/statements. aspx#mission.

Center for Academic Integrity, Clemson, North Carolina. Home page. http://www.academic integrity.org/fundamental_values_project/quotes_on_honesty.php.

Center for the Study of Boys Lives. "What Can We Expect of Boys." http://csbgl.org/articles/ expectofboys.php.

Chazan, Barry. "Jewish Education and Moral Development." In *Moral Development, Moral Education, and Kohlberg: Basic Issues in Philosophy, Psychology, Religion, and Education*, ed. by Brenda Munsey, 298–325. Birmingham, AL: Religious Education Press, 1980.

Clabaugh, Gary K., and Edward G. Rozycki. "Cheating Trends." 2003. http://www.newfound ations.com/PREVPLAGWEB/CheatingTrends1.html.

Cohen, Steven M., and Arnold M. Eisen. *The Jew Within: Self, Family and Community in America*. Bloomington: University of Indiana Press, 2000.

Coles, Robert. *The Moral Life of Children*. Boston: Atlantic Monthly Press, 1986.

Coles, Robert. *The Spiritual Life of Children*. Boston: Houghton Mifflin, 1990.

Coles, Robert. *The Story of Ruby Bridges*. New York: Scholastic, 1995.

Committee for Children. *Second Step: Student Success Through Prevention*. Seattle, WA: Committee for Children, 2008.

Confucius. *The Sayings of Confucius*. Edited and translated by James R. Ware. New York: Mentor/New American Library, 1955.

Csikszentmihalyi, Mihaly, and Reed Larson. *Being Adolescent: Conflict and Growth in the Teenage Years*. New York: Basic Books, 1986.

Csikszentmihalyi, Mihaly, Reed Larson, Kevin Rathunde, and Samuel Whalen. *Talented Teenagers: The Roots of Success and Failure*. Cambridge, UK: Cambridge University Press, 1993.

Dahl, Roald. 2002. *Fantastic Mr. Fox*. Rev. ed. New York: Alfred A. Knopf, 1970.

Damon, William, ed. *Bringing in a New Era in Character Education*. Stanford: Hoover Institution Press, Stanford University Press, 2002.

Damon, William. *The Moral Child: Nurturing Children's Natural Moral Growth*. New York: The Free Press, 1988.

Darsa, Jan. "Teaching the Holocaust." *Sh'ma* 36/630 (2006): 1.

"Darshona." *Ask Me Why I Write*. Columbus, GA: Zion, 2008.

Davidson, Matthew L., and Kelli E. Moran-Miller. "Character Development in Sport: An Ethnographic Study of Character Development in an Elite Prep-School Basketball Program." *Journal of Research in Character Education* 3(2) (2005): 121–38.

Dewey, John. *Moral Principles in Education*. New York: Philosophical Library, 1959.

Eger, Martin. "The Conflict in Moral Education: An Informal Case Study." *Public Interest* 63 (1981): 66–67.

Environmental Charter School in Los Angeles County. Home page. http://www.echsonline. org/.

Executive Office of the President. Office of National Drug Control Policy. "Drug Use Trends." Washington, DC: Executive Office of the President, Office of National Drug Control Policy, 2002. http://www.whitehousedrugpolicy.gov/publications/factsht/druguse/.

Fitzhugh, Louise. *The Long Secret*. New York: Dell, 1965.

Forster, E. M. *Howards End*. New York: Vintage, 1921.

Ghazi, Abidullah, and Tasneema Khatoon Ghazi. *Teachings of the Qur'an for Children: Islamic Morals and Manners*. Vol. 2. Chicago: IQRA' International Educational Foundation, 1995.

Gilligan, Carol. *In a Different Voice: Psychological Theory and Women's Development*. Cambridge: Harvard University Press, 1982.

Gillman, Neil. *Sacred Fragments: Recovering Theology for the Modern Jew*. Philadelphia: Jewish Publication Society, 1990.

Gilman School. Parent information home page. http://www.gilman.edu/parents/fornew parents.asp.

Ginsburg, Kenneth R. *A Parent's Guide to Building Resilience in Children and Teens: Giving Your Child Roots and Wings*. Elk Grove Village, IL: American Academy of Pediatrics, 2006.

Golding, William. *Lord of the Flies*. New York: Perigree, 1954.

Goodman, Joan F., and Howard Lesnick. *The Moral Stake in Education: Contested Premises and Practices*. New York: Addison Wesley Longman, 2001.

Goodrich, Frances, and Albert Hackett. "The Diary of Anne Frank." In *Prentice Hall Literature*, 776–869. Upper Saddle River, NJ: Pearson Prentice Hall, 2007.

Green Woods Charter School in Philadelphia. Home page. http://www.greenwoodscharter. org/.

Hansen, David T. *Exploring the Moral Heart of Teaching: Toward a Teacher's Creed*. New York: Teachers College Press, 2001.

Hartshorne, Hugh, and Mark May. *Studies in the Nature of Character*. New York: Macmillan, 1928–30.

Helprin, Mark. "Full Text of McCain's Alexandria Speech, April 10, 2008." http://thepage. time.com/excerpts-from-mccains-alexandria-speech/ (accessed August 31, 2008).

Hunter, James Davison. *The Death of Character: Moral Education in an Age Without Good or Evil*. New York: Basic Books, 2000.

Jackson, Philip W. Introd. to *The School and Society* and *The Child and the Curriculum*, by John Dewey. Chicago: The University of Chicago Press, 1990.

Jackson, Philip W., Robert E. Boostrom, and David T. Hansen. *The Moral Life of Schools*. San Francisco, CA: Jossey-Bass, 1993.

Joel, Billy. "Goodnight Saigon." *The Nylon Curtain*. Sony. Published, 1982 by Sony Records. Lyrics: http://www.seeklyrics.com/lyrics/Billy-Joel/Goodnight-Saigon.html (accessed July 28, 2008).

Kagan, Jerome, and Sharon Lamb, eds. *The Emergence of Morality in Young Children*. Chicago: University of Chicago Press, 1987.

Kant, Immanuel. 1785. *Grounding for the Metaphysics of Morals*. 2nd. ed. Translated by J. W. Ellington. Indianapolis, IN: Hackett Publishing Company, 1981.

Keohane, Nannerl. "Invitation." In *The Fundamental Values of Academic Integrity,* 2. Durham, NC: Duke University, Center for Academic Integrity, n.d.

Kohlberg, Lawrence. "Education for Justice: A Modern Statement of the Platonic View." In *Moral Education: Five Lectures,* 57–83. Cambridge, MA: Harvard University Press, 1970.

Kohlberg, Lawrence. *The Psychology of Moral Development.* Vol. II, *Essays on Moral Development.* New York: Harper & Row, 1984.

Larmore, Charles. *The Morals of Modernity.* Cambridge: Cambridge University Press, 1996.

Lawrence-Lightfoot, Sara. *The Good High School: Portraits of Character and Culture.* New York: Basic Books, 1983.

Lawrence-Lightfoot, Sara, and Jessica Hoffman Davis. *The Art and Science of Portraiture.* San Francisco, CA: Jossey-Bass, 1997.

LeCompte, Margaret D., and Judith Preissle. *Ethnography and Qualitative Design in Educational Research.* 2nd ed. San Diego, CA: Academic Press, 1993.

Levingston, Judd Kruger. "Jeffrey Schochet, Taking Center: A Moral Portrait." *Religious Education* 99, no. 4 (2004): 385–403.

Levingston, Judd Kruger. "Startlingly Moral: The Moral Outlooks of Jewish Adolescents." PhD diss., Jewish Theological Seminary, 2002.

Levingston, Judd Kruger. "Tamar Minick: A Moral Portrait of a Conservative Jewish Teenager." *Conservative Judaism* 56, no. 1 (2003): 90–106.

Levingston, Judd Kruger. "Three Moral Outlooks." *Journal of Thought* 39, no. 2 (2004): 61–76.

Levitt, Steven D., and Stephen J. Dubner. *Freakonomics: A Rogue Economist Explores the Hidden Side of Everything.* New York: William Morrow, 2005.

Lickona, Thomas. *Educating for Character.* New York: Bantam, 1991.

Lickona, Thomas. "The Power of Modeling in Children's Character Development." In *Parenting for Character: Five Experts, Five Practices,* ed. David Streight. Portland, OR: Council for Spiritual and Ethical Education, 2007.

Lickona, Thomas, and Matthew Davidson. *Smart and Good High Schools: Integrating Excellence and Ethics for Success in School, Work, and Beyond.* Cortland, NY: Center for the 4th and 5th Rs (Respect and Responsibility)/Washington, DC: Character Education Partnership, 2005.

Lyons, Nona. "Listening to Voices We Have Not Heard: Emma Willard Girls' Ideas about Self, Relationships, and Morality." In *Making Connections: The Relational Worlds of Adolescent Girls at Emma Willard School,* ed. Carol Gilligan, Nona P. Lyons, and Trudy J. Hanmer, 30–72. Cambridge, MA: Harvard University Press, 1989.

Mayer, Mercer. *Just Grandma and Me.* New York: Random House, 2001.

"Meiguo Chinese Academy." Home page. www.[meiguo]chinese.org.

National Alliance for Public Charter Schools. "Fact Sheet." Washington, DC: The National Alliance for Public Charter Schools, 2008. http://www.publiccharters.org/aboutschools/factsheet.

National Center for Education Statistics. "1.1 Million Homeschooled Students in the United States in 2003." Washington, DC: U.S. Department of Education, Institute of Education Sciences, National Center for Education Statistics, 2003. http://nces.ed.gov/nhes/homeschool.

National Heritage Academies. "Moral Focus." Grand Rapids, MI: National Heritage Academies, 2008. http://heritageacademies.com/our_schools/moral_focus/.

National Institute on Drug Abuse. "NIDA InfoFacts: High School and Youth Trends." Rev. ed. December 2007. http://www.nida.nih.gov/infofacts/HSYouthtrends.html.

Noddings, Nel. *The Challenge to Care in Schools.* New York: Teachers College Press, 1992.

Nucci, Larry P. *Education in the Moral Domain.* Cambridge: Cambridge University Press, 2001.

Nucci, Larry P., and Elliot Turiel. "Domain Theory: Distinguishing Morality and Convention." http://tigger.uic.edu/~lnucci/MoralEd/overview.html.

Nucci, Larry P., and Elliot Turiel. "The Moral and the Personal: Sources of Social Conflicts." In *Culture, Thought, and Development,* ed. Larry P. Nucci, Geoffrey B. Saxe, and Elliot Turiel, 115–37 Mahwah, NJ: Lawrence Erlbaum Associates, Publishers, 2000.

O'Brien, Tim. *The Things They Carried.* Boston: Houghton Mifflin, 1990.

PBS Newshour. (television show). Interview between Charlayne Hunter Gault and Ruby Bridges. February 18, 1997. http://www.pbs.org/newshour/bb/race_relations/jan-june97/bridges_2–18.html (accessed September 8, 2008).

Perrotti, Jeff, and Kim Westheimer. *When the Drama Club Is Not Enough: Lessons from the Safe Schools Program for Gay and Lesbian Students.* Boston: Beacon Press, 2001.

Piaget, Jean. *The Moral Judgment of the Child.* Trans. M. Gabain. New York: The Free Press, 1965.

Piercy, Marge. "Barbie Doll." In *Circles on the Water.* New York: Alfred E. Knopf, 1982.

Pipher, Mary. *Reviving Ophelia: Saving the Selves of Adolescent Girls.* New York: Putnam, 1994.

Power, F. Clark, Ronald J. Nuzzi, Darcia Narvaez, Daniel K. Lapsley, and Thomas C. Hunt. *Moral Education: A Handbook.* 2 vols. Westport, CT: Praeger, 2008.

Putnam, Robert. *Bowling Alone.* New York: Simon and Schuster, 2000.

Rampersad, Arnold. *Jackie Robinson: A Biography.* New York: Alfred A. Knopf, 1997.

Rawls, John. *A Theory of Justice.* Cambridge, MA: Harvard University Press, 1971.

Reichert, Michael C., Peter Kuriloff, and Brett Stoudt. "What Can We Expect of Boys? A Strategy to Help Schools Hoping for Virtue." Philadelphia, PA: The Center for the Study of Boys' and Girls' Lives, the University of Pennsylvania, 2008. http://csbgl.org/articles/expectofboys.php.

Ryan, Kevin, and Karen E. Bohlin. *Building Character in Schools: Practical Ways to Bring Moral Instruction to Life.* San Francisco, CA: Jossey-Bass, 1999.

Sandel, Michael. *Liberalism and the Limits of Justice.* Cambridge: Cambridge University Press, 1982.

Schwartz, Arthur. "Transmitting Moral Wisdom in an Age of the Autonomous Self." In *Bringing in a New Era in Character Education,* ed. William Damon, 1–21. Stanford, CA: Hoover Institution Press, Stanford University Press, 2002.

Schweder, Richard A., Manamohan Mahaptra, and Joan G. Miller. "Culture and Moral Development." In *The Emergence of Morality in Young Children,* ed. Jerome Kagan and Sharon Lamb, 1–83. Chicago: University of Chicago Press, 1987.

Shaiman, Barbara Greenspan. "Journey of a Champion." Teacher's Guide and Student Workbook. Villanova, PA: Champions of Caring, 2000.

Shumaker, David M., and Robert Heckel. *Kids of Character: A Guide to Promoting Moral Development.* Westport, CT: Praeger, 2007.

Sidgwick, Henry. 1906. *The Methods of Ethics.* 7th ed. Indianapolis, IN: Hackett Publishing Company, 1981.

Simon, Katherine G. *Moral Questions in the Classroom: How to Get Kids to Think Deeply about Real Life and Their Schoolwork.* New Haven, CT: Yale University Press, 2001.

Simon, Sidney B., Geri Curwin, and Marie Hartwell. "Teaching Values." In *Readings in Values Clarification*, 336–9. Minneapolis, MN: Winson, 1973.

Sommers, Christina Hoff. "How Moral Education Is Finding Its Way Back into America's Schools." In *Bringing in a New Era in Character Education*, ed. William Damon, 23–41. Stanford, CA: Hoover Institution Press, Stanford University Press, 2002.

Sprod, Tim. *Philosophical Discussion in Moral Education: The Community of Ethical Inquiry.* London: Routledge, 2001.

Strom, Paris S., and Robert D. Strom, "Cheating in Middle School and High School." *Educational Forum* 71, no. 2 (Winter 2007): 104–16.

Tan, Tian Yuan. "The Wolf of Zhongshan and Ingrates: Problematic Literary Contexts in Sixteenth-Century China." *Asia Major, Third Series* 20 (1) (2007): 105–31. http://www.ihp. sinica.edu.tw/~asiamajor/pdf/2007a/05%20chenwolf.pdf (accessed October 23, 2008).

Taylor, Charles. *Sources of the Self: The Making of Modern Identity.* Cambridge, MA: Harvard University Press, 1989.

Tough, Paul. "24/7 School Reform." *New York Times Magazine*, September 7, 2008, 17–20.

Turiel, Elliot. "Introduction." In *Education in the Moral Domain*, by Larry P. Nucci. Cambridge: Cambridge University Press, 2001.

UNICEF. "A League Table of Teenage Births in Rich Nations." Innocenti Report Card, July 2001. Reported in Charles M. Blow, "Let's Talk About Sex." *New York Times*, September 6, 2008, A17.

Villano, Matt. "Fighting Plagiarism: Taking the Work out of Homework." *T.H.E. Journal* 33, no. 15 (October 2006): 24–30.

Wisconsin Charter School Association. Home page. http://www.wicharterschools.org/ news.main.cfm?id=55.

Wolff, Tobias. *Old School.* New York: Vintage, 2003.

Wong, Harry K., and Rosemary T. Wong, *The First Days of School: How to Be an Effective Teacher.* Mountain View, CA: Harry K. Wong Publications, 2004.

Zion, Noam, and David Dishon. *A Different Night: The Family Participation Haggadah.* Jerusalem, Israel: The Shalom Hartman Institute, 1997.

Index

About the Author

JUDD KRUGER LEVINGSTON is a rabbi and educator. He heads the department of Jewish Studies at the Barrack Hebrew Academy and teaches at Temple University, Philadelphia. He has taught and served as an administrator in a variety of middle and high schools, including an all-girls school, an all-boys school, a boarding school, an Episcopalian school, and Jewish day schools. He received his rabbinic ordination and doctorate in moral education from the Jewish Theological Seminary in New York and he has undergraduate degrees from Harvard University and Beijing University.